T0305284

"Mark Tibergien is the Peter F. Drucker of the financial-advisory industry. Principals of advisory firms ignore his counsel at their peril. 'Value' is a word of many meanings. Whether you're a buyer or a seller of an advisory practice, Mark and Owen's book takes the mystery out of the transactions, giving the reader a complete road map through the process.

"Principals of financial-advisory firms often procrastinate on one of the most important decisions of their business life. Building value in your business and executing a transition are not easy. You have three options: a transition to a strategic party, to a financial buyer, or to the next generation. The fourth possibility—to do nothing and let your heirs worry about it—is not really an option. The transition can be made a lot less painful by following the advice in this book."

SCOTT D. ROULSTON
Chief Executive Officer, Fairport Asset Management, LLC

"Mark and Owen have done a wonderful job bringing together all aspects of valuing, buying, and selling a financial-advisory practice into one, comprehensive, easy-to-follow book. I wish I'd had this book when we made our first acquisition."

MARK C. SOEHN
Principal, Managing Director
Financial Solutions Advisory Group

"Tibergien and Dahl have delivered an excellent road map for financial-advisory firms seeking to avoid the critical mistakes that often result when deriving and realizing firm value. This comprehensive guide identifies the steps in the process and provides key insights on how to correctly identify and realize the value of your financial-advisory practice. Whether your focus is on buying and selling financial-advisory firms or on maximizing the value in your practice, this book will become an invaluable resource."

M. BRETT SUCHOR, CFA, ASA
President, Quist Valuation

How to
Value, Buy, or Sell
a Financial-Advisory
Practice

How to Value, Buy, or Sell a Financial-Advisory Practice

A Manual on Mergers, Acquisitions, and Transition Planning

MARK C. TIBERGIEN

and

OWEN DAHL

BLOOMBERG PRESS

NEW YORK

This publication contains the authors' opinions and is designed to provide accurate and authoritative information. It is sold with the understanding that the authors, publisher, and Bloomberg L.P. are not engaged in rendering legal, accounting, investment-planning, or other professional advice. The reader should seek the services of a qualified professional for such advice; the authors, publisher, and Bloomberg L.P. cannot be held responsible for any loss incurred as a result of specific investments or planning decisions made by the reader.

No ideas or examples offered in this book should be construed as legal advice. The authors are not licensed or qualified to provide legal advice, and individuals or entities contemplating a transaction should engage qualified legal counsel to review proposed transactions and to draft all documents.

First edition published 2006
3 5 7 9 10 8 6 4 2

ISBN-13: 978-1-57660-174-7

The Library of Congress has cataloged the earlier printing as follows:

Tibergien, Mark C.
    How to value, buy, or sell a financial-advisory practice : a manual on mergers, acquisitions, and transition planning / Mark C. Tibergien and Owen Dahl. -- 1st ed.
        p. cm.
    Includes bibliographical references and index.
    Summary: "A manual for financial advisers offering complete guidelines and techniques on the key issues related to valuing practices for sale, mergers, acquisitions, partnership, and transition planning. Special emphasis is given to ways to maximize and build value in a practice and to vital information related to valuation approaches, the marketplace, negotiations, due diligence, intermediaries, and buy-sell agreements"--Provided by publisher.
        ISBN 1-57660-174-9 (alk. paper)
    1. Financial planners--United States--Handbooks, manuals, etc. 2. Investment advisors--United States--Handbooks, manuals, etc. 3. Business enterprises--Valuation--United States--Handbooks, manuals, etc. 4. Sale of business enterprises--United States--Handbooks, manuals, etc. 5. Business enterprises--United States--Purchasing--Handbooks, manuals, etc. I. Dahl, Owen. II. Title.

HG179.5.T527 2006
338.8'30243326--dc22

                                                                                          2006009550

Acquired by Jared Kieling
Edited by Mary Ann McGuigan

To my parents, Co and Marian Tibergien,
for indulging me just enough to pursue my dreams.
—MT

To Mom and Dad, for teaching me that
client service is not a concept, but a calling.
—OD

Contents

Part I | Defining Value

Part II | Assessing Value

Part III | Coming to Terms

Part IV | Ounces of Prevention

Part V | Inside Stories

Part VI | The Marketplace

Acknowledgments

A REFERENCE BOOK that tackles a complex topic requires the help of many people, and *How to Value, Buy, or Sell a Financial-Advisory Practice* was no different. We would like to acknowledge the valuable guidance on legal issues we received from Tom Giachetti, who heads the securities practice for the law firm of Stark & Stark in Princeton, New Jersey; Dick Fohn, a partner at Moss Adams, for his guidance on the tax issues; and Jet Wales, a principal at Moss Adams Capital, for his insight and wisdom on the elements of negotiating and structuring a transaction.

We owe a special thank-you to Mary Ann McGuigan, our editor at Bloomberg Press, for the extraordinary patience she showed as we attempted to pull our thoughts together and put them into words and for her careful attention to how we phrased each thought.

Jennifer Long and Cathleen Mohr, two key administrative people on our team at Moss Adams, also deserve recognition for their diligence in herding us toward the goal and in checking our work and challenging us on our wording at each stage.

Stephanie Rodriguez and Sarah Denkewalter made important contributions to the development of our case studies and examples, and we greatly appreciate their work.

We've benefited from working with many interesting clients and friends in the business who have gone through complicated transactions and who have provided us with important insights into how best to approach each deal. Rusty Benton of Wealth Trust, Liz Nesvold of Berkshire Capital, and Scott Roulston of Fairport Asset Management have been especially helpful in sharing ideas with us, as have the many participants in the Schwab Transition workshops.

David DeVoe who runs the Schwab Transition program helped

us think through many of the unique challenges that registered investment advisers have experienced at each step of the process, as has David Goad, who was the creator of FP Transitions and now runs Succession Planning Consultants, a consulting business to help advisers plan for their succession.

We would like to make a special acknowledgement to Mari Wruble, a former colleague of ours who contributed in a meaningful way to the development of the case studies in this book and to some of the technical concepts. Her work has helped us to sharpen the message.

There are many others who, in many different ways, helped us to knit together ideas that we hope will better prepare those wrestling with the issues of valuation, mergers, acquisitions, and sales of advisory firms for the process. Our thanks to all of them.

— ◆ —

Early in my career, I was recruited to Seattle by Shannon Pratt of Willamette Management Associates, Inc. As an early leader in the valuation profession and a current icon, he has led the way for many. I had the special benefit of having Shannon as a tutor on valuation principles and owe him a big thanks for being my teacher and for being an early influence in my pursuit of a profession.

— MT

Thank you to Bernie and Deborah Dahl of Assante Wealth Management for providing a front row seat to watch as British Columbia's venerable Reimer Financial Services was sold. More than anything, your experiences helped to remind us that a successful transaction relies as much on humanity as it does on economics and good counsel.

— OD

Introduction

MUCH HAS BEEN WRITTEN in the trade press about the value of financial-planning, wealth-management, and investment-management firms. This coverage—as well as the interest in it—has expanded as many prominent professionals in the business negotiate purchases and sales of such practices. Although the details of each deal are kept close to the vest, the rumored price and terms create a buzz that advisers can't ignore.

Owners of financial practices view these transactions with both excitement and trepidation. The excitement comes from knowing that there are buyers willing to pay rich prices for such businesses; the trepidation comes from thinking that this may be a window of opportunity they have little choice but to capitalize on soon. But we believe that well-managed firms will always be appealing to willing buyers.

This book lays out a number of issues that should help both buyers and sellers make judgments about the value of businesses. We also identify valuation considerations in the event of internal transition, partner admission, gift and estate tax, divorce, and even shareholder litigation. Value—like beauty—is in the eye of the beholder, but the principles of valuation have been constant for many years. Our goal with this book is to explain how to examine each of the variables and each of the assumptions that can shape conclusions on valuation. We also identify areas that owners can work on to enhance the value of an advisory business, provided they have enough time to plan for an orderly transition.

Not all practices are equal. And although it may be tempting to rely on rules of thumb and industry benchmarks to define value, we've seen so many deals in which the multiple and the terms have been different that we tend to be fairly cynical about whether such models deserve much weight. The Financial Services consulting team at Moss Adams has consulted with more than 1,000 financial-services organizations on issues related to valuation, succession planning, practice management, and mergers and acquisitions, and we rarely encounter exactly the same assumptions and conclusions being used among these firms.

So even if you're inclined to rely on what other firms are bought and sold for as the basis for valuing your business (or one that you're buying), we believe you'll find *How to Value, Buy, or Sell a Financial-Advisory Practice* helpful in setting values regardless of the purpose of the valuation.

In the first six chapters, we offer a complete analysis of valuation theory and practice and present two case studies to help illustrate the key considerations. Our purpose here is not to give you an exact answer as to the multiple you should use but to demonstrate how to think critically about the differences in practices and therefore the differences in valuations. In chapters 7 through 11, we identify key considerations in negotiating an agreement and setting the terms of a deal. We follow these chapters with a discussion of integration after the sale and key issues to be considered in planning an internal transition.

You'll also find ideas on how to select intermediaries to help you through the sale process and our opinions regarding the state of the market. We close the book with a critical look at how to build value for your firm. The sample documents and checklists offered in the appendix will be useful to anyone contemplating a purchase or sale, although we emphasize that these samples should not be copied but used only as a reference. Only a qualified attorney familiar with both the law and the nuances of your firm's circumstances can assist you in drafting documents.

As you prepare for the process of selling a practice, several key matters require your attention:

1. Be clear on what your goals are.
2. Begin building a history of the business by gathering relevant documents for the last three to five years.
3. Begin benchmarking your business against relevant industry standards to see how yours stacks up.

4. When negative variances show up in your benchmarks, think about the steps you need to take to close these gaps so that you can enhance value.

5. Remember, valuation is more art than science—the firm's numbers tell a story but so does its potential. Position your business so that you can improve your cash flow, minimize your risk, and manage your growth.

As you prepare to buy a practice, there are critical issues you must consider:

1. Value is a function of future potential, not the past results.

2. All firms are not created equal; therefore, rules of thumb are insufficient gauges.

3. Do your own due diligence; the seller's facts are not always as they seem.

4. The devil is in the details; focus on all the terms, not just the price.

And as you progress toward a final agreement, remember that whether you're buying or selling, the trouble you take to confirm the value of the practice while the deal is negotiated can only ensure greater rewards once it's sealed.

Defining
Value

1. UNCOVERING TRUE WORTH
Defining Value

NVESTMENT OR FINANCIAL-PLANNING professionals—like many small-business owners—often have an inflated perception of the value of their practice. That's because they typically have 15, 20, or 30 years of blood, sweat, and tears invested in the enterprise, and it has been a fountain of economic rewards during their working years. And they have heard many people quote market multiples that they are certain apply to their practices. But when you assess the value of a practice, shortcuts don't tell the whole story. You must look more closely to understand nuances like the quality of the client base and the future potential of the practice. It's also important to understand whether the firm is profitable in its current form and whether that profitability is sustainable.

For a buyer, a realistic understanding of the worth of the practice is essential to paying a fair price. And clarity on these principles will make sellers more effective negotiators. This chapter outlines the valuation process and highlights the factors that drive practice value. Subsequent chapters will address the mechanics of valuation, deal structure, internal versus external transactions, and other factors that should help you prepare for this process regardless of which side of the deal you're on.

The Unruly Rule of Thumb

For a business as straightforward as financial planning, many ideas that circulate about how to value a financial-advisory practice are surprisingly convoluted. Each month, Moss Adams LLP receives scores of calls from advisers who want us to tell them the rule of thumb for valuing a practice. "Is it the multiple of gross?" they ask. "The multiple of assets under management? The multiple of EBITDA [earnings before interest, taxes, depreciation, and amortization]?"

Especially maddening is that some practices actually do sell for a rule-of-thumb price. That doesn't mean it's an appropriate price, but it happens nevertheless. The good news for sellers is that these rising multiples are enhancing the value of their practices every day, and consequently these advisers are in a unique position to capitalize in a big way on the businesses they've built. But some important issues are essential for both buyers and sellers to consider in determining value.

The rule-of-thumb methodology presumes that all advisory practices are equal. Such assumptions are just as faulty in comparing advisory firms as they are in comparing stocks. If the price of Starbucks falls below the price that Microsoft is selling for, does that make it a better buy? The question is obviously not relevant because their economics are different. What's more, each investor's perception of risk and growth is different.

The inclination to rely on a rule of thumb makes it clear that buyers and sellers of advisory practices view these transactions as they do the purchase and sale of a house. In real estate, one can look at a neighborhood, measure the square footage, see if it has a view and come up with a price. Buyers of homes don't usually calculate with accuracy what kind of return on investment they'll get with this purchase, because the whole point is to acquire an asset that they can live in and possibly sell for a gain down the road. Perhaps it's because buyers of advisory practices look at these firms as a means to an end, a necessary component for their lifestyle, a job, that they fall into this home buyer's approach to pricing them.

But advisory firms are not tangible assets like houses or cars; they're living, breathing entities with multiple nuances that could affect their value. What's the potential in the client base? How old are the clients? How profitable is the service model? Will clients accept the new adviser? What's the expense structure? What's the motivation of the buyer? of the seller?

Distorting Value

Rules of thumb tend to distort value. Even market comparables tend to distort value because of the unique characteristics of each business being sold, as well as the particular motivations of the buyers and sellers. We encountered an example of this when we were asked to evaluate a practice on behalf of a buyer–in fact, the buyer was in a bidding war to acquire the business. The owner of the practice had died suddenly, and his widow engaged a broker to find a buyer. The broker set the price at 2.5 times trailing 12 months' gross revenues. He advised our client not to bother offering anything less. In probing for the opportunity in this practice, we found that 40 percent of the clients were past the age of 70 and many were already withdrawing principal. None were contributing more cash to invest. Looking at the mortality rate of this client base gave the buyer enough pause not to step up to this multiple.

Oddly enough though, sometimes sellers don't realize what their firms have to offer. Again, relying on stated market rules of thumb, one adviser actually undervalued his practice. His average client was a business owner or executive, age 45, whose income was increasing each year and who was contributing substantial new assets yearly. The growth rate for the foreseeable future was exponential, and the practice was extraordinarily profitable, but by relying on the rule of thumb, the owner appraised his practice as "average." He now knows that the only time you should aspire to be average is when you are below it.

The Need for Valuation

Drawbacks aside, rules of thumb and market comparables come in handy as a starting point for a discussion of value. For the buyer, however, that figure should rarely be the end point. So many factors related to structure, financing, terms, and taxes go into a deal that there should be give-and-take in every situation. The key question the buyer of a practice should be asking is, "What is a reasonable rate of return on cash flow when I make this acquisition?" By beginning there, the buyer can move toward an understanding of the principles of business valuation.

It is unnecessary for buyers or sellers to obtain a formal valuation before entering into a merger or sale discussion. Sellers often have an idea of the price they want for the business regardless of economic reality. Buyers, however, will benefit from some form of valuation process. It provides a foundation for early negotiations and will help them put their thoughts through an economic filter. Since most people in the financial-advisory business are financially astute, the valuation process should be easy to relate to.

If a buyer or seller does go through a formal valuation process, the evaluator should consider key standards, such as:

1. Market prices of comparable publicly traded companies
2. Transaction values of similar entities
3. A discounted cash flow analysis of the business being valued
4. A detailed and specific analysis of the entity and the market conditions in which it operates

Typically, the first three benchmarks are given less weight than the specific analysis, but they're considered nonetheless. In using a rule of thumb—or market comparables—only one perspective is considered. Such a single-lens view is a little like making investment recommendations for your clients based on the last conference speaker you heard: compelling but incomplete.

Standards of Value

There are numerous ways to measure the value of a business. Two key questions are essential to beginning the valuation process:

1. What is the purpose?
2. What is being valued?

The answers to these questions determine the purpose of the valuation and dictate which standard of value applies and whether it's appropriate to consider discounts or premiums in deriving the value.

What Is the Purpose?

Fair market value and fair value. The standards of value relied on for tax, litigation, or contractual purposes are referred to as fair market value and fair value. Fair market value is the standard used in the context of gift and estate tax and sometimes applies in the division of assets in divorce. As promulgated by Revenue Ruling 59-60, fair market value defines a value at which an asset or business would change hands between a typical *willing buyer* and *willing seller*, neither party being under any obligation and both parties being fully informed of all the facts. Fair value is a standard usually defined by state law and is typically used in divorce, partnership, and shareholder disputes and sometimes in buy-sell agreements.

It's quite possible that valuing an asset for tax, divorce, or litigation purposes will result in a conclusion different from that which results in the process used to determine value for purchase or sale. In the case of litigation or divorce or estate tax, however, the emphasis is not on a real-life transaction. When a sale or purchase is contemplated, fair market value may be a starting point, but other factors, including the motivations of the buyers and sellers, could change the result. Another standard—investment value—may also come into play, however, because this standard considers the potential synergy of the two businesses, a measure that's quite useful for some owners and sellers.

Investment value. The term *investment value* as used here is defined in the American Society of Appraisers' *Business Valuation Glossary* as the value to a particular investor based on individual investment requirements and expectations. Investment value is different from fair market value, which is value to a typical buyer and seller, for various reasons, including:

♦ Economies of scale available with the buyer's operations
♦ Synergies available with the buyer's operations
♦ Differences in future earnings estimates
♦ Differences in perceived risk
♦ Differences in tax status

Using investment value as the primary premise of value is inappropriate in the sale of an advisory practice because the seller should not receive all of the synergistic value; nor should the seller expect to receive the full premium. That premium should be considered as part of the negotiation process.

What's Being Valued?

Many assume that what's being valued is the entire business. But there are situations in which portions of the business may have to be valued separately. The difference would influence whether one applies a control premium or a minority or nonmarketability discount to the price. It's all a function of rights.

The more rights the owner has—such as the right to liquidate the business, declare dividends, or sell major assets—the greater the premium applied. A discount is applied based on the transferability of the asset, lack of voting rights, or lack of a ready market. These matters become important to define in the context of litigation, shareholder disputes, divorce, or the admission of partners or when using stock as currency in a transaction (see *Figure 1.1*).

The factors related to defining value also play a role in translating market rules of thumb into your planning. We often see buy-sell agreements with multiple shareholders in which the value of each ownership interest is based on an enterprise value, meaning 100 percent control divided by the number of shares. The challenge with this

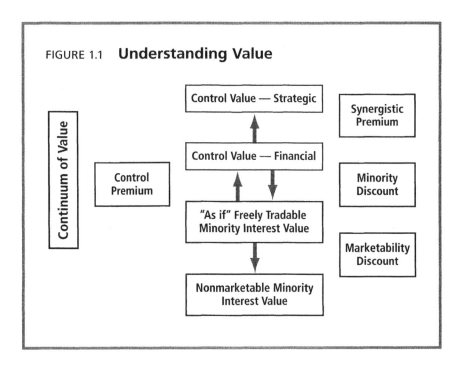

FIGURE 1.1   **Understanding Value**

approach is that most of the shareholders in these companies cannot do the things they could if they had control (usually 51 percent of the equity). Market multiples are generally on a minority, fully marketable basis, whereas transaction multiples are always based on control, so you must be careful to compare apples to apples.

The Valuation Process

In principle, the value of an investment equals the present value of expected future returns from the investment. Various methods may be used to estimate the value of a business-ownership interest. Broadly categorized, these methods separate into three approaches:

♦ **Cost- or asset-based approach.** In this method, the assets and liabilities of the business are restated from historical cost to fair market value.

♦ **Market approach.** This technique uses valuation ratios derived from market transactions involving companies that are similar to the business being valued. Past transactions, if any, involving the business are also considered.

♦ **Income approach.** In this method, expected future returns from an investment are discounted to present value at an appropriate rate of return for the investment.

Cost- or Asset-Based Approach

The cost or asset approach in this context refers to balance sheet assets, not assets under management (AUM). In the cost- or asset-based approach, net asset value is estimated by restating the value of assets and liabilities from historical cost to fair market value. Assets and liabilities can be valued either individually or collectively. Individual assets and liabilities of a business can be appraised using the cost, market, and income approaches to asset valuation.

Because most investment and financial-advisory practices do not have much in the way of tangible assets, accounts receivables, or work in process (WIP), this approach is not likely to have much weight in valuing such a practice.

The Market Approach

The market approach involves a comparison of the subject company to similar businesses, business ownership interests, securities that have been sold or are actively traded, and previous transactions involving the subject company. The method uses valuation ratios based on current market prices and historical (or projected) financial data for the guideline companies. Selected valuation ratios derived from the analysis—such as price/revenue, price/AUM, and price/EBITDA— are then applied to the subject company's adjusted historical (or projected) financial results to arrive at indications of value.

Most practitioners would like to have an easy formula—a rule of thumb—to determine the value of a practice. Typically the rule of thumb for the financial-advisory profession is a multiple of gross revenue or a percentage of assets under management. People often estimate the value of advisory firms at somewhere between one and two times gross revenue or between 1 percent and 2 percent of assets under management. We use the term *financial-advisory practice* generically here. Our observation is that commission-based practices tend to command multiples in the lower end of these ranges because their revenue is not as consistent and predictable.

As advisory firms become larger—for example, when they're responsible for more than $1 billion of assets under management— the multiples that buyers are willing to pay increase. That's because they perceive a lower risk and greater growth potential because of how the business has been institutionalized. According to Liz Nesvold, an investment banker with Berkshire Capital who specializes in wealth-management firms, multiples in the range of eight to 12 times EBITDA for larger firms are not uncommon.

The Income Approach

The method most likely to result in sound economic judgments in valuing an advisory practice is the income approach. There are two related income-approach valuation methods: capitalization of cash flow and discounted cash flow. *Capitalization of cash flow analysis* uses forecasted cash flow for the next period, which is converted to present value using an appropriate capitalization rate equal to a discount rate less the expected growth rate in perpetuity. In a *discounted*

FIGURE 1.2 **Capitalization of Cash Flow Calculation**

$$\text{Value} = \frac{\text{Adjusted Cash Flow}}{\text{Capitalization Rate}}$$

(Discount Rate – Growth Rate)

cash flow analysis, free cash flows are forecast for a discrete period of years (typically estimated over a three- to five-year period beginning on the valuation date). Beyond the five-year period, a terminal or residual value is calculated using an appropriate capitalization rate. The free cash flows and residual value are converted to present value using an appropriate discount rate or rate of return (see *Figure 1.2*).

Many professional buyers and investment bankers tend to rely less on discounted cash flow (DCF) as the basis for pricing. That's because they typically are in tune with the market, are experienced in their analysis of such businesses, and tend to find that market metrics serve as a better guide in their negotiations. This is not to diminish the value of the market approach but rather to acknowledge that those who have not bought or sold businesses before should force themselves to analyze the economics, because recognition of pitfalls in such transactions will not come as easily to them as it does to the experienced eye.

Tying It Together

The valuation process has many moving parts: market prices, rules of thumb, motives of both parties, cash flow potential, risk, transferability, and so on.

That's why business valuation can be more art than science. But regardless of how you approach it, there are three key points to remember when looking at the value of a financial-advisory practice:

1. What is not transferable does not have value.
2. Value ultimately is a function of future expectations.
3. Not all practices are created equal.

2. EVALUATING FISCAL HEALTH
Defining Value

BEFORE YOU CAN APPLY a valuation approach to a business, you need to have a thorough understanding of the business itself. That understanding must include not only the internal operations but also external factors, such as trends in the economy and the industry. The business analysis will indicate the level of risk the business entails, which is an integral part of valuing a company.

Evaluating a Firm's Fiscal Health

Measuring the Effects of Economic Conditions

Generally speaking, economic analysis is a key factor in the valuation of businesses that are affected by changes in economic conditions and provide services for which demand is highly elastic. To businesses that provide services considered essential, changes in the economy are far less important. But the financial-planning industry is definitely vulnerable to changes in the economy, so an economic analysis is a very important part of the valuation process.

Economic analysis provides insight into clients' propensity to save or spend money and other factors that affect a firm's profit margins. Key economic variables include but are not limited to gross domestic product, gross national product, disposable personal income, and interest rates. In addition, depending on the business, it may be necessary to analyze the local economies in which the firm operates. The broader the geographic market, the less risk sensitive a company is to one local economy. Local economies that are dominated by a particular industry or company can play a big role in the fortunes of financial advisers, especially to the extent the adviser's client base is drawn from individuals working for a single big employer or its vendors.

One demographic factor that makes income for advisory services less variable in the near term is the growing number of people nearing retirement and the trillions of dollars of concentrated wealth that will be distributed upon the death of its holders. The millennium market crash also caused many financial-planning "do-it-yourselfers" to recognize the value of advice, especially in a low- or zero-growth market environment. Between 2000 and 2004, the number of advisory firms doing more than $1 million in annual revenue doubled, according to the *2004 FPA Financial Performance Study of Financial Advisory Practices* sponsored by SEI Investments, and the number of advisory firms growing beyond $10 million is a major part of that trend.

That said, another market crash or an economy weakened by the country's unfavorable trade balance and the federal deficit could undermine the markets and, therefore, the net worth of individuals worldwide. So although there may be a demand for services, advisers whose primary source of income depends solely on the performance of assets under management could find their net revenues severely affected.

Understanding the Industry

The industry factor most important to the valuation process is the market outlook for that industry. Market outlook conveys the stage of growth the industry is experiencing—whether it's high growth, mature, stagnant, or declining. All things being equal, companies in a high-growth cycle are typically worth more than those in a declining or stagnant market.

There are several other key industry factors to consider: Who are the big players overall in the industry? Is the industry consolidating? Who are the company's primary competitors within its market? How do the company's strengths and weaknesses compare with those of its competitors? What threats do new entrants in the market present? What are the technological changes in the industry, and what potential impact or risk do they impose on the company? What is the regulatory environment like? Are the attitudes of regulators and legislators rapidly changing, thereby increasing the riskiness of the business? How is the company responding to the regulatory environment?

In examining the businesses of financial planning, investment management, securities and insurance brokerage, and wealth management, it's clear that all of these factors play a part in valuation. Studies by Tiburon Strategic Advisors (August 2004) and J.P. Morgan/ Fleming (June 2005) indicate that the advisory profession is on the precipice of a consolidation trend. The trend has been caused by rising operating costs, increasing pressure on compliance, and the aging of the adviser population in the face of greater demand for services. What's more, advisers today are faced with a shortage of qualified talent and increasing pressures on regulatory compliance, which make the marginal firms less appealing unless they can be folded into a larger practice that has systems in place to address both issues.

In spite of these margin, talent, client, and regulatory squeezes, it appears that at least for a while longer, it's a seller's market. Large institutional buyers and smaller independent firms see tremendous growth opportunities in the business and appear to believe they can achieve profitable growth while maintaining the personal touch through the acquisition of advisory firms. Eventually, of course, the selling prices firms can command will revert to the mean as economic logic takes root. But strategic buyers recognize the need to be quick to the market with high-impact acquisitions, a pattern that has caused the prices of practices to rise.

Reviewing Internal Operations

Analyzing internal operations is a qualitative process that involves evaluating how the firm operates in comparison with its peers and its own past performance. Certain characteristics of the business affect the future of the company and its performance relative to its history. Key factors in financial planning and wealth-management firms, for example, include such things as how the company charges for its services. Fee-only firms generate higher values than commission-only or fee-based practices, for example, but even how a firm structures its fees—retainers, asset-management fees, or hourly—makes a difference in the profitability and sustainability of the business. Other qualitative factors include:

♦ **Clearly defined strategy:** A more clearly defined and executed business strategy can reduce risk because the company is better able to focus on clients, services, markets, and personnel that fit within a framework. Strategies could include investing in a niche, such as evangelical Christians or the gay and lesbian market; being known for a technical specialty, such as executive stock-option planning; leveraging a unique sales method, such as formal strategic alliances; or being recognized as the lowest-cost provider.

♦ **Key personnel:** The more a company relies on a key employee or an owner, the greater the risk that the company will lose its client base if that person leaves the firm. This is especially true if no non-compete or other such agreements exist. The nature of the advisory profession lends itself to building a practice around an individual's technical skills and personality, but real value comes from transforming the practice into an enterprise whose value is transferable. In the first situation, what's for sale is a book of business, a list of clients; in the latter, one is selling an enterprise with people, systems, brand recognition, *and* clients.

♦ **Average age of client base:** The older the client base, the riskier the revenue source because revenue generated from aging clients generally declines as they get older. A buyer might pay a premium for a firm because he can envision a consistent cash flow for a long period of time. In firms where clients are beginning to withdraw principal and not contributing more assets (or, in the case of insurance practices, are no longer insurable), the future opportunities for that business are diminished and so, therefore, is its value.

♦ **Workforce:** Having a staff with less experience and education may be riskier than having employees with appropriate designations and experience, who can properly serve and advise the clients. In analyzing a practice, it's helpful to know which employees might remain with the firm and what their roles and potential contributions will be.

♦ **Average account size:** The larger the average account size, the easier it becomes to reach critical mass, which can lower risk in a company. Of course, if only a few large clients account for the majority of the firm's revenues, the risk associated with losing one or more of the clients is very significant. A key question to ask is, How have the average account sizes increased over time and why? Further, is this pattern likely to continue?

♦ **Economies of scale:** Larger companies can achieve efficiencies by appropriately leveraging staff, whereas a solo practice may achieve certain efficiencies through outsourcing.

♦ **Pricing policy:** Having a pricing policy in line with the firm's business strategy improves profitability overall, thereby increasing value. One challenge in selling a practice is finding a buyer whose pricing strategy is compatible with the seller's. Some advisers, for example, view commission practices as gold mines because they see the opportunity to increase margins dramatically by shifting how clients pay for services. But such a transition can be annoying if not traumatic to the clients and may result in high attrition.

♦ **Capacity:** Companies that have appropriate capacity, in terms of both facilities and employees, are better able to manage their current client base and growth than a company at or exceeding capacity. There is a physical limit to how many active client relationships any one adviser can manage. This ceiling limits growth unless the firm adds capacity. (This issue may also be a consideration for buyers: if the buyer does not have the capacity to digest the number of clients the firm is taking on, then the likelihood of attrition is high. Sellers should worry about this likelihood too if the ultimate payment is based on an earnout.)

♦ **Client turnover:** A study commissioned by Fidelity Investments in May 2005 estimated that the attrition rate among clients upon the sale of a practice can be as high as 40 percent. The history of client turnover in a practice may be an indicator of the extent to which the client base is at risk.

♦ **Client satisfaction:** As a matter of practice, every adviser contemplating the sale of his or her practice should be conducting client satisfaction surveys for several years prior to the sale. From a valuation standpoint, the buyer should evaluate through a similar process the performance of the advisory firm in serving its clients' needs. The result could raise or lower the buyer's confidence in the likelihood of retaining clients.

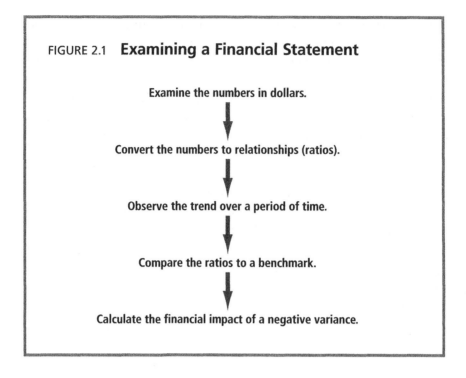

FIGURE 2.1 **Examining a Financial Statement**

Examine the numbers in dollars.

Convert the numbers to relationships (ratios).

Observe the trend over a period of time.

Compare the ratios to a benchmark.

Calculate the financial impact of a negative variance.

Analyzing the Financial Information

The process for analyzing an advisory firm's financial statements should be logical and linear.

The process depicted in *Figure 2.1* allows you to quickly assess problems and observe patterns. By converting numbers into ratios, you can translate the financials into a more meaningful analytical process. By calculating the financial impact of negative variances, you can measure the magnitude of the problem.

You'll need to organize the firm's financial statements in a way that makes it easier to interpret results. Ideally, the advisory firm would have both a balance sheet and an income statement. For the purpose of analysis, you'll want to look at financial statements for back-to-back years. The number of years that should be analyzed is largely dependent on the cyclicality of the business environment. If the industry has a 10-year cycle, then 10 years of financial performance should be analyzed. For financial-advisory firms, you would ideally analyze a minimum of three years and optimally five.

Evaluating the Income Statement

The income statement is the most revealing document in a financial-advisory practice because this is where you can isolate the management issues, such as poor productivity, poor pricing, or poor cost control. Observing the ratios in relationship to a benchmark and to a trend over several periods will help put the problem into context. Use industry benchmarks, such as those published by Moss Adams and the Financial Planning Association, or other relevant industry standards that are published by the CFA Institute, the Securities Industry Association (SIA), or the Risk Management Association (RMA). The firm's best year or some other objective target also makes a good benchmark or goal.

The income statement in *Figure 2.2* profiles a practice that generates $1 million in annual revenue. Let's assume it has one owner, one other financial adviser who's an associate, and four support staff. The compensation of the owner and financial adviser are charged to direct expense; the support staff salaries and all other overhead are charged to overhead. In this example, $250,000 is left over in operating profit, which the owner can choose to retain in the business, distribute as profit sharing to the staff, or pay out to himself as a dividend. This amount is the reward received over and above base compensation for labor in recognition of the special risks taken as the owner of the enterprise.

Analyzing at least three to five years of historical financial data renders the most meaningful results. The reliability of the financial statements themselves can also be an issue. Although it is uncommon

FIGURE 2.2 **Income Statement**

Revenue	$1,000,000	100%
Direct Expense	400,000	40
Gross Profit	600,000	60
Overhead Expense	350,000	35
Operating Profit	250,000	25

for smaller advisory firms to have reviewed or audited financial statements, such statements would be ideal because they follow generally
accepted accounting principles. Tax returns are adequate because
the Internal Revenue Service demands a greater level of accuracy,
but financial statements for tax purposes tend to produce a different
result than financial statements for management purposes. Internal
financial statements can also be quite problematic because they often
do not follow a standard, and costs and revenue are often booked in
creative ways to help the business owner achieve certain goals.

Ironically, one of the challenges in appraising financial-advisory
firms is that the quality of financial information is generally poor.
Often, firms do not have a balance sheet because it's mistakenly
believed that assets (and, in some cases, liabilities) do not exist in
advisory businesses. The income statement is usually presented as a
general ledger, which is not a meaningful management tool. There
tends to be a multitude of personal and unrelated expenses on the
statements as well. As owners begin to prepare for the review process,
they should do as much as they can to make these statements more
understandable to both their investment bankers or consultants and
prospective buyers.

The three categories on the income statement to evaluate are (1)
revenues, (2) gross profit margin, and (3) operating profit margin.

Revenues. Sources of revenue and how the company charges for
its services may vary significantly among financial-advisory firms.
Fee-only firms, for example, usually produce higher values than
commission-only firms, but a firm's fee structure—which can range
from retainers to hourly—affects a firm's value and potential. Trends
should be looked at carefully. Are the revenues growing over time?
Are they moving in a smooth and consistent fashion, or do they move
erratically up and down? Investors value predictability and prefer
more consistent movements over large swings.

Gross profit margin. Gross profit margin is what's left over after
fair compensation is paid to professional staff, including the owner.
These expenses are called *direct expenses* because they're directly
related to the generation of revenue. If this were a manufacturing
or retail business, a direct expense would be the same thing as a
cost of goods sold. When the compensation to owners has not been

clearly or fairly defined, it's best to plug in benchmark compensation data. Good sources for determining fair compensation are the Moss Adams *Compensation and Staffing Study* available through the Financial Planning Association, as well as the data compiled by the CFA Institute and by Salary.com. To whatever extent advisers in the business are paid a commission or some form of variable compensation, that compensation structure is likely to continue after the sale and these numbers should be left alone.

Gross profit margin is determined by dividing gross profit dollars by total revenue. For example, if your gross profit dollars are $600,000 and your revenues are $1,000,000, the result would be expressed as a 60 percent gross profit margin. Put another way, for every dollar of revenue, you're generating $0.60 in gross profit.

Operating profit margin. The operating profit margin is calculated by dividing operating profit by total revenue. For example, if your operating profit is $150,000 and your revenues are $1,000,000, your operating profit margin would be 15 percent. Expressed another way, you would be generating $0.15 of operating profit for every dollar of revenue generated.

A decline in operating profit can have as many as three causes:

1. A declining gross profit
2. Insufficient revenue volume to support the infrastructure expenses
3. Poor expense control

Common sizing. One technique for evaluating the cost-control problem is to use common sizing, in which an item is used as a base value and all other accounts in the financial statement are compared to this base value. On the balance sheet, total assets equal 100 percent, and each asset is stated as a percentage of total assets. Similarly, total liabilities and stockholders' equity are assigned 100 percent, with a given liability or equity account stated as a percentage of total liabilities and stockholders' equity. On the income statement, 100 percent is assigned to net sales, with all revenue and expense accounts related to it expressed as percentages. Common sizing helps identify anomalies and trends from year to year and eases the process of comparing the firm to other companies within the industry.

FIGURE 2.3

	Financial Planner Income Statement		Benchmarks — Averages from FPA Study			
			$1MM–$2.5MM in Revenue		High Profit Ensembles	
Revenue:						
Asset Management Fees	$1,180,000	91.5%	$1,074,737	70.0%	$1,403,581	74.6%
Planning & Consulting Fees	10,000	0.8	139,510	9.1	168,594	9.0
Securities Commissions	—	0.0	108,878	7.1	84,884	4.5
Insurance Commissions	—	0.0	68,461	4.5	51,265	2.7
Trails & Renewals	100,000	7.8	95,769	6.2	97,866	5.2
Other Revenue		0.0	47,931	3.1	74,598	4.0
Total Revenue	**$1,290,000**	**100.0%**	**$1,535,287**	**100.0%**	**$1,880,788**	**100.0%**
Direct Expenses:						
Professional Salaries	$400,000	31.0%	$283,030	18.4%	$337,434	17.9%
Commissions Paid (Contract Adv Fees)			78,971	5.1	28,232	1.5
Owner's Draws or Base Compensation	350,000	27.1	272,939	17.8	336,521	17.9
Total Direct Expense	**$750,000**	**58.1%**	**$634,939**	**41.4%**	**$702,187**	**37.3%**
Gross Profit	**$540,000**	**41.9%**	**$900,348**	**58.6%**	**$1,178,601**	**62.7%**
Overhead Expenses:						
Advertising/Public Relations/Marketing	$7,000	0.5%	$20,456	1.3%	$23,027	1.2%
Auto Expenses	—	0.0	10,546	0.7	9,007	0.5
Charitable Contributions	—	0.0	2,661	0.2	3,274	0.2
Client Appreciation	4,000	0.3	6,355	0.4	6,409	0.3
Depreciation/Amortization	—	0.0	20,907	1.4	23,086	1.2
Dues – Clubs	3,000	0.2	1,823	0.1	1,750	0.1
Dues – Professional	8,000	0.6	4,071	0.3	4,641	0.2
Employee Benefits	81,000	6.3	52,143	3.4	71,697	3.8
Equipment Leases/Purchases	6,000	0.5	13,673	0.9	12,959	0.7
Insurance	25,000	1.9	21,830	1.4	22,840	1.2
Office Expense	19,000	1.5	29,056	1.9	34,370	1.8
Other Salaries	89,000	6.9	161,236	10.5	178,604	9.5
Payroll Taxes	50,000	3.9	50,530	3.3	46,401	2.5
Professional Services	47,000	3.6	24,374	1.6	29,047	1.5
Rent	53,000	4.1	81,052	5.3	88,568	4.7
Repairs & Maintenance	1,000	0.1	5,158	0.3	3,543	0.2
Software/Hardware Expense	24,000	1.9	19,077	1.2	20,415	1.1
Tax & Licenses	—	0.0	7,093	0.5	10,036	0.5
Training & Continuing Education	11,000	0.9	7,894	0.5	8,165	0.4
Travel & Entertainment	48,000	3.7	20,161	1.3	19,403	1.0
Utilities/Phone/Fax/Online Service	19,000	1.5	18,044	1.2	17,111	0.9
All Other Expenses	3,000	0.2	42,765	2.8	36,463	1.9
Total Overhead Expense	**$498,000**	**38.6%**	**$620,904**	**40.4%**	**$670,814**	**35.7%**
Operating Income	**$42,000**	**3.3%**	**$279,444**	**18.2%**	**$507,787**	**27.0%**
Other Income/Expense:						
Other Income	$—	0.0%	$8,071	0.5%	$6,093	0.3%
Other Expense (–)	(2,000)	–0.2	(15,819)	–1.0	(13,375)	–0.7
Owner's Bonus	(30,000)	–2.3	(94,263)	–6.1	(135,701)	–7.2
Total Other Income (Expense)	**$(32,000)**	**–2.5%**	**$(102,012)**	**–6.6%**	**$(142,983)**	**–7.6%**
Profit Before Tax	**$10,000**	**0.8%**	**$177,432**	**11.6%**	**$364,804**	**19.4%**

Source: © Moss Adams, 2004 FPA Financial Performance Study of Financial Advisory Practices (SEI Investments and Financial Planning Association, September 2004)

Figure 2.3 compares the one-year, common-size income statement for one financial-advisory firm to industry benchmarks from the annual *FPA Financial Performance Study of Financial Advisory Practices* conducted by Moss Adams.

In evaluating the income statement, common sizing means that all costs are expressed as a percentage of revenue. In financial analysis, it's helpful to observe the trends in that percentage over a period of time (three to five years). If costs are rising as a percentage of revenue—especially when revenues are rising—the business has a problem with expense control. Such trends beg for an explanation. Is it because the owner is investing in infrastructure? Or has she had to add administrative staff to serve a larger client base? From a valuation perspective, the bigger question is whether that high overhead cost base is reasonable and sustainable.

When gross profit is the culprit in lower profitability, the cause is invariably one of five factors:

1. Poor pricing
2. Poor productivity
3. Poor service or product mix
4. Poor client mix
5. Poor payout

In an optimal practice, the advisory firm should be maintaining an overhead expense ratio of no greater than 35 percent of revenue, meaning that for every $1.00 of revenue, the firm spends $0.35 on things like rent, administrative and management salaries, marketing, and other overhead. Ideally, the firm would also be maintaining a gross profit margin in the range of 60 percent, meaning that for every $1.00 of revenue, the business is not spending more than $0.40 on professional compensation and referral fees. For many practice valuations, adjustments will have to be made to reflect fair compensation to the professional staff, especially in cases where the owner of the practice is also an adviser (which is most of the time).

Other adjustments include nonrecurring or nonoperating items. These are "unusual" expenses that are not always directly related to ongoing operations. Some companies list such items almost every year. How do these reflect on the earnings quality? For income tax

---

FIGURE 2.4 **Profitability Ratio Calculations**

- ◆ Gross profit margin % = Gross profit / Revenue
- ◆ Operating profit margin % = Operating profit / Revenue
- ◆ Pretax profit margin % = Profit before tax / Revenue
- ◆ Net margin % = Profit after tax / Revenue
- ◆ EBIT margin % = Earnings before interest and taxes / Revenue
- ◆ EBITDA margin % = Earnings before interest, taxes, depreciation, and amortization / Revenue

---

FIGURE 2.5 **Productivity Ratio Calculations**

- ◆ Number of clients per staff = Number of clients / Number of full-time equivalent staff
- ◆ Number of clients per professional = Number of clients / Number of professionals (including owners)
- ◆ Assets under management (AUM) per staff = AUM / Number of full-time equivalent staff
- ◆ AUM per professional = AUM / Number of professionals (including owners)
- ◆ Revenue per staff = Revenue / Number of full-time equivalent staff
- ◆ Revenue per professional = Revenue / Number of professionals (including owners)
- ◆ AUM per client = AUM / Number of clients at year-end
- ◆ AUM per active client = AUM / Number of active clients at year-end
- ◆ Revenue per client = Revenue / Number of clients at year-end
- ◆ Revenue per active client = Revenue / Number of active clients at year-end
- ◆ Operating profit per client = Operating profit / Number of clients at year-end
- ◆ Operating profit per active client = Operating profit / Number of active clients at year-end

---

purposes, owners may include expenses other than those directly related to the business. To lower his tax basis, one owner included expenses that belonged to a building he owned outside of the com-

---

FIGURE 2.6   **Liquidity and Solvency Ratios**

♦ Current ratio = Current assets / Current liabilities. This is a measure of liquidity, the ability to pay one's bills.
♦ Debt-to-equity ratio = Total liabilities / Equity. This is a measure of solvency, the ability to withstand adversity.

---

pany. Another owner, whose firm was a C corporation, paid out significant bonuses at year-end to zero out the tax basis. Nonrecurring items may include one-time moving expenses, legal fees associated with a lawsuit, or consulting services related to conversion to a new software package. These items should be removed for valuation purposes.

Profitability and productivity ratios. Certain other ratios should also be computed to spot trends and compare the firm with others in the industry (see *Figures 2.4* and *2.5*). Important ratios in the financial-planning industry include profitability and productivity ratios. If balance sheets are available, then efficiency, liquidity, and solvency ratios should also be analyzed (see *Figure 2.6*).

The linear process suitable to analyzing financial statements for valuation includes these steps:

1. **Examine the numbers:** Are the actual dollar amounts growing or shrinking?

2. **Convert the numbers into ratios:** By considering each number in relation to another, it's easier to observe patterns.

3. **Observe trends.** Ratios by themselves are interesting, but it's even more critical to observe the trend in these ratios over a period of three to five years to detect improvement or deterioration.

4. **Compare with benchmarks:** Often, it's best to compare a firm's performance with its own best year or an average of previous years; however, the true measure of success is how the firm's ratios compare with the industry standards. This may lead to an adjustment of the valuation up or down.

5. **Calculate the impact of negative variance:** Translating the negative variance into a dollar amount reveals the magnitude problem. For

example, if the benchmark for operating profit is 25 percent, but the subject practice has a profit margin of 20 percent, you can calculate the size of the problem by multiplying the 5 percent variance times the total revenue of the practice (example .05 × $1,000,000 = $50,000). This may also give you a sense of whether the business has hidden economic opportunity. But this should be done only after adjustments have been made for nonrecurring and nonoperating items.

For more detail on the financial management of a financial-advisory practice, please see *Practice Made Perfect: The Discipline of Business Management for Financial Advisers* by Mark Tibergien and Rebecca Pomering (Bloomberg Press, 2005). The book walks advisers through examples of how to apply benchmark data and how to interpret financial results in a way that can make them more effective at analyzing practice performance.

Real-Time Ratios

Figure 2.7 compares the vital profitability and productivity ratios of a financial-advisory firm compared with those of benchmark firms from an FPA study.

Compared with the companies in its industry peer group shown in Figure 2.7, this firm's clients appear to have more assets under management. But this apparent advantage should be further analyzed to determine the true makeup of the client base. If the company has one or two clients holding the majority of AUM, that makes it a much riskier firm than a company that has the majority of its clients in its sweet spot of $1 million of AUM each.

Revenue per client for this company is significantly higher than the industry average, but operating profit is well below. It may be that the company uses more professional staff, who are paid more than administrative staff, than is typical in the industry.

In *Figure 2.8,* company A is an example of a practice that has shown good year-to-year revenue growth but declining profits. What is the source of this declining profitability? Is it a cost-control problem? Or is it a productivity problem?

The reason for company A's declining operating profit is its declining gross profit margin. In a valuation of this advisory firm, you must determine the cause of this decline—whether it's pricing, productivity,

FIGURE 2.7 **Median Operational Ratios**
Ensemble Practices by Income per Owner

	Financial Planner	FPA Study $1MM–$2.5MM	High Profit Ensembles
Assets Under Management	$225,000,000	$190,000,000	$200,000,000
Revenue	$1,290,000	$1,408,918	$1,300,000
Clients (by family, could be multiple clients & accounts)	138	251	250
Median Gross Margin	41.9%	58.8%	61.6%
Median Operating Profit Margin	3.3%	12.2%	22.8%
Pretax Income	$10,000	$227,363	$327,000
Staff Head Count:			
Principals	2.0	2.0	2.0
Professionals	3.5	2.0	2.0
Reps/Contractors	0.0	0.0	0.0
Support Staff	2.0	3.0	2.0
Admin Staff	0.5	2.0	2.0
Total Head Count (sum of above)	**8.0**	**9.0**	**8.0**
Clients per Principal & Professional	25	63	125
Clients per Principal, Professional & Support	18	36	42
Revenue per Principal & Professional	$234,545	$352,230	$325,000
Revenue per Principal, Professional & Support	$172,000	$201,274	$216,667
AUM per Principal & Professional	$40,909,091	$47,500,000	$50,000,000
AUM per Principal, Professional & Support	$30,000,000	$27,142,857	$33,333,333
Revenue per Client	$9,348	$5,613	$5,200
AUM per Client	$1,630,435	$756,972	$800,000
Operating Profit per Client	$304	$944	$1,440

FIGURE 2.8 **Company A's Financial Statement**

	2004	% of Revenue	2005	% of Revenue
Revenue	$1,680,000	100%	$1,730,000	100%
Direct Expense	789,000	47	899,000	52
Gross Profit	891,000	53	831,000	48
Overhead Expense	655,000	39	675,000	39
Operating Profit	236,000	14	156,000	9

client mix—before you can evaluate the quality of the business and its sustainability. When the gross profit margin is deteriorating, the uncertainty of an enterprise's achieving acceptable levels of return is increased. More important, the analysis provides insight into the quality of management, a factor that may be even more relevant to consider if a merger of practices is planned.

This case of declining operating profit is a good example of why it isn't prudent to base valuations on a multiple of revenue or a percentage of assets. Generating revenue is the easy part; translating that revenue into a financial return is another matter.

Once the full business analysis is complete, a much better picture emerges of the riskiness of the business in relation to companies within the industry and you get a much better sense of what the future of the practice looks like. The framework is now set to move on to the nuts and bolts of valuation.

3. THE INCOME APPROACH TO VALUATION
Defining Value

MANY INVESTMENT BANKERS and business brokers prefer simpler methods of valuation, such as a multiple of revenue, a multiple of assets under management, or even a simple multiple of EBITDA (earnings before interest, taxes, depreciation, and amortization). Although these methods are useful when comparing transactions, they are insufficient for making a judgment on an investment. The method most suitable to valuing a financial-planning or advisory practice is the income approach. Two related valuation methods are based on the income approach—capitalization of cash flow and discounted cash flow. The basic difference between the two methods is that the capitalization process is more of a default forecast that assumes a normalized rate of growth from the base year. It is essentially a shortcut in the valuation process.

The Calculations

When you use the income approach to valuation, you forecast cash flow for the next period—generally the next fiscal year—and convert it to present value using an appropriate capitalization rate equal to a discount rate less the expected growth rate in perpetuity. (We'll define cash flow later in this chapter.) This exercise is called capitalization of cash flow analysis (see *Figure 3.1*).

When you calculate discounted cash flow, you're forecasting a specific year-to-year performance. The discounted future cash flow approach is useful and perhaps more realistic because it allows

---

FIGURE 3.1   **Capitalization of Cash Flow Calculation**

$$\text{Value} = \frac{\text{Adjusted Cash Flow}}{\text{Capitalization Rate}}$$

where Capitalization Rate = Discount Rate – Growth Rate

---

you to account for any expected attrition or dramatic growth. In a discounted cash flow analysis, you forecast free cash flows for a discrete period of years (typically a three- to five-year period beginning on the valuation date). Beyond the three- to five-year period, you calculate a terminal, or residual, value using an appropriate capitalization rate. The free cash flows and residual value are converted to present value, using an appropriate discount rate, or rate of return (see *Figure 3.2*).

FIGURE 3.2   **Discounted Cash Flow Calculation**

Value = Cash Flow + Cash Flow + ... + Cash Flow + Cash Flow

$$\frac{\text{Year 1}}{(1+d)^1} \qquad \frac{\text{Year 2}}{(1+d)^2} \qquad \frac{\text{Year 5}}{(1+d)^5} \qquad \frac{\text{Year N}}{(1+d)^N}$$

where d = Discount Rate or Required Rate of Return

In both income methods—the discounted cash flow calculation and the capitalization of cash flow calculation—you must determine free cash flow and a discount rate.

Calculating Free Cash Flow

Free cash flow is defined as:

Earnings before interest & taxes (EBIT)

− **Income taxes on EBIT**

+ **Noncash expenses (i.e., depreciation)**

± **Adjusted working capital changes**

− **Capital expenditures**

= **Free cash flow**

Essentially, free cash flow is the amount of return the practice generates once these key factors have been considered. To calculate free cash flow, follow these steps:

Revenue (gross income from the practice)

− **Direct expenses**

= **Gross profit**

− **Overhead expenses**

= **Earnings before interest & taxes (EBIT)**

Step 1. Begin by looking at EBIT, the earnings of the practice before interest and taxes, which is calculated as:

Direct expenses include fair compensation to professional staff (including the owners and any other staff directly responsible for generating revenue), plus benefits. Overhead expenses are all reasonable and necessary expenses required for the operation of the practice. Adjustments are frequently made to EBIT when determining free cash flow.

Adjustments to EBIT. Certain adjustments need to be made to the historical financial statements to normalize the returns. These adjustments include all nonrecurring, nonoperating, and discretionary items during the period. Adjustments are typically made to both the level of compensation for the owner (a component of direct expense) and to overhead or general and administrative expenses that are not likely to recur or are unnecessary or extraordinary.

Because most of the practice's profits are typically paid out in compensation to the practitioner, an owner's compensation is typically adjusted to determine the true profitability of the practice. If the owner is not paid a salary, it's necessary to determine a market rate of compensation for the owner as an employee of the firm—the amount he or she would get paid for doing the job. To make this adjustment, it's necessary to compare the income of the practitioner to the salaries of similar employees with the same credentials performing similar work at similar firms. This is often a difficult concept for owners of practices to relate to because they tend to distribute all the profits. But for the purpose of this analysis, it's helpful to differentiate between what someone would be paid as a key employee of the business versus what an owner's distribution would be.

One relevant comparison is the payout of brokers within wirehouses such as Merrill Lynch. Such brokers are employees of the wirehouse, just as a practitioner is an employee of his or her own firm. Top producers in most wirehouses receive a payout equal to a range of 30 percent to 45 percent of revenue.

A principal in a financial-advisory firm is usually paid differently—and more—than a planner who's not an owner of the firm. What would fair compensation be if the principal were not an owner? The difference between the amount the principal receives and fair compensation for employees performing the same functions is attributed to the profit of the practice. Generally, fair compensation to all professional staff, including the owner, should be in the range of 30 percent to 45 percent of revenue, though research by Moss Adams in recent years is helping to establish measurable salary ranges for key people at all levels within a firm. The percentage calculation described here serves as a proxy in the absence of comparable salary data.

Examples of other acceptable adjustments to a practice's expenses that could improve the profitability in the eyes of a prospective buyer include:

- ◆ Rent (especially if a related party owns the building and lease payments are not at market rates)
- ◆ Travel and entertainment
- ◆ Nonbusiness-related legal expenses
- ◆ Certain support staff salaries

After these adjustments are made, a more realistic picture of the earnings of the practice emerges. Keep in mind, however, that EBIT does not take into account the interest expense of the practice. Because some practices are leveraged and others are debt-free, ignore for valuation purposes how the practice is being financed (equity or debt) and do not subtract interest expense from EBIT to determine free cash flow.

Step 2. In formal valuations, the prevailing tax rates for a C corporation would be applied to EBIT because it's generally assumed that a C corporation would be buying the business, and this is a way of recognizing tax as a cost of doing business. What's more, capitalization-rate comparables are almost always based on C corporation rates.

Step 3. Any noncash expenses, such as depreciation and amortization, are added back because they do not represent an actual outflow of cash and because practices may account for the acquisition of fixed assets in different ways.

Step 4. In valuations of more traditional businesses, an adjustment would be made to account for changes in working capital (current assets less current liabilities). Because most financial-advisory practices use a cash basis of accounting, however, they do not show accounts receivable or accounts payable, or in many cases they generate no balance sheet at all. For that reason, adjustments for working capital changes may not be accounted for in valuing financial-advisory practices.

Step 5. The capital expenditures the practice makes—investments in computers, software, and equipment required to do business efficiently and to support growth—must also be subtracted from EBIT to determine free cash flow.

Calculating the Discount Rate

Once free cash flow is calculated, the next step in assessing discount-ed cash flow, or capitalized cash flow, is to determine a discount rate, or required rate of return. The discount rate selected should reflect the degree of uncertainty or risk associated with the future returns of the practice for sale as well as returns available from alternative invest-ments. Greater uncertainty or risk leads to a higher expected rate of return, producing a lower value for the investment. Choosing a discount rate is a somewhat subjective process, and usually the buyer and seller will have differing opinions.

Following are some of the factors that should be considered when determining a discount rate for an investment-advisory or financial-planning practice:

♦ Return available on alternative investments
♦ Volatility or stability of income
♦ Amount and quality of competition
♦ Size of the practice
♦ Condition of the economy
♦ Quality and nature of the book of business

For example, if the book of business consists solely of limited partnership interests and life insurance for clients who are all over the age of 65, the degree of uncertainty about its future income potential will be very high. However, if most of the financial adviser's clients are between 35 and 55 years old, affluent, pay a fee for an annual plan update, and have their assets under management, then the risk is less. The big unknown, which must be quantified in either case, is the ease with which this book of business can be transferred to a new practitioner.

The buildup approach. One common method of determining a discount rate is called the buildup approach. To use this method, start with a risk-free rate (generally assumed to be the 20-year Treasury bond rate) and add risk premiums based on the perceived and unique risks of the practice being valued. *Figure 3.3* illustrates the discount-rate buildup formula.

FIGURE 3.3 **The Buildup Formula**

The discount rate is defined as

$$K_e = R_f + R_e + R_s + R_c$$

where R_f = risk-free rate

R_e = equity risk premium

R_s = small-stock risk premium

R_c = subject-practice risk premium

Risk Premiums

Risk premiums for equity investments are published every year by Ibbotson Associates in its *Annual Yearbook on Stocks, Bonds, Bills and Inflation*. At the end of 2005, for example, rates were approximately as indicated in *Figure 3.4*.

The *risk-free rate* is the rate of return of an investment with no—or low—risk, generally the 20-year Treasury bond rate. Even though there is more inherent risk in using the 20-year Treasury bond versus the short-term Treasury bill rate, the 20-year bond is more commonly used for two primary reasons: it more closely matches the expected

FIGURE 3.4 **Risk Premiums**

Risk-free rate (R_f)	4.7%
+ Equity risk premium (R_e)	7.2%
+ Small-stock risk premium (R_s)	4.0%
Market-based return	16.0% (rounded)

life of the investment, and it tends to fluctuate less over time for the same period.

The *equity risk premium* is the premium required for investing in large, publicly traded equities. Equity investment exposes the investor to a greater risk; accordingly, the investment needs to generate a higher return to be acceptable.

The *small-stock risk premium* is the premium required for investing in a small publicly traded company. Smaller companies are more risky and hence have historically commanded a premium over the return required for larger companies.

Based on the historical data, the calculation in Figure 3.4 indicates that those who invest in small-cap common stocks *expect* an average return of 16.0 percent. The key word is expect. That return may or may not be achieved, but if it is not, either expectations will be lowered or investments will flow out of such equities.

Another risk premium taken into account when calculating the discount rate is called the *subject-practice risk premium*. Since the market-based return calculated in Figure 3.4 is the expected return for investments in publicly traded companies, it's appropriate to add an additional risk premium—that is, the subject-practice risk premium—for the specific financial-advisory practice being valued. This measure is the most subjective element of the process, but it allows you to take into account many factors in defining your required rate of return.

Critical elements or unique risks that can *add or detract* from value and that help determine the subject-company risk premium include:

♦ Transferability of the book of business
♦ Profile of the client base
♦ Average client portfolio size
♦ Nature of the investments
♦ Sources and consistency of income
♦ Cost and method of marketing to procure clients
♦ Turnover of clients
♦ Opportunities for additional income
♦ Geographic location
♦ Economic climate and related factors affecting the practice
♦ Niche or specialization

♦ Client satisfaction scores or record of client complaints
♦ Systems and staff in place
♦ Overhead expense structure
♦ Dependence on key personnel

The subject-practice risk premium for most financial-advisory firms ranges from 5 percent to 15 percent. As shown in Figure 3.3, the sum of the risk-free rate and the risk premiums (the equity risk premium, small-stock risk premium, and subject-practice risk premium) will give you the discount rate:

$$K_e = R_f + R_e + R_s + R_c.$$

If you are *discounting* the practice's projected annual cash flows (that is, doing a discounted cash flow analysis), you'll use this discount rate to discount the projected cash flows back to present value, as outlined in Figure 3.2.

If you are *capitalizing* the practice's cash flow, you'll need to calculate the capitalization rate.

Calculating the Capitalization Rate

The capitalization rate is the expected return that a buyer requires to be persuaded to invest in a particular business. The capitalization rate takes the discount rate one step further by subtracting an expected growth rate into perpetuity.

To calculate the capitalization rate (C), subtract the assumed growth rate into perpetuity (G) from the discount rate calculated in Figure 3.3, that is, $C = (K_e - G)$. Then calculate capitalized cash flow by dividing one year's forecasted free cash flow by the capitalization rate (see Figure 3.1). To determine value by capitalizing the practice's cash flow, divide next year's estimated free cash flow by the capitalization rate (C).

The capitalization rate reflects both the unique risks of the practice and a reasonable and normalized rate of growth in free cash flow. It's also the reciprocal of the price/earnings multiple (that is, a 25 percent capitalization rate is four times earnings; a 20 percent capitalization rate is five times earnings). Service businesses, particularly financial-advisory firms, are typically valued using capitalization rates that range from 15 percent to 30 percent, though there have been examples of even lower required rates of return.

The Growth Rate

The growth rate used in the capitalization-rate formula and the normalized rate of growth used in the discounted cash flow calculation both refer to the assumption of growth in free cash flow into perpetuity—not 1, 5, or 10 years, but *forever*. When estimating a growth rate in perpetuity, most practitioners are very aggressive and insist, "This practice will grow at least 10 percent (or 20 percent or 30 percent) a year." The critical concept here is *forever*. Thirty percent growth every year forever is just not feasible, no matter how strong the practice. Eventually, all books of business experience natural attrition as retired clients begin reducing the appreciation in their assets for living expenses. And through boredom, burnout, or market penetration, the practitioner will not continue to add new clients indefinitely.

Calculating discounted cash flow (instead of simply capitalizing cash flow) allows you to project more aggressive growth rates over the term of your forecast, but the terminal growth rate in the discounted cash flow calculation—and the growth rate in the capitalization-rate formula—represent the expected growth of the practice in perpetuity.

Having worked with hundreds of financial-advisory practices and studied the short- and long-term trends in the industry, Moss Adams normally uses 5 percent as the *highest* sustainable long-term growth rate. Negotiators in a deal may argue among themselves about this rate and come to an agreement on a different set of assumptions, but for the purpose of valuation, it would be very difficult to justify a higher rate.

Tangible Assets

The value calculated using the income approach is the total value of the practice, tangible and intangible. It is inappropriate to add the value of any hard assets to this value. The operating assets are required to generate the income that was capitalized, so the income-approach calculation accounts for them in that way—with one exception: any nonoperating assets should be added to the value indicated by the income approach. Nonoperating assets are assets that could be liquidated without impairing the company's operations. Examples of nonoperating assets include the cash surrender value of life insurance, cash, cash equivalents, and marketable securities in excess of what is needed for operations of the company.

Goodwill

Goodwill is often discussed in valuing a financial-advisory practice. But how can goodwill be identified and valued? There are many interpretations of goodwill and as many components. There is a mistaken notion that just because someone has worked at the same business for 15 or 20 years, somehow the practice has aged like fine wine into an extraordinary value. Blood, sweat, and tears do not constitute goodwill value. In fact, one element of goodwill in a practice often depends on the reputation of the owner, and that reputation is usually difficult to transfer with the sale. In objective terms, goodwill exists in a practice if it allows the adviser to earn above-average income. The valuation calculation does not have a separate amount included for goodwill, although goodwill is relevant in the purchase agreement when establishing values for the tax reporting of the sale.

Revenue and Valuation

The reliability and predictability of a firm's future revenue are critical to its valuation. Different income streams have different margins, different degrees of predictability, different growth opportunity, and different transferability characteristics. Those differences are why every practice should be valued based on its particular mix of revenue, not just by taking total revenue times some generic multiple drawn from a rule of thumb.

Practices that generate revenue from fees charged on assets under management tend to be valued more highly than those that generate revenue from commissions. That's because the ongoing revenue stream is more predictable in a fee-based practice. Conversely, revenues from commission-based practices are less certain because they depend on future transactions.

For buyers shopping for insurance practices—which include some major players in the consolidation market—the critical consideration in valuing a firm that emphasizes the sale of insurance is, "Are the renewals transferable to the buyer?" If the renewals cannot be transferred, they have no value. For most insurance firms, removing the renewal income from forecasted revenue leaves very little to consider when examining future cash flow. However, if the firm has not harvested all of the opportunity from these clients, buyers may be willing to pay on an earnout basis to acquire the book of business— a relatively risk-free way to acquire prospects.

A Valuation Example

To illustrate the concepts and calculations that are part of this valuation process, let's look at an example. Kelly Clark's practice has been growing steadily during the last several years. She is considering selling her practice and has had initial discussions with someone she considers to be a suitable potential buyer. She wants to estimate the value of her practice before talking further with the interested buyer. Her firm's revenues were about $1.4 million in 2005. She expects to grow revenues by 25 percent next year, and by 35 percent and 20 percent in the following two years.

FIGURE 3.5	**EBIT Projections**		
	2006	2007	2008
Revenue	$1,800,000	$2,430,000	$2,920,000
− Direct Expense	(1,080,000)	(970,000)	(1,160,000)
Gross Profit	$ 720,000	$1,460,000	$1,760,000
− Overhead Expense	(540,000)	(730,000)	(875,000)
Earnings Before Interest & Taxes	$ 180,000	$ 730,000	$ 885,000
Adjustments:			
Owner's Compensation	360,000	0	0
Rent	(20,000)	(20,000)	(20,000)
Travel	25,000	0	0
Adjusted Earnings Before Interest & Taxes	**$545,000**	**$710,000**	**$865,000**

Recognizing that her personal compensation in 2005 and her projected compensation for 2006 are higher than market rates and that some of the travel she has budgeted for 2006 is not entirely business related, she made some adjustments to her projected EBIT. She also made an adjustment to rent, knowing that she pays lower than market rates by renting office space from her father. Kelly's projections for EBIT and adjusted EBIT over the next three years are shown in *Figure 3.5*.

Following the procedures outlined in steps 1–5 in calculating free cash flow, Kelly calculated her adjusted cash flows for the three years as shown in *Figure 3.6*.

FIGURE 3.6 **Adjusted Cash Flows**

	2006	2007	2008
Adjusted Earnings Before Interest & Taxes	$545,000	$710,000	$865,000
Apply Tax Rate @ 34%	(185,300)	(241,400)	(294,100)
Earnings Before Interest & After Taxes	$359,700	$468,600	$570,900
+ Depreciation	25,000	25,000	25,000
± Working Capital Changes	15,000	15,000	15,000
− Normalized Capital Expenditures	(5,000)	(5,000)	(5,000)
= **Adjusted Cash Flow**	**$394,700**	**$503,600**	**$605,900**

FIGURE 3.7 **The Discount Rate**

Risk-free rate (R$_f$)	4.7%
+ **Equity risk premium (R$_e$)**	7.2%
+ **Small-stock risk premium (R$_s$)**	4.0%
+ **Subject-practice risk premium (R$_s$)**	9.0%
Discount Rate	**25.0% (rounded)**

FIGURE 3.8   **Discounted Cash Flow**

$$\text{Value} = \frac{\$400,000}{(1 + 25\%)^1} + \frac{\$500,000}{(1 + 25\%)^2} + \frac{\$600,000}{(1 + 25\%)^3} + \frac{(\$600,000\ /\ 20\%)}{(1 + 25\%)^3} =$$

$$\$320,000 + \$320,000 + \$307,000 + \$1,536,000 = \mathbf{\$2,483,000}$$

Having determined free cash flow, Kelly uses the buildup formula to compute a discount rate, as shown in *Figure 3.7.*

Kelly assumed a long-term growth rate of 5 percent, yielding a capitalization rate of 20 percent (the discount rate of 25 percent less the long-term growth rate of 5 percent). To calculate her practice's capitalized cash flow, Kelly divided next year's cash flow of $400,000 (rounded) by the capitalization rate of 20 percent: value = $400,000 / 20% = $2,000,000.

She calculated the practice's discounted cash flow by discounting back her three years of projected cash flows (rounded), as shown in *Figure 3.8.*

After working through her numbers, Kelly felt comfortable enough with the basic concepts of valuation to know which issues to prepare for in negotiating with the potential buyer.

It's important to understand that no approach to valuation that relies solely on a purely mathematical calculation can truly capture a practice's value. Analysis must be done case by case to identify the unique qualities and circumstances of the business. The exercise presented here highlights critical assumptions used in valuation and gives buyers and sellers a framework for negotiation. Those areas of negotiation will center largely on:

♦ **Direct expense:** What are reasonable adjustments for compensation to principals and professional staff?

♦ **Overhead expense:** Which expenses are likely to transfer, and which are reasonable operating expenses going forward?

♦ **Discount rate:** What is the rationale for a range of expected rates of return?

♦ **Growth rate:** What is a reasonable expectation for cash flow in the foreseeable future and for the long term?

It's also important to understand that although certain advisers, brokers, and investment bankers prefer to rely on a standard multiple, they are essentially forecasting by default. By understanding this process, you can test the assumptions that buyers and sellers are making in their expectations of future cash flow and their required rate of return when they use this type of analysis.

The Market Approach

The market approach to valuing an advisory business hinges on analyzing the prices at which the stock in businesses similar to the company being valued has changed hands. In its simplest form, this approach is based on the principle of substitution. Transaction data used in this approach are taken from publicly traded companies and acquired or merged companies. In addition, prior transactions involving the company itself are analyzed. The method uses valuation ratios based on current market prices and historical (or projected) financial data for the guideline companies. Selected valuation ratios derived from the analysis—such as price/revenue, price/AUM, and price/EBITDA—are then applied to the company's adjusted historical (or projected) financial results to arrive at value indicators.

A Basis of Comparison

Market analysis looks at stock market transactions involving publicly traded companies that are similar in nature to the business being valued. The guideline companies should generally be influenced by similar business and economic conditions, meaning comparable in terms of business description, market positioning, product line, diversification, customer base, capital structure, earning capacity, and liquidity. They may be considered alternative investment opportunities. The steps that are key to making this analysis work are to select appropriate companies, compute valuation ratios, make adjustments to the ratios, and compute values.

Select Guideline Companies

One major problem with the market approach to valuing a business is the difficulty of finding publicly traded companies that are exactly like the firm in question. Publicly traded companies are generally much larger and more diversified than private companies. If no public companies exactly match the company being valued, expand the search to include companies that operate in the same region, have a similar client base, or have similar processes.

Sources for underlying data can be obtained from SEC filings for public companies, which contain a wealth of information, including historical financial statements and descriptions of the business, assets, management, competition, and financial condition. One benefit of using financial statements for public companies is that they're prepared in accordance with generally accepted accounting principles (GAAP) and are therefore of high quality, and they generally are consistent from company to company. It's important to make adjustments to the guideline company's financial statements similar to those made to the financial statements in the income approach. Typical adjustments are nonrecurring items, such as extraordinary items, or changes in accounting methods.

Once you've made the financial-statement adjustments, you can compare the publicly traded companies to your firm. How does it compare in terms of operations, size, historical growth, profitability, leverage, efficiency, productivity, and solvency? These yardsticks will help you determine the risk of the company relative to those of the public companies and help determine the magnitude of adjustments, if any, to the multiples.

Compute Valuation Ratios

Valuation ratios show the embedded value in stocks and are used by investors as a screening device before making investments. Popular valuation ratios include:

♦ Price-to-earnings (P/E) ratio = current market price per share / after-tax earnings per share
♦ Dividend yield = annual dividends per share / current market price per share

When analyzing stocks, some may regard a high P/E ratio as a sign of overpricing. When the markets are bullish (optimistic) or if investor sentiment is optimistic about a particular stock, the P/E ratio will tend to be high. The Internet bubble is a prime example of this. In the late 1990s, Internet stocks tended to have extremely high P/E ratios, despite the lack of profits (sometimes even beyond a five-year pro forma period), reflecting investors' optimism about the future prospects of these companies. The bursting of the bubble showed us that such confidence was misguided.

Conversely, a low P/E ratio may indicate that the company has a poor track record. However, the stock may simply be priced too low based on its potential earnings, and further investigation is required to determine whether the company would be a good investment.

For purposes of evaluating a company, valuation ratios can be broadly categorized into two types: total equity and total capital (debt and equity) multiples. There is a third category—asset multiples—but we will not address that here. Commonly used total equity ratios in this industry include the ratios of market value of total equity to assets under management, pretax income, and net

FIGURE 4.1   **Financial Planner Corp. Guideline Company Analysis Multiples**

	Market Value of Equity			Market Value of Invested Capital		
	AUM	Pretax Income	Net Income	Revenue	EBITDA	EBIT
American	0.02	6.35	11.26	2.25	4.65	5.65
National	0.04	5.72	7.72	1.75	5.12	6.35
Optimum	0.02	6.65	8.53	1.80	5.65	6.95
Principal Group	0.07	7.01	9.76	3.20	6.20	8.20
Investors Group	0.03	4.25	6.21	1.15	4.95	5.15
Mean	0.04	6.00	8.70	2.03	5.31	6.46
Median	0.03	6.35	8.53	1.80	5.12	6.35
Range	0.02–0.07	4.25–7.01	6.21–11.26	1.15–3.20	4.65–6.20	5.15–8.20
Coefficient of Variation	0.576	0.181	0.222	0.375	0.116	0.184

income. Total capital multiples include the ratios of market value of invested capital (MVIC) to revenue, EBITDA, and EBIT. *Figure 4.1* illustrates the results of the computation of the multiples.

Adjust Market-Derived Valuation Ratios

The valuation ratios derived in the analysis represent values for relatively fast-growing, large, publicly traded companies. In comparison, the typical financial-planning firm likely has less growth potential, is generally significantly smaller, and may have unique risks. As a result, adjustments may need to be made to the selected valuation ratios to account for these factors.

Continuing the example of Kelly Clark's practice from chapter 3, it was determined that a 40 percent discount was appropriate from the median valuation ratios, as shown in *Figure 4.2*, because of less growth potential, the firm's smaller size, less diversification, and various other factors.

Compute Values and Summarize

Once the necessary adjustments to the valuation ratios have been made, the ratios can be applied to the corresponding normalized earnings, cash flow, revenue, or total assets under management to produce an indication of value—either equity value or total capital value, depending on the type of valuation ratio employed. The most current 12-month period is typically used as the basis if it's representative of the firm's near-term financial results.

FIGURE 4.2   **Kelly Clark–Guideline Company Analysis ($000)**

	Market Value of Equity			Market Value of Invested Capital		
	AUM	Pretax Income	Net Income	Revenue	EBITDA	EBIT
Median	0.03	6.35	8.53	1.80	5.12	6.35
Adjustment Downward (40%)	× 0.60	× 0.60	× 0.60	× 0.60	× 0.60	× 0.60
Adjusted Ratio	0.018	3.810	5.118	1.080	3.072	3.810

For the MVIC multiples, interest-bearing debt (if any) is subtracted to arrive at estimates of equity value. The values estimated from the total equity multiples need no further adjustment.

The results then need to be weighted, depending on the coefficient of variation. The coefficient of variation, which is the sample standard deviation divided by the sample mean, measures relative variability, that is, variability relative to the magnitude of the data. More weight should be given to results with a lower coefficient of variance. In Figure 4.1, the coefficients of variation for the computed valuation multiples were fairly close, except those for assets under management and revenue, which had a greater degree of variability and should be given less weight.

When we apply the weighted average multiples to Kelly Clark's 2005 figures, the result is a value of $2.0 million, as shown in *Figure 4.3*, which is similar to the results of the capitalization of earnings method in the income approach but slightly lower than the $2.5 million value indicated by the discounted cash flow analysis. Remember that the market approach takes into account only the historical nature of the earnings and does not account for future growth expectations.

FIGURE 4.3   **Kelly Clark–Guideline Company Analysis ($000)**

	Market Value of Equity			Market Value of Invested Capital		
	AUM	Pretax Income	Net Income	Revenue	EBITDA	EBIT
2005 Basis	$180,000	$545	$360	$1,800	$570	$545
× Adjusted Ratio	0.018	3.810	5.118	1.080	3.072	3.810
Indicated Value	$3,240	$2,076	$1,841	$1,944	$1,751	$2,076
– Interest-Bearing Debt	NA	NA	NA	$0	$0	$0
Indicated Equity Value	$3,240	$2,076	$1,841	$1,944	$1,751	$2,076
× Weighting	0.050	0.225	0.225	0.050	0.225	0.225
Weighted Value	$162	$467	$414	$97	$394	$467
Total Value	**$2,001**					

The Merger-and-Acquisition Approach

This approach to valuation analyzes merger and acquisition transactions involving companies that are similar in nature to the business being evaluated. The more recent the transaction, the more relevant the transaction becomes. The approach also becomes more relevant as the number of transactions increases. The steps are the same as those used in market analysis based on similar public companies: select appropriate companies, compute valuation ratios, make adjustments to the ratios, and compute values.

Many problems arise in attempting this analysis. It can be difficult to obtain information about private transactions, and even if the information is available, it's often nearly impossible to verify, which reduces its reliability.

Several merger-and-acquisition databases have been compiled, such as Mergerstat/Shannon Pratt's Control Premium Study, Pratt's Stats, Bizcomps, IBA Market Database, and Done Deals, but the amount, type, and quality of information each provides vary greatly. These variations significantly affect the reliability of the valuation ratios derived from each source. Because merger-and-acquisition data cannot be independently verified, and it's not clear whether reported financial results conform to GAAP. In addition, the different data sources use varying definitions of *earnings* and *cash flow*, and so valuation ratios are often not comparable across different sources. Another difficulty is that the acquired companies usually don't disclose the accounting conventions they used, so earnings may not be reported consistently from company to company. Quality issues aside, financial data for acquired companies are usually very limited, which precludes the financial ratios from being directly comparable to those of the company being valued.

Sources of data on small-company acquisitions do not define price clearly, which is a significant problem. The definition of *price* depends on whether a transaction is a stock deal (an acquisition of stock) or an asset deal (an acquisition of certain assets, net of assumed liabilities). None of the sources of small-company deals denotes which transactions are asset deals and which are stock deals. Although these sources claim that it's safe to assume that most of the deals are asset purchases, some estimate that 10 to 20 percent of transactions are actually stock deals. As a result, that assumption, which is necessary to make the data usable, will be inaccurate for a certain number of transactions, reducing the reliability of the data.

What's more, none of the data sources defines which assets are included in the asset deals. As a result, the asset deal price refers to the price paid for some unknown group of assets, net of unknown assumed liabilities. The various data sources generally assume that acquired assets include furniture, fixtures, and equipment; any leases, goodwill, and intangible assets; plus inventory and exclude real estate, cash and cash equivalents, accounts receivable, prepaid expenses, nonoperating assets, and all liabilities. This assumption further limits the reliability of the data because the assets acquired (and liabilities assumed) actually vary from deal to deal. Finally, it isn't possible to determine whether the acquisition price reflects synergistic or buyer-specific value, because the terms of the deal are often undisclosed. These problems clearly reduce the reliability of the merger-and-acquisition analysis.

Comparing the Drawbacks

Although the market approach is useful, it has its drawbacks. The concept is largely oriented to historical results rather than to future performance. So if a company currently has a very poor year, the indicated value will be significantly skewed.

The publicly traded companies used as the guideline companies for the financial-planning industry are generally incredibly large, diversified companies whose stocks are actively traded on the major exchanges, making a direct comparison to most privately held financial-advisory firms difficult. The significant adjustments that need to be made for factors like growth, size, differences in such operating factors as market conditions, customers, management and labor issues, products and services, and financial factors reduce the reliability of this approach.

The merger-and-acquisition approach is also unreliable given the difficulty in obtaining information related to the transactions and the difficulty of verifying the information. In addition, price and earnings may be defined differently across transactions. These transactions may also indicate investment value that includes premiums for such factors as synergies or economies of scale.

Reconciling Values

Once the three approaches to valuation—income, market, and merger and acquisition—have been applied, it is necessary to reconcile the values derived from each. Generally, the income approach is given significant weight because it provides a value based on projected cash flows of the business. The market approaches, however, provide values based on current market transactions and conditions, and their results cannot be disregarded. Careful consideration should be given to results derived from all of the approaches and can be weighted based on relevance and reliability. Or, rather than arbitrarily applying weights to the results and coming up with one number for the firm's value, the varying results can be viewed as a range of values, which can be especially useful in the negotiations of a transaction.

The next chapter presents some examples that will provide a better understanding of how valuation concepts apply to financial-advisory firms.

Assessing Value

5. THE MULTIPLE-PARTNER FIRM
Assessing Value

REGARDLESS OF THE methodology used to value a business, key factors must be considered. Nevertheless, no single methodology is adequately suited to the range of advisory firms now represented in the industry. Value is likely to be far more sharply defined if viewed through three lenses: the income approach, the market approach (including the guideline company and the merger-and-acquisition approaches), and the asset-based approach.

In this chapter and the next, we bring these approaches to life. Valuing a business can often come off as an academic exercise, out of touch with the reality of the marketplace. Business brokers often dismiss the discipline as a "black box" mystery: the appraiser throws a bunch of assumptions into a mixer, stirs it up, and arrives at a value that, in their opinion, could have been determined by simply looking at market comparables. Although there is some mystery surrounding the valuation process—it is more art than science in some cases—the discipline of valuation gives both buyers and sellers a foundation for evaluating the true economics of a practice and negotiating in terms of a reasonable set of assumptions. The process is not perfect. Indeed, it is much like financial planning: you can't predict the future with accuracy, but that doesn't stop you from giving your clients advice based on a set of assumptions valid at the time.

This chapter presents an example of the process of valuing a multiple-partner financial advisory firm; the next chapter offers an example of valuing a solo practitioner. Our goal is to help you learn not merely how to lock in on a simple number that captures value but

also how to recognize that there are a number of nuances that arise
in negotiating price and terms.

The Basics

Multipartner Firm, a registered investment-advisory firm, is an S corporation located in a state with no sales tax, thus taxes are applied at
the federal corporate rate only. The firm offers wealth-management
services, serving high-net-worth clients with more than $1 million
in assets under management. The firm transitioned to a fee-only
structure in 2001 and currently enjoys recurring revenues of approximately 90 percent. One of the shareholders has been with the firm
since its inception and is considered a rainmaker, although some of
the other shareholders are responsible for bringing in new clients and
the professionals work in a team. Neither the shareholders nor the
employees have signed noncompete or nonsolicitation agreements.

Figures 5.1 and *5.2* present the historical common-size income
statement and balance sheet of Multipartner for the years ended
December 31, 2001 through 2004. Again, the income statement
should reflect both direct expenses (professionals' and owners' salaries)
and operating expenses. *Figure 5.3* presents the cash flow statement.

After all the company documents, financial and otherwise, have
been reviewed and the economy and industry in which the company
operates have been analyzed, the historical common-size financial
statements of the company need to be analyzed to identify trends
and possibly identify any unusual or nonoperating items that need to
be adjusted. As discussed in chapter 3, examples of acceptable adjustments to a practice's expenses that could improve the profitability in
the eyes of a prospective buyer could include:

♦ Rent (especially if the adviser owns the building)
♦ Compensation
♦ Travel and entertainment
♦ Nonbusiness-related or nonrecurring legal expenses
♦ Certain support staff salaries
♦ Taxes applied to adjusted earnings
♦ Interest expense
♦ Depreciation and amortization

FIGURE 5.1   **Multipartner Firm**
              Historical Common-Size Income Statement

Fiscal Year Ended December 31	Internal 2001	%	Internal 2002	%	Internal 2003	%	Internal 2004	%	Average % FY 01–04
Revenue	$3,850,000	100.0%	$5,100,000	100.0%	$6,000,000	100.0%	$6,400,000	100.0%	100.0%
Professional Salaries	1,600,000	41.6	2,025,000	39.7	2,400,000	40.0	2,500,000	39.1	40.1
Total Direct Expense	1,600,000	41.6	2,025,000	39.7	2,400,000	40.0	2,500,000	39.1	40.1
Gross Profit	2,250,000	58.4	3,075,000	60.3	3,600,000	60.0	3,900,000	60.9	59.9
Operating Expenses:									
Advertising/Marketing	2,100	0.1	10,000	0.2	15,000	0.3	11,300	0.2	0.2
Depreciation & Amortization	27,000	0.7	17,000	0.3	16,500	0.3	16,700	0.3	0.4
Employee Benefits	14,500	0.4	88,600	1.7	84,000	1.4	120,000	1.9	1.3
Insurance	9,000	0.2	22,000	0.4	54,000	0.9	46,000	0.7	0.6
Office Expense	65,500	1.7	54,500	1.1	56,000	0.9	47,500	0.7	1.1
Salaries – Other	380,000	9.9	413,000	8.1	593,000	9.9	680,000	10.6	9.6
Payroll Taxes	83,000	2.2	76,000	1.5	92,000	1.5	107,000	1.7	1.7
Professional Fees	66,000	1.7	9,000	0.2	63,000	1.1	34,000	0.5	0.9
Rent	200,000	5.2	225,000	4.4	240,000	4.0	260,000	4.1	4.4
Software/Hardware Expense	30,000	0.8	35,000	0.7	57,000	1.0	90,000	1.4	1.0
Taxes & Licenses	65,000	1.7	105,000	2.1	120,000	2.0	130,000	2.0	1.9
Travel & Entertainment	120,000	3.1	95,000	1.9	100,000	1.7	113,000	1.8	2.1
Utilities	25,000	0.6	22,000	0.4	30,000	0.5	29,000	0.5	0.5
Other Expenses	186,400	4.8	193,100	3.8	236,000	3.9	296,000	4.6	4.3
Total Operating Expense	1,273,500	33.1	1,365,200	26.8	1,756,500	29.3	1,980,500	30.9	30.0
Operating Income/(Loss)	976,500	25.4	1,709,800	33.5	1,843,500	30.7	1,919,500	30.0	29.9
Other Income (Expense):									
Other Income	6,000	0.2	26,000	0.5	30,500	0.5	32,400	0.5	0.4
Other Expense (–)	(800)	(0.0)	(8,000)	(0.2)	(6,000)	(0.1)	0	0.0	(0.1)
Interest Expense (–)	0	0.0	0	0.0	0	0.0	0	0.0	0.0
Total Other Income (Exp.)	5,200	0.1	18,000	0.4	24,500	0.4	32,400	0.5	0.4
Pretax Profit	981,700	25.5	1,727,800	33.9	1,868,000	31.3	1,951,900	30.5	30.3
Total Income Taxes	0	0.0	0	0.0	0	0.0	0	0.0	0.0
Net Income	$981,700	25.5%	$1,727,800	33.9%	$1,868,000	31.1%	$1,951,900	30.5%	30.3%

Revenues for Multipartner grew substantially during the four-year period, from $3.9 million in 2001 to $6.4 million in 2004, a compound annual growth rate of 18.5 percent. Such growth is substantial, especially given the effects of the technology bust and the

FIGURE 5.2   **Multipartner Firm Historical Common-Size Balance Sheet**

Fiscal Year Ended December 31	Internal 2001	%	Internal 2002	%	Internal 2003	%	Internal 2004	%	Average %FY 01–04
Current Assets:									
Cash & Equivalents	$109,000	11.9%	$76,000	6.2%	$474,000	28.6%	$726,000	32.4%	19.8%
Trade Accounts Receivable	640,000	70.1	795,000	64.6	1,099,000	66.3	1,430,000	63.8	66.2
Other Current Assets	113,000	12.4	174,000	14.1	700	0.0	0	0.0	6.6
Prepaid Expenses	6,000	0.7	155,800	12.7	27,700	1.7	45,700	2.0	4.3
Total Current Assets	868,000	95.1	1,200,800	97.5	1,601,400	96.7	2,201,700	98.3	96.9
Fixed Assets:									
Net Fixed Assets	45,100	4.9	30,700	2.5	55,200	3.3	38,500	1.7	3.1
Total Assets	$913,100	100%	$1,231,500	100.0%	$1,656,600	100.0%	$2,240,200	100.0%	100.0%
Current Liabilities:									
Trade Accounts Payable	$11,000	1.2%	$66,800	5.4%	$87,000	5.3%	$110,800	4.9%	4.2%
Other Account Payable	407,000	44.6	424,400	34.5	467,300	28.2	550,300	24.6	33.0
Accrued Expenses	17,100	1.9	134,500	10.9	228,500	13.8	153,400	6.8	8.4
Total Current Liabilities	435,100	47.7	625,700	50.8	782,800	47.3	814,500	36.4	45.5
Total Liabilities	435,100	47.7	625,700	50.8	782,800	47.3	814,500	36.4	45.5
Equity:									
Beginning Equity	263,000	28.8	478,000	38.8	605,800	36.6	873,800	39.0	35.8
Distributions	0	0.0	(1,600,000)	(129.9)	(1,600,000)	(96.6)	(1,400,000)	(62.5)	(72.3)
Current Year Income	215,000	23.5	1,727,800	140.3	1,868,000	112.8	1,951,900	87.1	90.9
Total Equity	478,000	52.3	605,800	49.2	873,800	52.7	1,425,700	63.6	54.5
Total Liabilities & Equity	$913,100	100.0%	$1,231,500	100.0%	$1,656,600	100.0%	$2,240,200	100.0%	100.0%

terrorist attacks, which affected the financial-advisory industry and the economy during 2001 and 2002.

An analysis of Multipartner's expenses appears to show that the company may have had some unusual professional fees during 2001 and 2003. Indeed, management confirmed that the company had unusual attorney fees and that a normal level of professional fees for this firm is approximately $30,000 per year.

Pretax profit margins grew steadily from approximately $1.0 million in 2001 to $2.0 million in 2004, a compound annual growth rate of 25.7 percent. This growth is substantial, exceeding even the growth rate of revenues.

Total assets are primarily cash and trade accounts receivable

FIGURE 5.3 **Multipartner Firm Historical Cash Flow**

Fiscal Year Ended December 31	Internal 2002	Internal 2003	Internal 2004	Fiscal Year Average
Cash Flows From Operating Activities:				
Net Income After Tax	$1,727,800	$1,868,000	$1,951,900	$1,849,233
Adjustments to Reconcile Net Income to Net Cash Provided by Operating Activities:				
+ Depreciation & Amortization	17,000	16,500	16,700	16,733
− (Gains)/Losses on Sale of Assets	0	0	0	0
Gross Cash Flow	1,744,800	1,884,500	1,968,600	1,865,967
Change in Assets and Liabilities:				
Trade Accounts Receivables − Decr. (Incr.)	(155,000)	(304,000)	(331,000)	(263,333)
Prepaid Expenses − Decr. (Incr.)	(149,800)	128,100	(18,000)	(13,233)
Other Current Assets − Decr. (Incr.)	(61,000)	173,300	700	37,667
Trade Accounts Payable − Incr. (Decr.)	55,800	20,200	23,800	33,267
Other Accounts Payable − Incr. (Decr.)	17,400	42,900	83,000	47,767
Accrued Expenses − Incr. (Decr.)	117,400	94,000	(75,100)	45,433
Other Noncurrent Liabilities − Incr. (Decr.)	0	0	0	0
Operating Cash Flow	**1,569,600**	**2,039,000**	**1,652,000**	**1,753,533**
Cash Flows From Investing Activities:				
Capital Expenditures (−)	(25,000)	(20,000)	(20,000)	(21,667)
Proceeds From Sale of Assets	22,400	(21,000)	20,000	7,133
Investing Cash Flow	**(2,600)**	**(41,000)**	**0**	**(14,533)**
Cash Flow Before Financing	1,567,000	1,998,000	1,652,000	1,739,000
Cash Flows From Financing Activities:				
Notes Payable − Incr. (Decr.)	0	0	0	0
Long Term Debt − Incr. (Decr.)	0	0	0	0
Debt Financing Cash Flow	0	0	0	0
Cash Flow Before Equity Financing	1,567,000	1,998,000	1,652,000	1,739,000
Capital Stock − Incr. (Decr.)	0	0	0	0
Dividends or Distributions	(1,600,000)	(1,600,000)	(1,400,000)	(1,533,333)
Adjustment to Retained Earnings	0	0	0	0
Equity Financing Cash Flow	(1,600,000)	(1,600,000)	(1,400,000)	(1,533,333)
Financing Cash Flow	**(1,600,000)**	**(1,600,000)**	**(1,400,000)**	**(1,533,333)**
Beginning Cash	109,000	76,000	474,000	219,667
Operating Cash Flow	1,569,600	2,039,000	1,652,000	1,753,533
Investing Cash Flow	(2,600)	(41,000)	0	(14,533)
Financing Cash Flow	(1,600,000)	(1,600,000)	(1,400,000)	(1,533,333)
Comprehensive Cash Flow	(33,000)	398,000	252,000	205,677
Ending Cash	**$76,000**	**$474,000**	**$726,000**	**$425,333**

and increased from \$900,000 in 2001 to \$2.2 million in 2004, a 34.9 percent compound annual increase. No nonoperating assets were identified. In addition, this company did not have any interest-bearing debt during the period under review. Capital expenditures averaged \$20,000 each year, and the company paid an average of \$1.5 million per year in S corporation distributions.

Industry Comparisons

When analyzing a firm for valuation purposes, it is helpful to compare the subject company's operating performance with a benchmark as discussed in chapter 3. This analysis is presented in *Figure 5.4.* Industry comparisons are from the *2004 FPA Financial Performance Study,*[1] published by the Financial Planning Association and produced by Moss Adams for companies considered "elite ensembles," and from the *Annual Statement Studies 2004/2005,*[2] published by the Risk Management Association (RMA). The medians shown are for SIC Code 6282, "Investment Advice," with sales in the same size range as the practice being valued. SIC codes, or standard industrial classification codes, are four-digit numerical codes assigned by the U.S. government to business establishments to identify the primary business of the establishment. The classification was developed to facilitate the collection, presentation, and analysis of data; and to promote uniformity and comparability in the presentation of statistical data collected by various agencies of the federal government, state agencies, and private organizations.

Multipartner's gross profit margin averaged 59.9 percent during the 2001–2004 period, below the FPA median of 66.8 percent. This suggests that the company is paying compensation that's higher than the industry average. However, when we analyze the company in more detail, we can see that the firm has more professionals on average to support its model and growth. This is also evidenced by the Multipartner's lower number of clients per professional than the FPA median. Therefore, an adjustment in this case is unwarranted. In this instance, we compared salaries as a percentage of revenue rather than looking at what salaries for comparable positions should be. Ideally, more specific compensation information would be provided for individuals working in these roles.

FIGURE 5.4   **Multipartner Firm
Historical Financial Ratios**

Fiscal Year Ended December 31	Internal 2001	Internal 2002	Internal 2003	Internal 2004	Average FY 01–04	FPA Study 2004 Elite Firms	RMA 2004/2005 SIC 6282[*] $3–5M
Growth Rates:							
Revenue Growth	NA	32.5%	17.6%	6.7%	18.5%[b]	NA	NA
Pretax Income Growth	NA	76.0%	8.1%	4.5%	25.7%[b]	NA	NA
Total Asset Growth	NA	34.9%	34.5%	35.2%	34.9%[b]	NA	NA
Profitability (% of Sales):							
Net Sales	100.0%	100.0%	100.0%	100.0%	100.0%	100.0%	100.0%
Gross Profit	58.4%	60.3%	60.0%	60.9%	59.9%	66.8%	0.0%
Operating Expenses	33.1%	26.8%	29.3%	30.9%	30.0%	44.3%	75.6%
Operating Profit	25.4%	33.5%	30.7%	30.0%	29.9%	22.5%	24.4%
All Other Income/(Expenses)	0.1%	0.4%	0.4%	0.5%	0.4%	(8.5%)	(0.9%)
Pretax Profit	25.5%	33.9%	31.1%	30.5%	30.3%	14.0%	23.5%
Net Income	25.5%	33.9%	31.1%	30.5%	30.3%	13.6%	NA
Liquidity Ratios:							
Current Ratio	2.0	1.9	2.0	2.7	2.2	NA	1.7
Quick Ratio	1.7	1.4	2.0	2.6	1.9	NA	1.3
Solvency Ratios:							
Debt to Worth	0.9	1.0	0.9	0.6	0.9	NA	1.1
Long-Term Debt to Total Capital[a]	0.0%	0.0%	0.0%	0.0%	0.0%	NA	61.3%
Productivity Data:							
Number of Employees	NA	NA	NA	26	NA	15	NA
Number of Professionals	NA	NA	NA	13	NA	6.5	NA
AUM ($000)	NA	NA	NA	781,000	NA	$360,146	NA
Active Clients	NA	NA	NA	320	NA	287	NA
Productivity Ratios:							
AUM per Professional + Support ($000)	NA	NA	NA	41,105	NA	$40,079	NA
AUM per Professional ($000)	NA	NA	NA	60,077	NA	$66,068	NA
Revenue per Professional + Support	NA	NA	NA	336,842	NA	$261,057	NA
Revenue per Professional	NA	NA	NA	492,308	NA	$480,001	NA
Total Revenue/AUM	NA	NA	NA	0.82%	NA	0.70%	NA
Active Clients per Professional + Support	NA	NA	NA	17	NA	33	NA
Active Clients per Professional	NA	NA	NA	12	NA	56	NA

NA = not applicable; AUM = assets under management
* SIC 6282 = Investment Advice; medians
a Estimated RMA ratios
b Compound annual growth rates

However, Multipartner's operating margin averaged 29.9 percent during the 2001–2004 period, above the FPA and RMA medians. The above-average operating profit margin was due to the company's increase in sales relative to its increase in operating expenses. This company has done an exceptional job of managing costs while growing and has surpassed its critical mass. It now has the appropriate infrastructure in place to profitably manage even more growth.

Liquidity ratios measure a company's ability to meet its current obligations as they come due. As measured by the current ratio (current assets divided by current liabilities) and quick ratio (cash and equivalents plus trade receivables divided by total current liabilities), liquidity was better than industry norms during the 2001–2004 period.

Solvency ratios are used to measure a company's ability to meet interest and principal payments on long-term debt and other obligations as they become due. These ratios analyze leverage, debt coverage, and long-term profitability. As previously mentioned, Multipartner used no interest-bearing debt during the period under review.

Productivity ratios were mixed, compared with the average for the industry. In 2004, AUM per professional and support staff of $41 million was in line with the industry, but AUM per professional at $60 million was below. Both the revenue per professional and support staff and the revenue per professional were above industry norms. The number of clients per professional and support staff and of clients per professional were below the industry levels. Revenue per AUM at 0.82 percent in 2004 was slightly higher than the industry median of 0.70 percent.

Historical Financial Ratios

Often, financial advisory firms don't have balance sheets to provide an adequate comparison. But in this case, we assumed one existed in order to give you the proper perspective. *Figure 5.5* presents Multipartner's historical working capital (which is equal to current assets less current liabilities) in terms of dollars and as a percentage of revenues. Any nonoperating assets or liabilities would need to be

FIGURE 5.5 **Multipartner Firm**
Historical Working Capital Analysis ($000)

Fiscal Year Ended December 31	2001	2002	2003	2004	Average FY 01–04	Weighted Average FY 01–04	RMA 2004/2005 SIC 6282* $3–5M	Selected % Sales[d]
Net Working Capital (NWC)	433	575	819	1,387	NA	NA	NA	NA
− Nonoperating Assets	0	0	0	0	NA	NA	NA	NA
+ Current Interest-Bearing Debt	0	0	0	0	NA	NA	NA	NA
Adjusted Net Working Capital (ANWC)	433	575	819	1,387	NA	NA	NA	NA
Working Capital Ratios:[a]								
Sales/Net Working Capital	8.9	8.9	7.3	4.6	7.4	6.7	9.2	NA
Net Working Capital/Sales	11.2%	11.3%	13.7%	21.7%	14.5%	16.1%	10.9%	NA
Sales/Adjusted NWC	8.9	8.9	7.3	4.6	7.4	6.7	4.6[b]	4.6
Adjusted NWC/Sales	11.2%	11.3%	13.7%	21.7%	14.3%	16.1%	21.7%[b]	21.7%
Account Analysis:[a]								
Cash & Equivalents/Sales	2.8%	1.5%	7.9%	11.3%	5.9%	7.5%	14.3%[c]	11.3%
Trade Accounts Receivables/Sales	16.6%	15.6%	18.3%	22.3%	18.2%	19.2%	14.0%[c]	22.3%
Other Accounts Receivables/Sales	0.0%	0.0%	0.0%	0.0%	0.0%	0.0%	NA	0.0%
Inventories/Sales	0.0%	0.0%	0.0%	0.0%	0.0%	0.0%	1.0%[c]	0.0%
Prepaid Expenses/Sales	0.2%	3.1%	0.5%	0.7%	1.1%	1.1%	NA	0.7%
Other Current Assets/Sales	2.9%	3.4%	0.0%	0.0%	1.6%	1.0%	2.5%[c]	0.0%
Trade Accounts Payable/Sales	0.3%	1.3%	1.5%	1.7%	1.2%	1.4%	2.0%[c]	1.7%
Other Accounts Payable/Sales	10.6%	8.3%	7.8%	8.6%	8.8%	8.5%	NA	8.6%
Taxes Payable/Sales	0.0%	0.0%	0.0%	0.0%	0.0%	0.0%	1.0%[c]	0.0%
Accrued Expenses/Sales	0.4%	2.6%	3.8%	2.4%	2.3%	2.7%	NA	2.4%
Other Current Liabilities/Sales	0.0%	0.0%	0.0%	0.0%	0.0%	0.0%	7.0%[c]	0.0%
Adjusted Net Working Capital	11.2%	11.3%	13.6%	21.7%	14.5%	16.1%	21.9%[c]	21.7%

NA = not available/not applicable
* SIC 6282 = Investment Advice
[a] Annualized where applicable
[b] Estimated based on RMA percentage of total assets ratios
[c] Estimated based on RMA sales to total assets ratio of 2.1
[d] Based on FY 2004 unless noted

adjusted out, but none were identified. Also, any current interest-bearing debt the company had would be removed, as the cash flows are on a debt-free basis. As shown in Figure 5.5, the 2004 working capital as a percentage of revenue is selected as an appropriate level for future requirements.

Adjustments to the historical income statement are made in

FIGURE 5.6   Multipartner Firm
Earnings Analysis and Adjustments ($000)

Fiscal Year Ended December 31	2001	2002	2003	2004
Revenue	$3,850	$5,100	$6,000	$6,400
Direct Expense:				
Actual Direct Expense	1,600	2,025	2,400	2,500
Adjusted Direct Expense	1,600	2,025	2,400	2,500
Operating Expense Adjustments:				
Operating Expenses	1,274	1,365	1,757	1,981
− Depreciation Expense[a]	(27)	(17)	(17)	(17)
− Nonrecurring Items Attorney Fees	(30)	0	(30)	0
Adjusted Operating Expenses	1,217	1,348	1,710	1,964
Other Income (Expense) Adjustments:				
Other Income (Expense)	5	18	25	32
Adjusted Other Income (Expense)	5	18	25	32
Depreciation Expense Summary:				
Depreciation in Operating Exp.	27	17	17	17
Total Depreciation Expense	27	17	17	17

Note: As reported in financial statements unless noted
[a] Reclassified

Figure 5.6. Nonrecurring attorney fees were removed in 2001 and 2003, as management indicated a level of $30,000 for professional fees is expected in the future. No adjustment was made for salaries, as discussed earlier. Depreciation was removed and treated separately.

Figure 5.7 is a restatement of the income statement reflecting the adjustments in Figure 5.6.

Figure 5.8 presents the calculation of the discount rate and the capitalization rate, which were discussed in greater detail in chapter 3, "Defining Value: The Income Approach to Valuation." Based on the comparison of Multipartner with companies in the financial-advisory industry, a subject company risk premium of 7 percent was selected.

Important negative factors include:

♦ The firm's small size (it is smaller than the micro-cap companies

FIGURE 5.7 **Multipartner Firm Adjusted Income Statement and Cash Flow ($000)**

Fiscal Year Ended December 31	2001	%	2002	%	2003	%	2004	%	Weighted Average FY 01–04
Revenue[a]	$3,850	100.0%	$5,100	100.0%	$6,000	100.0%	$6,400	100.0%	100.0%
Direct Expense[a]	1,600	41.6	2,025	39.7	2,400	40.0	2,500	39.1	39.8
Gross Profit	2,250	58.4	3,075	60.3	3,600	60.0	3,900	60.9	60.2
Operating Expenses:									
Operating Expenses[a]	1,217	31.6	1,348	26.4	1,710	28.5	1,964	30.7	29.3
Depreciation Expense[a]	27	0.7	17	0.3	17	0.3	17	0.3	0.3
Operating Income	1,007	26.1	1,710	33.5	1,874	31.2	1,920	30.0	30.6
Other Income (Expense):									
Other Income (Expense)[a]	5	0.1	18	0.4	25	0.4	32	0.5	0.4
Earnings Before Interest & Taxes (EBIT)	1,012	26.3	1,728	33.9	1,898	31.6	1,952	30.5	30.9
Interest Expense	0	0.0	0	0.0	0	0.0	0	0.0	0.0
Pretax Income	1,012	26.3	1,728	33.9	1,898	31.6	1,952	30.5	30.9
Income Tax (*Effective Rate*)[b]	344	*34.0*	587	*34.0*	645	*34.0*	664	*34.0*	*34.0*
Net Income	668	17.3	1,140	22.4	1,253	20.9	1,288	20.1	20.4
Plus: Depreciation & Amortization	27	0.7	17	0.3	17	0.3	17	0.3	0.3
Gross Cash Flow	**$695**	**18.0**	**$1,157**	**22.7**	**$1,269**	**21.2**	**$1,305**	**20.4**	**20.8%**
Debt-Free Data:									
Earnings Before Interest, Taxes, Depreciation & Amortization (EBITDA)	$1,039	27.0%	$1,745	34.2%	$1,915	31.9%	$1,969	30.8%	31.3%
Less: Depreciation & Amortization	27	0.7	17	0.3	17	0.3	17	0.3	0.3
Earnings Before Interest & Taxes (EBIT)	1,012	26.3	1,728	33.9	1,898	31.6	1,952	30.5	30.9
Income Taxes on EBIT (*Effective Rate*)[b]	344	*34.0*	587	*34.0*	645	*34.0*	664	*34.0*	*34.0*
Net Income (Debt Free)	668	17.3	1,140	22.4	1,253	20.9	1,288	20.1	20.4
Depreciation & Amortization	27	0.7	17	0.3	17	0.3	17	0.3	0.3
Cash Flow (Debt Free)	**$695**	**18.0%**	**$1,157**	**22.7%**	**$1,269**	**21.2%**	**$1,305**	**20.4%**	**20.8%**

[a] Adjusted as shown in Figure 5.6
[b] At federal corporate income tax rates

included in the small-stock risk premium discount, therefore an additional discount for size is appropriate)

♦ Its slight reliance on one key shareholder
♦ The mixed productivity results
♦ The absence of noncompete or nonsolicitation agreements

FIGURE 5.8 **Multipartner Firm
Discount Rate and Capitalization
Rate Analysis**

Discount Rate—Buildup Method:

Risk-Free Rate (20-Year Government Bond)	4.9%
Equity Risk Premium[a]	+ 7.2%
Small-Stock Risk Premium (Size Premium)[b]	+ 4.0%
Subject Company Risk Premium	+ 7.0%
Discount Rate	= 23.1%
Capitalization Rate:	
Discount Rate (see above)	23.1%
Growth Rate (into perpetuity)	− 5.0%
Capitalization Rate	= 18.1%

[a] This represents the premium demanded by investors in equity securities over and above the risk-free rate as published by Ibbotson Associates in *Stocks, Bonds, Bills & Inflation (SBBI) 2005 Yearbook*

[b] This represents the premium for size demanded by investors in small-capitalization stocks over and above the premium demanded by equity investors, as published by Ibbotson Associates in *SBBI 2005 Yearbook*

Positive factors that partially offset the negatives include:

♦ Above-average financial performance
♦ A high-net-worth client base
♦ A recurring revenue stream

As shown in Figure 5.8, a discount rate of 23.1 percent was calculated, which translates into a capitalization rate of 18.1 percent, after subtracting growth into perpetuity of 5 percent.

As we've explained, there are two approaches to value in the income approach: a discounted cash flow analysis and a capitalization of cash flow analysis. In the discounted cash flow analysis, future cash flows are discounted to present value using an appropriate discount rate or rate of return. Cash flows are forecasted for a discrete period of years and then projected to grow at a constant rate in perpetuity. The capitalization of cash flow analysis uses forecasted cash flow for the next period, which is converted to present value using an appropriate capitalization rate, equal to the discount rate less the expected growth rate in perpetuity.

A discounted cash flow analysis is appropriate for Multipartner rather than a capitalization of cash flows analysis, since the company expects strong future growth. If it's determined that the most current year is representative of the future earnings potential of the company, than a capitalization of cash flows would be appropriate to use. Cash flow is defined as:

Earnings before interest & taxes

− Income taxes

= Net income (debt free)

+ Depreciation

± Change in working capital

− Capital expenditures

= Cash flow (debt free)

The discounted cash flow analysis is presented in *Figure 5.9*. Five years of cash flows are projected for Multipartner. A residual period, otherwise called a terminal year, must also be projected. This is the cash flow that is expected into perpetuity. When creating a pro forma analysis, underlying assumptions are critical. If strong growth is projected without a history of growth or a reasonable basis for the growth of the company, then the riskiness of the cash flows increases and the discount rate should be adjusted accordingly. Another way to offset some risk of projecting strong growth is to create more than one scenario: worst case, most likely, and best case. Also, the premise of this analysis is fair market value, which should only be used as a starting point. If you're buying or selling a practice, assumptions can be changed based on knowledge of economies of scale and synergies of the transaction.

The assumptions used in Figure 5.9 are as follows:

♦ Revenues are expected to increase 15 percent in 2005 and 10 percent in 2006 through 2008 based on 5 percent growth in

FIGURE 5.9   **Multipartner Firm**
Income Approach—Discounted Cash Flow
Analysis ($000)

Forecast Year Ending December 31	Adjusted[a] 2004	Projected 2005	Projected 2006	Projected 2007	Projected 2008	Projected 2009	Residual
Revenue	$6,400	$7,360	$8,096	$8,906	$9,797	$10,287	$10,801
Direct Expense	2,500	2,875	3,163	3,479	3,827	4,018	4,219
Gross Profit	3,900	4,485	4,933	5,427	5,970	6,269	6,582
Operating Expenses:							
Operating Exp.–Excluding Dep.	1,964	2,101	2,248	2,405	2,573	2,705	2,841
Depreciation Expense	17	18	16	18	20	21	22
Operating Income	1,920	2,367	2,669	3,004	3,377	3,543	3,719
Other Income (Expense):							
Other Income (Exp.)–Excluding Interest Expense	32	31	41	45	50	52	55
Earnings Before Interest & Taxes	1,952	2,398	2,710	3,049	3,427	3,595	3,774
Income Taxes on EBIT[b]	664	815	921	1,037	1,165	1,222	1,283
Net Income (Debt Free)	1,288	1,583	1,789	2,012	2,262	2,373	2,491
Depreciation & Amortization	17	18	16	18	20	21	22
Cash Flow (Debt Free)	1,305	1,600	1,805	2,030	2,282	2,394	2,513
Adj. Working Capital Changes	NA	(210)	(160)	(176)	(193)	(106)	(112)
Capital Expenditures	NA	(18)	(16)	(18)	(20)	(21)	(22)
Free Cash Flow (Debt Free)	**NA**	**$1,373**	**$1,629**	**$1,836**	**$2,069**	**$2,267**	**$2,379**
Assumptions:[c]							
Revenue Growth Rate	6.7%	15.0%	10.0%	10.0%	10.0%	5.0%	5.0%
Direct Expense	39.1%	39.1%		39.1%	39.1%	39.1%	39.1%
Gross Profit Margin	60.9%	60.9%	60.9%	60.9%	60.9%	60.9%	60.9%
Operating Expenses:							
Operating Exp.–Excluding Dep.[d]	30.7%	28.5%	27.8%	27.0%	26.3%	26.3%	26.3%
Depreciation Expense	0.3%	0.2%	0.2%	0.2%	0.2%	0.2%	0.2%
Other Income (Exp.)–Excluding Interest Expense	0.5%	0.5%	0.5%	0.5%	0.5%	0.5%	0.5%
Earnings Before Interest & Taxes	30.5%	32.6%	33.5%	34.2%	35.0%	34.9%	34.9%
Effective Tax Rate–Taxes on EBIT	34.0%	34.0%	34.0%	34.0%	34.0%	34.0%	34.0%
Adjusted Net Working Capital	21.7%	21.7%	21.7%	21.7%	21.7%	21.7%	21.7%
Adjusted Net Working Capital[e]	$1,387	$1,597	$1,757	$1,933	$2,126	$2,232	$2,344
Capital Expenditures	NA	0.2%	0.2%	0.2%	0.2%	0.2%	0.2%

[a] Adjusted per Figure 5.7
[b] At federal corporate income tax rates
[c] All assumptions, excluding sales growth and effective tax rate, are stated as a percentage of sales
[d] Operating expenses are projected to increase 7% per year through 2008
[e] Required working capital level based on 2004 working capital

existing AUM and growth in new clients, then 5 percent in 2009 and thereafter based on long-term industry and economic trends.

♦ Direct expense is projected based on adjusted 2004 direct expense as a percentage of sales, which is indicative of future results and incorporates the firm's philosophy of the team approach to client service.

♦ Operating expenses are projected based on adjusted 2004, growing at a 7 percent rate through 2008. Multipartner has already invested in the infrastructure requirements for growth, so improvements in the operating margin are reasonable.

♦ Other income/expense is projected based on adjusted 2004 as a percentage of sales.

♦ Capital expenditures and depreciation were forecasted at 0.2 percent of revenue, based on discussions with Multipartner's management, and are in line with the firm's historical levels.

♦ Working capital is set equal to 2004 as a percentage of revenue.

Once the cash flows are projected, they must be discounted to present value. *Figure 5.10* presents the discounted cash flow summary. Since the cash flows do not tend to come in only at the end of the year, this analysis uses a midyear convention, which assumes that the cash flows will come in throughout the year. The formula for discounting the cash flows is as follows:

$$\frac{\text{CF Year 1}}{1/(1+r)^{\wedge}1} + \frac{\text{CF Year 2}}{1/(1+r)^{\wedge}2} + \frac{\text{CF Year n}}{1/(1+r)^{\wedge}n} + \frac{\text{CF perpetuity}/(r-g)}{1/(1+r)^{\wedge}n}$$

where CF = cash flow
n = periods deferred
r = discount rate
g = growth rate in perpetuity

The present value of the cash flows in each period and the residual are added together to produce a total capital value of Multipartner of $10,571,000. Total capital is the value to both debt and equity

FIGURE 5.10   **Multipartner Firm**
               Income Approach—Discounted Cash Flow
               Analysis ($000)

Forecast Year Ending December 31	Projected 2005	Projected 2006	Projected 2007	Projected 2008	Projected 2009	Residual
Free Cash Flow (Debt Free)	$1,373	$1,629	$1,836	$2,069	$2,267	$2,379
Residual Capitalization Rate						÷ 18.1%
Future Value of Free Cash Flows	$1,373	$1,629	$1,836	$2,069	$2,267	$13,144
Number of Periods Deferred	0.50	1.50	2.50	3.50	4.50	4.50
Present Value Factor*	× 0.9013	× 0.7322	× 0.5948	× 0.4832	× 0.3925	× 0.3925
Present Value of Free Cash Flows	$1,237	$1,193	$1,092	$1,000	$890	$5,159

DISCOUNTED CASH FLOW SUMMARY	
Present Value of FY 2005–2009 Free Cash Flows	$5,412
+ Present Value of Residual	+ 5,159
Indicated Total Capital Value	10,571
– Interest Bearing Debt	– 0
Indicated Equity Value	$10,571
+ Nonoperating Assets	+ 0
Concluded Income Approach Value (Majority Interest)	**$10,571**

* Present Value Factor = $1/(1 + \text{discount rate})^{\text{nth period}}$

holders. To determine the value of the stockholder's equity, subtract total interest-bearing debt from the total capital value and add the value of nonoperating assets. Since Multipartner has neither, the income approach produces an equity value of $10,571,000.

In the market approach to valuation, there are three main methods: a public company analysis, a merger-and-acquisition transaction analysis, and a prior-transaction analysis. A prior-transaction analysis involves analyzing prior transactions of Multipartner's stock. Since there have been no transactions in the stock in the past five years, this analysis was not employed.

Public Company Analysis

The publicly traded guideline company analysis uses stock market transactions involving publicly traded companies that are similar

FIGURE 5.11 **Multipartner Firm Market Approach—Public Company Analysis Financial Ratio Analysis, Latest 12 Months ($MM)**

Company	American Financial Company	East Coast Consulting	Financial Planning Group	Investment Advisors	Money Managers Corp.	Northern Planners Group	Retirement Specialists	Southern Wealth Builders	West Coast Planners
Latest Fiscal Year	Dec. 04	Dec. 04	Oct. 04	Dec. 04	Dec. 03	Dec. 03	Dec. 04	Dec. 03	Dec. 03
Latest Quarter	Dec. 04	Dec. 04	Oct. 04	Dec. 04	Sep. 04	Sep. 04	Dec. 04	Sep. 04	Sep. 04
Size ($MM):									
Sales*	659,997	725,311	661,813	846,964	250,297	495,281	1,280,349	133,217	503,748
Total Assets	1,933,421	1,145,235	743,566	954.688	744,323	1,016,289	1,928,825	141,952	644,635
Shareholder Equity*	707,692	768,352	449,506	457,753	396,116	545,951	1,697,300	121,554	205,957
Pretax Income*	244,617	298,634	221,658	330,415	95,407	246,413	533,783	58,352	163,519
Compound Annual Growth Rates:**									
Sales	9.5%	11.1%	11.4%	5.6%	3.8%	6.4%	1.4%	(11.5%)	6.4%
Pretax Income	11.0%	7.5%	4.3%	4.3%	25.9%	9.9%	3.9%	(17.0%)	(10.4%)
Total Assets	24.9%	20.8%	14.5%	7.9%	31.9%	15.2%	7.0%	18.0%	14.0%
Profitability:*									
Gross Profit Margin	60.9%	41.0%	34.6%	43.3%	41.1%	52.7%	44.2%	71.3%	44.6%
Operating Profit Margin	40.6%	38.2%	33.6%	41.1%	40.7%	50.1%	41.0%	43.8%	34.4%
Pretax Profit Margin	37.1%	41.2%	33.5%	39.0%	38.1%	49.8%	41.7%	43.8%	32.5%
Dividends/Net Income*	NA	NA	26.6%	22.5%	0.0%	36.0%	30.3%	127.7%	50.6%
Liquidity:*									
Current Ratio	2.1	2.6	4.2	1.8	NMF	9.2	2.8	NA	1.5
Quick Ratio	1.9	2.6	4.1	1.7	NMF	9.2	2.8	NA	1.4
Productivity Data:									
AUM ($ Millions)	129,800	342,000	94,300	179,300	28,700	115,500	235,200	9,300	38,700
Number of Employees	822	973	686	1,385	197	627	4,139	105	1,476
Productivity Ratios:									
Total Revenue per Employee	0.8	0.7	1.0	0.6	1.3	0.8	0.3	1.3	0.3
AUM per Employee ($ Millions)	157.9	351.5	137.5	129.5	145.7	184.2	56.8	88.6	26.2
Total Revenue/ Total AUM	0.51%	0.21%	0.70%	0.47%	0.87%	0.43%	0.54%	1.43%	1.30%

* Based on adjusted historical financial data
** Based on latest fiscal year
NA = not available/applicable
NMF = not meaningful

FIGURE 5.12 **Multipartner Firm**
Market Approach—Public Company
Analysis Valuation Ratios

Company	Equity/AUM	Equity/Pretax Income	Equity/Net Income	MVIC/ EBITDA	MVIC/ EBIT
American Financial Co.	0.02	8.6	27.2	9.9	10.7
East Coast Consulting	0.01	16.3	22.6	15.2	16.3
Financial Planning Group	0.04	15.1	24.1	14.6	15.1
Investment Advisors	0.02	9.9	16.5	9.6	10.1
Money Managers Corp.	0.05	15.3	24.4	15.5	15.6
Northern Planners Group	0.03	14.0	22.9	14.5	15.3
Retirement Specialists	0.03	14.9	23.5	13.8	14.8
Southern Wealth Builders	0.11	17.6	19.9	15.7	17.9
West Coast Planners	0.05	11.9	18.6	12.3	13.0
Median	**0.03**	**14.9**	**22.9**	**14.5**	**15.1**
Maximum	0.11	17.6	27.2	15.7	17.9
Minimum	0.01	8.6	16.5	9.6	10.1

Equity = market value of total stockholders' equity
MVIC = Market Value of Invested Capital Price (dept and equity capital)
EBITDA = earnings before interest, taxes, depreciation, and amortization
EBIT = earnings before interest and taxes

in nature to the financial-advisory business being valued. The steps necessary to employ this analysis are to select appropriate companies, compute valuation ratios, make adjustments to the ratios, and compute values.

Figure 5.11 presents the publicly traded companies that were found in SIC Code 6282, "Investment Advice." Although the companies found for this valuation are not exactly like Multipartner, they provide alternative-investment opportunities for an investor in this industry.

After choosing the publicly traded guideline companies, it's necessary to make adjustments to the financial statements to account for any differences in accounting methods and nonrecurring or extraordinary items. Many of these items can be found in annual reports and SEC filings, especially Form 10-K filings of these companies.

As shown in Figure 5.11, nine companies were identified. Financial ratios similar to those calculated in the income approach

FIGURE 5.13   **Multipartner Firm
Market Approach—Public Company
Analysis Valuation Summary ($000)**

Valuation Ratios	Market Derived Valuation Ratio	Upward/ (Downward) Adjustment[a]	Adjusted Valuation Ratio[b]	Subject Company Financial Basis	Indicated Value	Subtract Debt[c]	Indicated Equity Value	Weight
Total Equity Multiples (Latest 12 Months):								
Assets Under Management	0.03	(60%)	0.01	$781,000	$7,810	NA	$7,810	20%
Pretax Income	14.87	(60%)	5.95	$1,952	$11,614	NA	$11,614	20%
Net Income	22.93	(60%)	9.17	$1,288	$11,811	NA	$11,811	20%
MVIC Multiples (Latest 12 Months):								
EBITDA	14.50	(60%)	5.80	$1,969	$11,420	$0	$11,420	20%
EBIT	15.05	(60%)	6.02	$1,952	$11,751	$0	$11,751	20%
Weighted Average Equity Value							$10,881	
+ Nonoperating Assets						+	$0	
Concluded Value–Public Company Analysis (Majority Interest)							**$10,881**	

NA = not available/applicable
[a] The MVIC adjustment is equal to total adjustment multiplied by the Ratio of Total Equity to Invested Capital
[b] Adjusted Valuation Ratio = Market Derived Valuation Ratio (1 + Adjustment)
[c] For Total Equity Multiples: not applicable (NA), for MVIC Multiples: subtract interest bearing debt
Total equity = market value of total stockholders' equity
MVIC = Market Value of Invested Capital Price (debt and equity capital)
EBITDA = earnings before interest, taxes, depreciation, and amortization
EBIT = earnings before interest and taxes

to make comparisons with these companies easier. These companies are much larger, more diversified, more profitable, and have higher liquidity on average than Multipartner. However, Multipartner has grown at a faster rate historically than these companies. Productivity measures were mixed compared with the publicly traded guideline companies.

Valuation ratios are then calculated as presented in *Figure 5.12*. Two types of ratios can be developed: stockholder's equity (price) or market value of invested capital (MVIC), which is interest-bearing debt plus stockholder's equity. This analysis used five ratios: equity to AUM; price to pretax income; price to net income; MVIC to earnings before interest, taxes, depreciation, and amortization; and MVIC to earnings before interest and taxes. There are many more ratios that can be calculated, but these are the most common.

These ratios then need to be adjusted upward or downward based on the comparison analysis. As noted earlier, Multipartner is much smaller, less diversified, and less profitable. It also has lower-than-average liquidity compared with the guideline companies. Although Multipartner has grown at a faster rate than the guideline companies, on average the guideline companies are expected to grow at a faster rate than Multipartner. Analysts' estimates for earnings per share and growth rates for publicly traded companies can be found in such publications as Standard & Poor's *S&P Earnings Guide*.[3] Overall, the ratios are adjusted downward 60 percent based on these factors.

Figure 5.13 presents the summary of publicly traded guideline company analysis. The ratios shown are the medians calculated in Figure 5.12. The adjusted ratio is applied to Multipartner's most recent financial basis, which is 2004 in this case. Interest-bearing debt needs to be subtracted from the MVIC ratios only. Results from the ratios then need to be weighted based on the reliability and variation of the ratios. In this case, equal weight is given to the ratios. Nonoperating assets, if any, then need to be added to determine the value of stockholder's equity. Multipartner does not have any nonoperating assets; therefore, the value indicated by the public company analysis is $10,881,000.

M&A Transaction Analysis

The second market approach analysis is the merger-and-acquisition transaction analysis. This analysis uses merger-and-acquisition transactions involving companies similar in nature to the business being valued. The steps are the same as those for the public company analysis: select appropriate transactions, compute valuation ratios, make adjustments to the ratios, and compute values.

Figure 5.14 presents the sixteen transactions and computed valuation ratios that were identified in this industry. Sources for finding merger-and-acquisition data include Form 8-K filings of publicly traded companies, industry trade journals, and various databases described in chapter 4, "Defining Value: Other Approaches to Valuation." Data for mergers and acquisitions can be difficult to find. Because of that difficulty, only three valuation ratios were calculated:

FIGURE 5.14   **Multipartner Firm**
               Market Approach—Merger & Acquisition
               Analysis ($ MM)

Date Effective	Equity Value	MVIC	Revenue	Net Earnings	EBITDA	EBITDA/ Revenue	Price/ Earnings	MVIC/ Revenue	MVIC/ EBITDA
01/16/04	$321.3	$321.3	$103.3	($177.4)	($179.3)	−173.5%	(1.8)*	3.1	(1.8)*
10/31/03	$3,000.0	$3,145.6	$622.4	$107.7	$252.9	40.6%	27.8	5.1	12.4
07/01/03	$475.0	$1,523.3	$376.7	$107.4	$129.3	34.4%	4.4	4.0	11.8
05/05/03	$26.0	$27.4	$11.2	($8.7)	($7.4)	−65.9%	(3.0)*	2.4	(3.7)*
08/02/02	$6.8	$6.8	$11.3	($0.1)	$0.1	0.6%	(52.3)*	0.6	97.1*
08/01/02	$140.0	$160.8	$29.8	($7.8)	$5.1	17.0%	(17.0)*	5.4	31.8
07/15/02	$485.6	$485.6	$278.9	$157.7	$163.9	58.8%	3.1	1.7	3.0
07/13/02	$245.2	$245.3	$64.1	$4.8	$11.0	17.2%	51.3	3.8	22.2
05/10/02	$5.2	$10.0	$33.2	($4.5)	($11.3)	−34.0%	(1.1)*	0.3	(0.9)*
04/29/02	$15.0	$29.7	$322.8	($51.3)	$48.1	14.9%	(0.3)*	0.1	0.6
01/04/02	$3.9	$4.1	$2.3	$0.0	$0.1	3.9%	393.0*	1.7	45.1*
10/31/01	$241.0	$241.0	$90.8	$60.2	NA	NA	4.0	2.7	NA
10/01/01	$132.7	$132.7	$24.8	$4.2	NA	NA	31.5	5.4	NA
07/17/01	$222.0	$222.0	$62.8	$37.9	$38.1	60.7%	5.9	3.5	5.8
04/10/01	$780.2	$780.2	$185.0	$19.8	NA	NA	39.4	4.2	NA
01/11/01	$300.4	$334.1	$305.5	$33.9	$116.0	38.0%	8.9	1.1	2.9
Median	$231.5	$231.5	$157.8			17.0%	8.87	2.88	8.80
Maximum	$3,000.0	$3,145.6					393.0	5.4	97.1
Minimum	$3.9	$4.1					3.1	0.1	0.6

* Nonmeaningful ratio eliminated from calculations based on standard deviation analysis

price to earnings where earnings equal net income, MVIC to revenue, and MVIC to EBITDA.

Figure 5.15 presents the summary of the merger-and-acquisition analysis. Because of the range of ratios, median ratios are the most applicable, because the medians smooth the variation in the multiples. As in the public company analysis, the ratios need to be adjusted upward or downward depending on the comparison factors. The companies included in the transaction analysis are larger and more diversified on average than Multipartner, whereas Multipartner was more profitable on average. Therefore, the ratios were adjusted downward 30 percent.

FIGURE 5.15   **Multipartner Firm**
               Market Approach—Merger & Acquisition
               Analysis Summary ($000)

	Market Derived Valuation Ratio	Upward/ (Downward) Adjustment	Adjusted Valuation Ratio*	Subject Company Financial Basis[a]	Indicated Value	Subtract Debt	Indicated Equity Value	Weight
Equity Multiples:								
Net Income	8.87	(30%)	6.21	$1,288	$8,000	NA	$8,000	33.3%
MVIC Multiples:								
Revenue	2.88	(30%)	2.02	$6,400	$12,928	$0	$12,928	33.3%
EBITDA	8.80	(30%)	6.16	$1,969	$12,127	$0	$12,127	33.3%
Indicated Weighted Average Value – Merger & Acquisitions Analysis							$11,018	
+ Nonoperating Assets						+	$0	
Concluded Value–Public Company Analysis (Rounded)							**$11,018**	

NA = not available/applicable
* Adjusted Valuation Ratio = Market Derived Valuation Ratio × (1 + Adjustment)
[a] Adjusted, as per Figure 5.9

The adjusted ratios are then applied to Multipartner's adjusted 2004 financial basis. Interest-bearing debt needs to be subtracted from the MVIC ratios only. Results from the ratios then need to be weighted based on the reliability and variation of the ratios. In this case, equal weight is given to the ratios. Nonoperating assets, if any, are then added to determine the value of stockholder's equity. Multipartner does not have any nonoperating assets; therefore, the value indicated by the public company analysis is $11,018,000.

The Valuation Summary

The final step in the valuation process requires a review of each valuation approach and a reconciliation of these approaches to reach a final value conclusion. In a specific appraisal situation, the weight given to each approach depends on the valuation function and purpose, the value premise and definition, the quantity and quality of available data, and the reliability of the analysis. *Figure 5.16* presents the valuation summary for Multipartner Firm.

FIGURE 5.16   **Multipartner Firm Valuation Summary**

	Indicated Value	Weight
Concluded Income-Approach Value	$10,571,000	80%
Concluded Market-Approach Value —Publicly Traded Guideline Companies	$10,881,000	10%
Concluded Market-Approach Value —M&A Transactions	$11,018,000	10%
Concluded Value	**$10,647,000**	

The income approach was given significant weight (80 percent) because it represents the amount a prudent investor would pay for Multipartner's expected future cash flows, based on current market rates of return and Multipartner's specific risks.

In the market approach, the public company analysis was given some weight (10 percent) because it reflects current stock market pricing for reasonably comparable businesses that represent alternative investment opportunities. However, significant adjustments were made to the valuation ratios, which reduce the reliability of this approach.

In addition, the merger-and-acquisition analysis in the market approach was given some weight (10 percent) because it reflects recent merger and acquisition prices for reasonably comparable companies that represent alternative investment opportunities. However, the quality of the underlying data and the adjustments made to the valuation ratios reduce the reliability of this approach.

Based on these weightings, the fair market value of Multipartner Firm as of December 31, 2004 is $10,647,000.

Chapter Notes

1. Moss Adams, *2004 FPA Financial Performance Study of Financial Advisory Practices* (SEI Investments and Financial Planning Association, September 2004).

2. The Risk Management Association (RMA), *Annual Statement Studies: Financial Ratio Benchmarks 2004/2005* (The Risk Management Association).

3. Standard & Poor's, *Earnings Guide January 2006* (The McGraw-Hill Companies, Inc., 2006).

THERE IS AN important difference between a business and a book of business. Put simply, a business is a systematic, leveraged enterprise that is not solely dependent on its owner to thrive. A book of business is literally an asset—a client list—that's managed by a solo practitioner and depends on that solo practitioner to remain viable. Ensemble firms tend to command higher multiples than solo practices because of this reduced dependency, which translates as reduced risk. What's more, ensembles tend to have greater potential to grow, whereas in solo practices, there is a physical limit to the number of clients one owner can manage. In this chapter, we'll evaluate a solo practice and highlight the differences in relation to the ensemble firm profiled in chapter 5.

The Basics

Solo Practitioner, a registered investment-advisory firm, is an S corporation located in a state with no sales tax, thus taxes are applied at the federal corporate rate. The firm is a financial-planning firm, serving clients of modest net worth who have investable assets greater than $200,000. This is a fee-based firm that currently enjoys recurring revenues of approximately 75 percent. By definition, there is only one shareholder. The other two employees provide administrative support only. The employees have not signed noncompete and/or nonsolicitation agreements.

Figure 6.1 presents the historical common-size income statement

FIGURE 6.1   **Solo Practitioner**
              Historical Common-Size Income Statement
              (Cash Basis)

Fiscal Year Ended December 31	Tax Return 2001	%	Tax Return 2002	%	Tax Return 2003	%	Internal 2004	%	Average FY 01–04
Revenue	$520,000	100.0%	$410,000	100.0%	$425,000	100.0%	$530,000	100.0%	100.0%
Officers' Compensation	80,000	15.4	90,000	22.0%	115,000	27.1	120,000	22.6	21.8
Gross Profit	440,000	84.6	320,000	78.0	310,000	72.9	410,000	77.4	78.2
Operating Expenses:									
Advertising	2,900	0.6	2,800	0.7	2,300	0.5	2,800	0.5	0.6
Education	800	0.2	900	0.2	700	0.2	950	0.2	0.2
Depreciation	0	0.0	4,000	1.0	4,000	0.9	4,000	0.8	0.7
Dues & Subscriptions	2,300	0.4	6,000	1.5	5,800	1.4	5,600	1.1	1.1
Employee Benefits	2,200	0.4	2,400	0.6	3,400	0.8	4,200	0.8	0.7
Insurance	3,500	0.7	3,600	0.9	3,650	0.9	8,000	1.5	1.0
Miscellaneous Expense	2,700	0.5	12,500	3.0	7,900	1.9	8,100	1.5	1.7
Office Expense	6,800	1.3	15,000	3.7	6,500	1.5	17,600	3.3	2.5
Professional Fees	3,300	0.6	3,700	0.9	4,000	0.9	4,500	0.8	0.8
Rent	22,000	4.2	22,660	5.5	23,340	5.5	24,040	4.5	4.9
Salaries – Other	70,000	13.5	74,000	18.0	82,000	19.3	90,000	17.0	16.9
Supplies	3,200	0.6	3,000	0.7	4,000	0.9	3,800	0.7	0.8
Taxes & Licenses	1,200	0.2	1,900	0.5	1,000	0.2	1,200	0.2	0.3
Telephone	3,200	0.6	4,500	1.1	5,800	1.4	7,900	1.5	1.1
Travel & Entertainment	1,200	0.2	600	0.1	300	0.1	700	0.1	0.1
Utilities	600	0.1	400	0.1	1,800	0.4	1,900	0.4	0.2
Vehicle	1,900	0.4	1,900	0.5	1,900	0.4	1,900	0.4	0.4
Total Operating Expense	127,800	24.6	159,860	39.0	158,390	37.3	187,190	35.3	34.0
Pretax Profit	312,200	60.0	160,140	39.1	151,610	35.7	22,810	42.0	44.2
Total Income Taxes	0	0.0	0	0.0	0	0.0	0	0.0	0.0
Net Income	**$312,200**	**60.0%**	**$160,140**	**39.1%**	**$151,610**	**35.7%**	**$222,810**	**42.0%**	**44.2%**

of Solo Practitioner for the years ended December 31, 2001 through 2004. Again, the income statement should reflect both direct expenses (professional and owner's salaries) and operating expenses. *Figure 6.2* presents the balance sheet as of December 31, 2004, the only year the balance sheet data were available.

Revenues for Solo Practitioner fell from $520,000 in 2001 to $410,000 in 2002 because of the tech bust and the terrorist attacks,

FIGURE 6.2   **Solo Practitioner**
               Historical Common-Size Balance Sheet

Fiscal Year Ended December 31	Internal 2004	%
Current Assets:		
Cash	$33,000	27.4%
Prepaid Expenses	12,700	10.5
Total Current Assets	45,700	37.9
Fixed Assets:		
Net Fixed Assets	72,000	59.8
Other Noncurrent Assets:		
Security Deposit	2,800	2.3
Total Other Noncurrent Expenses	2,800	2.3
Total Assets	$120,500	100.0%
Current Liabilities:		
Accrued Expenses	$44,500	33.6%
Other Current Liabilities	0	0.0
Total Current Liabilities	40,500	33.6
Total Liabilities	40,500	33.6
Equity:		
Retained Earnings	80,000	66.4
Total Equity	80,000	66.4
Total Liabilities & Equity	$120,500	100.0%

which affected the financial-advisory industry and the economy during 2001 and 2002. Revenues then increased to $530,000 in 2004. Over the four-year period, revenues were essentially flat, increasing at only a 0.5 percent compound annual rate. According to the firm's shareholder, Solo Practitioner is at capacity with its existing infrastructure; therefore, it is not expecting to grow significantly in the foreseeable future.

Solo Practitioner moved offices in 2002 and incurred unusual expenses of $25,000 as a result. In addition, the shareholder indicated that personal expenses of $8,000 in 2002 and $10,000 in 2004 were being run through the company. These expenses will need to be adjusted for in the valuation.

Pretax profit margins declined from $312,000 in 2001 to $223,000 in 2004, an 8.1 percent compound annual decline. Assets consisted of cash, prepaid expenses, leasehold improvements, and deposits. Solo Practitioner had no interest-bearing debt in 2004. S corporation distributions averaged $200,000 per year during the four-year period.

Industry Comparisons

A comparison of Solo Practitioner with the industry is presented in *Figure 6.3*. Again, industry comparisons are from the *2004 FPA Financial Performance Study*,[1] produced by Moss Adams for companies considered "virtuoso," and *Annual Statement Studies 2004/2005*,[2] published by the Risk Management Association (RMA). The medians shown are for SIC Code 6282, "Investment Advice" (see chapter 5 for definition), with sales in the same size range as Solo Practitioner's.

Solo Practitioner's gross profit margin averaged 78.2 percent during the 2001–2004 period, above the FPA median of 66.8 percent. This suggests that the owner of the practice is taking less compensation than average for comparable practices. Therefore, an adjustment in this case is warranted.

Operating profit margins averaged 44.2 percent during the 2001–2004 period, which was above the FPA and RMA medians. The above-average operating margin was a result of the above-average gross margin and the shareholder's ability to keep costs down relative to the industry.

Liquidity ratios were in line with industry norms during 2004.

Solvency ratios are used to measure a company's ability to meet interest and principal payments on long-term debt and other obligations as they become due. These ratios analyze leverage, debt coverage, and long-term profitability. As mentioned, Solo Practitioner used no interest-bearing debt during the period under review.

Productivity ratios were mixed compared with the industry. The AUM per professional and support staff was $18 million in 2004, below the industry average, whereas AUM per professional at $55 million was above. Revenue per professional and support staff was below the industry norm, whereas revenue per professional was above in 2004. Revenue per AUM at 0.96 percent in 2004 was higher than the industry median of 0.75 percent.

FIGURE 6.3   **Solo Practitioner
Historical Financial Ratios**

Fiscal Year Ended December 31	Tax Return 2001	Tax Return 2002	Tax Return 2003	Internal 2004	Average FY 01–04	FPA Study 2004 Elite Firms	RMA 2004/2005 SIC 6282* $0–1M
Growth Rates:							
Revenue Growth	NA	(21.2%)	3.7%	24.7%	0.5%[b]	NA	NA
Pretax Income Growth	NA	(48.7%)	(5.3%)	47.0%	(8.1%)[b]	NA	NA
Profitability (% of Sales):							
Net Sales	100.0%	100.0%	100.0%	100.0%	100.0%	100.0%	100.0%
Gross Profit	84.6%	78.0%	72.9%	77.4%	78.2%	66.8%	0.0%
Operating Expenses	24.6%	39.0%	37.3%	35.3%	34.0%	44.3%	75.6%
Operating Profit	60.0%	39.1%	35.7%	42.0%	44.2%	22.5%	24.4%
All Other Income/(Expenses)	0.0%	0.0%	0.0%	0.0%	0.0%	(8.5%)	(4.5%)
Pretax Profit	60.0%	39.1%	35.7%	42.0%	44.2%	14.0%	19.9%
Net Income	60.0%	39.1%	35.7%	42.0%	44.2%	13.6%	NA
Liquidity Ratios:							
Current Ratio	NMF	NMF	NMF	1.1	1.1	NA	1.2
Quick Ratio	NMF	NMF	NMF	0.8	0.8	NA	0.9
Solvency Ratios:							
Debt to Worth	NMF	NMF	NMF	0.5	0.5	NA	5.0
Long-Term Debt to Total Capital[a]	NMF	NMF	NMF	0.0%	0.0%	NA	144.8%
Productivity Data:							
Number of Employees	2	2	3	3	3	3	NA
Number of Investment Managers	1	1	1	1	1	1	NA
AUM (Assets Under Management $000)	NA	NA	NA	55,000	55,000	50,400	NA
Productivity Ratios:							
AUM per Professional + Support ($000)	NA	NA	NA	18,333	18,333	24,564	NA
AUM per Professional ($000)	NA	NA	NA	55,000	55,000	45,700	NA
Revenue per Professional + Support	29,624	66,109	92,267	167,004	88,751	207,596	NA
Revenue per Professional	59,248	132,218	276,802	501,011	242,320	357,000	NA
Total Revenue/AUM	NA	NA	NA	0.96%	0.96%	0.75%	NA

Ratios are annualized where applicable
NA = not applicable; NMF = not meaningful; EBIT = earnings before interest and taxes
* SIC 6282 = Investment Advice
[a] Estimated RMA ratios
[b] Compound annual growth rates

FIGURE 6.4   **Solo Practitioner**
              Historical Working Capital Analysis ($000)

Fiscal Year Ended December 31	2004	RMA 2004/2005 SIC 6282* $0–1M	Selected % Sales[d]
Net Working Capital (NWC)	5	NA	NA
− Current Nonoperating Assets	0	NA	NA
+ Current Interest-Bearing Debt	0	NA	NA
Adjusted Net Working Capital (ANWC)	5	NA	NA
Working Capital Ratios:[a]			
Sales/Net Working Capital	101.9	84.6	NA
Net Working Capital/Sales	1.0%	1.2%	NA
Sales/Adjusted NWC	101.9	(42.8)[b]	101.9
Adjusted NWC/Sales	1.0%	(2.3%)	1.0%
Account Analysis:[a]			
Cash & Equivalents/Sales	6.2%	9.8%[c]	6.2%
Trade Accounts Receivables/Sales	0.0%	3.4%[c]	0.0%
Other Accounts Receivables/Sales	0.0%	NA	0.0%
Inventories/Sales	0.0%	0.0%[c]	0.0%
Prepaid Expenses/Sales	2.4%	NA	2.4%
Other Current Assets/Sales	0.0%	1.5%[c]	0.0%
Trade Accounts Payable/Sales	0.0%	0.8%[c]	0.0%
Other Accounts Payable/Sales	0.0%	NA	0.0%
Taxes Payable/Sales	0.0%	0.0%[c]	0.0%
Accrued Expenses/Sales	7.6%	NA	7.6%
Other Current Liabilities/Sales	0.0%	7.9%[c]	0.0%
Adjusted Net Working Capital	1.0%	6.0%[c]	1.0%

NA = not applicable
* SIC 6282 = Investment Advice
[a] Annualized where applicable
[b] Estimated based on RMA percentage of total assets ratios
[c] Estimated based on RMA sales to total assets ratio of 4.1
[d] Based on FY 2004 unless noted

Historical Financial Ratios

Figure 6.4 presents Solo Practitioner's historical working capital (which is equal to current assets less current liabilities) in terms of dollars and as a percentage of revenues. Any nonoperating assets or liabilities would need to be adjusted out, but none were identified. Also, any current interest-bearing debt the company had would

FIGURE 6.5 Solo Practitioner Earnings Analysis and Adjustments ($000)

Fiscal Year Ended December 31	2001	2002	2003	2004
Sales	$520	$410	$425	$530
Direct Expense Adjustments:				
Direct Expenses	80	90	115	120
+ Adjust Compensation to Industry Level[a]	90	88	72	77
Adjusted Direct Expense	170	178	187	197
Operating Expense Adjustments:				
Operating Expenses	128	160	158	187
− Depreciation Expense[b]	0	(4)	(4)	(4)
− Nonrecurring Items				
Moving Expenses	0	(25)	0	0
Personal Expenses	0	(8)	0	(10)
Adjusted Operating Expenses	128	123	154	173
Depreciation Expense Summary:				
Depreciation in Cost of Sales	0	0	0	0
Total Depreciation Expense	0	4	4	4

Note: As reported in financial statements unless noted
[a] Owner's compensation adjusted to industry level provided by the *2003 FPA Compensation and Staffing Study*
[b] Reclassified

be removed, because the cash flows are first adjusted to a debt-free basis. As shown in Figure 6.4, the 2004 working capital as a percentage of revenue is selected as an appropriate level for future requirements.

Adjustments to the historical income statement are made in *Figure 6.5*. The owner's compensation was adjusted to the industry level based on the *2003 FPA Compensation and Staffing Study*.[3] Nonrecurring moving expense was removed in 2002, and personal expenses were removed in 2002 and 2004. Depreciation was removed and treated separately.

Figure 6.6 is a restatement of the income statement reflecting the adjustments in Figure 6.5.

Solo Practitioner's owner indicated that the firm has essentially reached its capacity for properly servicing new clients and does not expect significant growth in revenue or expenses for the foreseeable

---

FIGURE 6.6   **Solo Practitioner**
             Adjusted Income Statement and
             Cash Flow ($000)

Fiscal Year Ended December 31	2001	%	2002	%	2003	%	2004	%	Weighted Average FY 01–04
Sales[a]	$520	100.0%	$410	100.0%	$425	100.0%	$530	100.0%	100.0%
Direct Expense[a]	170	32.7	178	43.5	187	44.1	197	37.1	39.8
Gross Profit	350	67.3	232	56.5	238	55.9	333	62.9	60.2
Operating Expenses:									
Operating Expenses[a]	128	24.6	123	30.0	154	36.3	173	32.7	32.0
Depreciation Expense[a]	0	0.0	4	1.0	4	0.9	4	0.8	0.7
Operating Income	222	42.7	105	25.5	79	18.7	156	29.5	27.4
Other Income (Expense):									
Other Income (Expense)[a]	0	0.0	0	0.0	0	0.0	0	0.0	0.0
Earnings Before Interest & Taxes (EBIT)	222	42.7	105	25.5	79	18.7	156	29.5	27.4
Interest Expense[a]	0	0.0	0	0.0	0	0.0	0	0.0	0.0
Pretax Income	222	42.7	105	25.5	79	18.7	156	29.5	27.4
Income Tax (*Effective Rate*)[b]	70	*31.5*	24	*23.0*	15	*19.2*	44	*28.3*	*25.0*
Net Income	152	29.3	81	19.7	64	15.1	112	21.1	20.3
+ Depreciation & Amortization	0	0.0	4	1.0	4	0.9	4	0.8	0.7
Gross Cash Flow	**$152**	**29.3%**	**$85**	**20.6%**	**$68**	**16.0%**	**$116**	**21.9%**	**21.0%**
Debt-Free Data:									
Earnings Before Interest, Taxes, Depreciation & Amortization (EBITDA)	$222	42.7%	$109	26.5%	$83	19.6%	$160	30.2%	28.2%
– Depreciation & Amortization	0	0.0	4	1.0	4	0.9	4	0.8	0.7
Earnings Before Interest & Taxes (EBIT)	222	42.7	105	25.5	79	18.7	156	29.5	27.4
Income Taxes on EBIT (*Effective Rate*)[b]	70	*31.5*	24	*23.0*	15	*19.2*	44	*28.3*	*25.0*
Net Income (Debt Free)	152	29.3	81	19.7	64	15.1	112	21.1	20.3
Depreciation & Amortization	0	0.0	4	1.0	4	0.9	4	0.8	0.7
Cash Flow (Debt Free)	**$152**	**29.3%**	**$85**	**20.6%**	**$68**	**16.0%**	**$116**	**21.9%**	**21.0%**

[a] Adjusted as shown in Figure 6.5
[b] At federal corporate income tax rates

---

future. Therefore, using the capitalization of cash flows is reasonable in this instance. *Figure 6.7* presents the calculation of the discount rate and the capitalization rate, which was discussed in greater detail in chapter 3, "Defining Value: The Income Approach to Valuation" Based on how Solo Practitioner compared with the

FIGURE 6.7   **Solo Practitioner**
              Discount Rate and Capitalization
              Rate Analysis

Discount Rate – Buildup Method:

Risk-Free Rate (20-Year Government Bond)	4.9%
Equity Risk Premium[a]	+ 7.2%
Small-Stock Risk Premium (Size Premium)[b]	+ 4.0%
Subject-Company Risk Premium	+ 10.0%
Discount Rate	= **26.1%**
Capitalization Rate:	
Discount Rate (See Above)	26.1%
Growth Rate (Into Perpetuity)	− 5.0%
Capitalization Rate	= **21.1%**

[a] This represents the premium demanded by investors in equity securities over and above the risk-free rate as published by Ibbotson Associates in *Stocks, Bonds, Bills & Inflation (SBBI) 2005 Yearbook*

[b] This represents the premium for size demanded by investors in small-capitalization stocks over and above the premium demanded by equity investors, as published by Ibbotson Associates in *SBBI 2005 Yearbook*

companies in the financial-advisory industry, a subject-company risk premium of 10 percent was selected for these reasons:

♦ Small size (it is much smaller than the micro-cap companies included in the small-stock risk premium discount; therefore, an additional discount for size is appropriate)

♦ Significant reliance on one key shareholder

♦ Mixed productivity results

♦ No noncompete or nonsolicitation agreements

Positive factors partially offset the negatives:

♦ Above-average financial performance

♦ Length of the client relationships and the low average age of the client base

♦ Recurring revenue stream of 75 percent

As shown in Figure 6.7, a discount rate of 26.1 percent was calculated, which translates into a capitalization rate of 21.1 percent, after subtracting growth into perpetuity of 5 percent.

FIGURE 6.8 **Solo Practitioner
Income Approach—Capitalization of
Cash Flow Analysis ($000)**

Forecast Year Ending December 31	Adjusted[a] 2004	Projected Cash Flow
Sales	$530	$557
Direct Expense	197	207
Gross Profit	333	350
Operating Expenses:		
Operating Exp.–Excluding Dep.	173	182
Depreciation Expense	4	5
Operating Income	156	163
Other Income (Expense):		
Other Income (Exp.)–Excluding Interest Expense	0	0
Earnings Before Interest & Taxes	156	163
Income Taxes on EBIT[b]	44	47
Net Income (Debt Free)	112	116
Depreciation & Amortization	4	5
Cash Flow (Debt Free)	116	121
Adj. Working Capital Changes	NA	(1)
Capital Expenditures	NA	(5)
Free Cash Flow (Debt Free)	**NA**	**$115**
Assumptions:[c]		
Sales Growth Rate	24.7%	5.0%
Direct Expense	37.1%	37.1%
Gross Profit Margin	62.9%	62.9%
Operating Expenses:		
Operating Exp.–Excluding Dep.	32.7%	32.7%
Depreciation Expense	0.8%	0.9%
Other Income (Exp.)–Excluding Interest Expense	0.0%	0.0%
Earnings Before Interest & Taxes	29.5%	29.3%
Effective Tax Rate–Taxes on EBIT	*28.3%*	*28.8%*
Adjusted Net Working Capital	1.0%	1.0%
Adjusted Net Working Capital[d]	$5	$6
Capital Expenditures	NA	0.9%

[a] Adjusted per Figure 6.6
[b] At federal corporate income tax rates
[c] All assumptions, excluding sales growth and effective tax rate, are stated as a percentage of sales
[d] Required working capital level based on 2004 working capital

FIGURE 6.9   **Solo Practitioner
Income Approach—Capitalization of
Cash Flow Analysis ($000)**

Cash Flows (per Figure 6.8)		$115
÷ by Capitalization Rate (Discount Rate – Growth)	÷	21.1%
Indicated Total Capital Value		546
– Interest Bearing Debt	–	0
Indicated Equity Value (Majority Interest)		546
+ Nonoperating Assets	+	0
Concluded Income-Approach Value (Majority Interest)		**$546**

The capitalization of cash flow analysis is presented in *Figure 6.8*. Revenues are projected to grow at a 5 percent rate into perpetuity. All other assumptions are based on Solo Practitioner's adjusted 2004 results as a percentage of sales.

Figure 6.9 presents the capitalization of cash flow summary. The $115,000 of free cash flows from Figure 6.8 is divided by the 21.1 percent capitalization rate to produce a value of $546,000. Total interest-bearing debt must then be subtracted and nonoperating assets added to determine the value of the common stock. Because Solo Practitioner has no interest-bearing debt or nonoperating assets, the value of its common stock based on the income approach value is $546,000.

Public Company Analysis

The same nine publicly traded guideline companies used for the valuation of Multipartner Firm in Figure 5.11 in chapter 5 are also appropriate companies for the valuation of Solo Practitioner. Although these companies are not exactly like Solo Practitioner, they provide alternative investment opportunities for an investor in this industry. These companies have grown faster, are much larger, more diversified, and have higher liquidity on average than Solo Practitioner. However, Solo Practitioner has had higher profitability on average. Productivity measures were mixed compared with the publicly traded guideline companies.

FIGURE 6.10   **Solo Practitioner**
Market Approach—Public Company
Analysis Valuation Summary ($000)

Valuation Rates	Market Derived Valuation Ratio	Upward/ (Downward) Adjustment[a]	Adjusted Valuation Ratio[b]	Subject-Company Financial Basis	Indicated Value	Subtract Debt[c]	Indicated Equity Value	Weight
Total Equity Multiples (Latest 12 Months):								
Assets Under Management	0.03	(75%)	0.01	$55,000	$550	NA	$550	20%
Pretax Income	14.87	(75%)	3.72	$156	$580	NA	$580	20%
Net Income	22.93	(75%)	5.73	$104	$596	NA	$596	20%
MVIC Multiples (Latest 12 Months):								
EBITDA	14.50	(75%)	3.63	$160	$581	$0	$581	20%
EBIT	15.05	(75%)	3.76	$156	$587	$0	$587	20%
Weighted Average Equity Value							$579	
+ Nonoperating Assets						+	$0	
Concluded Value–Public Company Analysis (Majority Interest)							**$579**	

[a] The MVIC adjustment is equal to total adjustment multiplied by the ratio of total equity to invested capital
[b] Adjusted Valuation Ratio = Market Derived Valuation Ratio × (1 + Adjustment)
[c] For Total Equity Multiples: not applicable (NA), for MVIC Multiples: subtract interest-bearing debt
Total equity = market value of total stockholders' equity
MVIC = Market Value of Invested Capital Price (debt and equity capital)
EBITDA = earnings before interest, taxes, depreciation, and amortization
EBIT = earnings before interest and taxes

Valuation ratios were calculated in Figure 5.12 of chapter 5. The same five ratios—equity to AUM; price to pretax income; price to net income; market value of invested capital to earnings before interest, taxes, depreciation, and amortization; and market value of invested capital to earnings before interest and taxes—are applicable to Solo Practitioner.

These ratios then need to be adjusted upward or downward based on the comparison analysis. As noted earlier, Solo Practitioner has less growth potential, is much smaller, is less diversified, and has lower than average liquidity compared with the guideline companies. However, Solo Practitioner has been more profitable than the guideline companies on average. Overall, the ratios are adjusted downward 75 percent based on these factors.

Figure 6.10 presents the summary of publicly traded guideline com-

FIGURE 6.11 **Solo Practitioner**
Market Approach—Merger & Acquistion
Analysis Summary ($000)

	Market-Derived Valuation Ratio	Upward/ (Downward) Adjustment	Adjusted Valuation Ratio*	Subject-Company Financial Basis	Indicated Value	Subtract Debt	Indicated Equity Value	Weight
Equity Multiples:								
Net Income**	8.87	(45%)	4.88	$112	$546	NA	$546	33%
MVIC Multiples:								
Revenue	2.88	(45%)	1.58	$530	$837	$0	$837	33%
EBITDA**	8.80	(45%)	4.84	$160	$775	$0	$775	33%
Indicated Weighted Average Value – Merger & Acquisitions Analysis							$719	
Add: Nonoperating Assets						+	$0	
Concluded Value–Public Company Analysis (Rounded)							$719	

NA = not applicable
 * Adjusted Valuation Ratio = Market Derived Valuation Ratio × (1 + Adjustment)
** Adjusted, as per Figure 6.6

pany analysis. The ratios shown are the medians calculated in Figure 5.12. The adjusted ratio is applied to Solo Practitioner's most recent financial basis, which is 2004 in this case. Interest-bearing debt needs to be subtracted from the MVIC ratios only. Results from the ratios then need to be weighted based on the reliability and variation of the ratios. In this case, equal weight is given to the ratios. Nonoperating assets, if any, then need to be added to determine the value of stockholder's equity. Solo Practitioner has no nonoperating assets; therefore, the value indicated by the public company analysis is $579,000.

M&A Transition Analysis

The 16 transactions used in the merger and acquisition transaction analysis are the same as those used in the Multipartner valuation and are presented in Figure 5.14 in chapter 5. Also, the three calculated valuation ratios, price to net income, MVIC to revenue, and MVIC to EBITDA, are also applicable to Solo Practitioner.

Figure 6.11 presents the merger-and-acquisition analysis summary for Solo Practitioner. Although the companies included in the transaction analysis are much larger and more diversified on average than Solo Practitioner, Solo Practitioner was more profitable on average, so the valuation ratios are adjusted downward 45 percent.

The adjusted ratios are then applied to Solo Practitioner's adjusted 2004 financial basis. Interest-bearing debt needs to be subtracted from the MVIC ratios only. Results from the ratios then need to be weighted based on the reliability and variation of the ratios. In this case, equal weight is given to the ratios. Nonoperating assets, if any, are then added to determine the value of stockholder's equity. Solo Practitioner does not have any nonoperating assets; therefore, the value indicated by the public company analysis is $719,000.

Valuation Summary

Figure 6.12 presents the valuation summary for Solo Practitioner. As in the valuation of Multipartner Firm, the income approach was given significant weight (80 percent) because it represents the amount a prudent investor would pay for Solo Practitioner's expected future cash flows based on current market rates of return and Solo Practitioner's specific risks.

In the market approach, the public company analysis was given some weight (10 percent) because it reflects current stock market pricing for reasonably comparable businesses that represent alternative investment opportunities. However, significant adjustments were made to the valuation ratios, which reduce the reliability of this approach.

In addition, the merger and acquisition analysis in the market approach was given some weight (10 percent) because it reflects recent merger and acquisition prices for reasonably comparable companies that represent alternative investment opportunities. However, the quality of the underlying data and the adjustments made to the valuation ratios reduce the reliability of this approach.

Based on these weightings, the fair market value of Solo Practitioner as of December 31, 2004 is $567,000.

We did not take into account a control premium in either of these examples. If the cash flows are adjusted for items such as owner's

FIGURE 6.12   **Solo Practitioner Valuation Summary**

	Indicated Value	Weight
Concluded Income-Approach Value	$546,418	80%
Concluded Market-Approach Value —Publicly Traded Guideline Cos.	$579,000	10%
Concluded Market-Approach Value —M&A Transactions	$719,000	10%
Concluded Value	**$567,000**	

compensation, rent, and discretionary items, then a control premium generally is not warranted because the cash flows are those available to a controlling purchaser already. However, if no adjustments are made to the cash flows that a controlling purchaser would make, then a control premium may be appropriate. There are several control-premium studies, such as those by Mergerstat and Houlihan Lokey Howard and Zukin, that can provide a basis for control-premium adjustments.

The two examples show that no two companies are alike and thus should not be treated the same way in terms of value as rules of thumb indicate. A great deal of analysis goes into a formal valuation, and randomly applying certain metrics, or rules of thumb, to determine value generally does not capture the value of an advisory practice.

It's important to emphasize the importance of fair market value and investment value. No adjustments have been made for possible synergies or economies of scale. These examples were conducted under the premise of fair market value, which should be used only as a starting point for negotiations in a transaction.

Chapter Notes

1. Moss Adams, *2004 FPA Financial Performance Study of Financial*

Advisory Practices, sponsored by SEI Investments and the Financial Planning Association, September 2004.

2. The Risk Management Association (RMA), *Annual Statement Studies: Financial Ratio Benchmarks 2004/2005* (The Risk Management Association).

3. Moss Adams, *2003 FPA Compensation and Staffing Study*, sponsored by SEI Investments and the Financial Planning Association, September 2003.

Coming
to Terms

7. THE ART OF NEGOTIATION
Coming to Terms

VALUE IS KEY, but other, equally important considerations affect whether an agreement will be negotiated successfully. For both buyers and sellers, the focus should be on such things as net price after taxes, financing terms, and the time value of money. Consider the risk, for example, of a buyout period that's too long or too expensive. How long will it take for the buyer to actually earn back his payment to the seller, and will there be sufficient cash flow from the practice to allow the buyer to buy it without dipping too deeply into his own pocket? How long is the buyer willing to have the seller around? Often, sellers are like fish and relatives: you want them out of your house as quickly as possible. How rigid will the payment schedule be? And what is the seller's recourse in case of default? Does the buyer have any personal guarantees in the transaction? These are just a few of the questions that must be raised.

Digging Deeper

Fortunately, most purchases of advisory practices are based on some performance expectations and the deal is often structured as an earnout, which hinges on how many clients actually transfer. This structure allows the buyer to hedge his risk. But surprises often await the buyer: How were the clients serviced? What was their level of satisfaction and trust with the original adviser? How much will it cost to deliver the services to which the client has become accustomed? What is the potential income for the firm from these clients, and how old are they? In some cases, there may even be compliance risks, which is why the complaint record of the selling adviser should always be checked before the final papers are signed.

Many of these issues may come up in early negotiations or be uncovered during the due-diligence process, but it's the buyer's challenge to know which questions to ask and what key information to look for. If the buyer isn't careful, he could be out the down payment at a minimum, and perhaps even a substantial portion of the purchase price, before the depth of the problem becomes clear.

We recommend that both the buyer and seller be prepared to articulate their "deal killers" early in the process rather than at the end, so that the other party can consider ways to navigate around this obstacle. When the deal-killer bomb is dropped at the end, it can force the negotiations back to square one.

Getting Answers

To remain organized in negotiations and keep a cool head about price and terms, be prepared to understand the following:

♦ How many other buyers may be interested in buying this practice?

♦ What is a reasonable value to the buyer or seller?

♦ What is the motivation of the buyer or seller?

♦ What is the buyer or seller's required rate of return (and is it reasonable)?

♦ How prepared are the employees on both sides for this transition?

♦ Is the timetable for closing the acquisition in sync on both sides of the transaction?

Although many subjective elements are involved in negotiating the purchase of a financial-advisory practice, understanding certain rational economic principles is absolutely essential when initiating negotiations and as a gauge for the reasonableness of the agreed value between buyer and seller.

Transferability

Evaluating a financial-advisory practice as an economic entity for sale necessarily leads to the question of what exactly is being sold. Not all the value in a practice may be transferable. Consider a typical small practice with a staff of three, including the principal/adviser: The firm has approximately 110 clients, representing more than $13 million of assets under management. The firm's gross professional income in the most recent year amounted to $175,000, including $50,000 of noncommission, fee-based income. A potential buyer, usually another practicing adviser, would likely want the practice because of its capacity to generate revenue. Given a practice like the one in this example, the key question becomes, What portion of the firm's revenue-generating capacity can be transferred to the purchaser?

In a manufacturing business, significant value rests principally with the products produced, but the capacity of an advisory firm to generate revenue is not tied to a tangible product or to any other tangible business assets. When products or other tangible assets are more readily identifiable and transferable within a business, it's easier to impute their value.

When evaluating the sale or purchase of a practice, to determine how easily a business's value can be transferred, you must examine the practice's revenue mix. Fee income, for example, is more consistent and predictable than commission income, which helps to justify a higher value. For many advisers, fee-based income is basically drawn from the consulting associated with the development and ongoing services required in a financial-planning relationship. Other types of fee income, such as supervisory or management fees to oversee clients' investment portfolios, are more closely tied to the client base.

On the other hand, the practice may generate primarily commission income, which is directly tied to the adviser's efforts. Despite the risk of oversimplification, these commissions (including any overrides) can appropriately be viewed as a function of the "captive" client base of the practice. Even though it's undoubtedly true that the seller's personal relationships with clients play an important part in generating the commission income, it's possible (with careful arrangements) for the acquiring adviser to step in and service the existing client base without triggering a major loss of clients. In other words, a captive client base has greater transferability value because of its demonstrated capacity to generate revenue.

When reviewing commission income, be sure to note the mix of income and how much of it is recurring. For example, the commissions may be from mutual fund class A shares, which means the front-end load fee was already paid and all that's being transferred are the commission trails (or 12b-1 fees). If the value is based on the annual gross, the revenue potential will be exaggerated because that income is not likely to recur at the same level. Conversely, if the funds are class C shares, for which the adviser receives a 1 percent trail, it should be regarded as the recurring revenue. But in either case, the buyers should closely scrutinize the nature of the trailing fees being paid, which may put pressure on the value of such practices.

This lack of transferability is one reason so many advisers have moved to a fee-only or fee-based model that looks and feels more like that of a classic registered investment adviser. The desire to enhance transferability is another reason why there is a movement to create larger advisory firms that are less dependent on one person. Small, transaction-based practices provide minimal opportunity for buyers, though they may have a handful of appealing clients. Larger, fee-driven practices produce more consistent, predictable income and can be more systematic in how they procure and serve clients.

From the purchaser's perspective, the client base represents a book of ongoing business from which he can immediately benefit after purchase. Because the client base is transferable and has measurable revenue-generating capacity, it should be awarded value in a sale.

Evaluating Return

Part of the challenge in both assessing practice value and negotiating the purchase price comes down to understanding and evaluating the return generated by the target practice. Two critical elements determine whether an advisory practice generates an adequate return:

1. Fair compensation for labor
2. Fair reward for ownership

Fair Compensation for Labor

Most sole practitioners take as personal income the amount that remains after all their business expenses are covered and therefore show limited or no profits in the business. This practice makes it difficult to discern whether the owner is being adequately compensated for his labor and how much earnings the practice is generating over and above that compensation.

Consider this: If you purchase a practice across town, you still need to work with that practice's clients to maintain the relationships and to generate income from them. Even if fees are based on assets under management, it's incorrect to assume that you will not have to expend any effort to maintain the client relationships. As a result, you would want to be paid fairly by the business for managing those relationships. In other words, as a prospective buyer you will expect the practice to generate adequate compensation for the effort (labor) required to generate income from the book of business.

For a commission-oriented practice, here's a good way to measure the earnings a business should generate. The owner of a practice has a choice: She can work as an employee of a wirehouse such as Merrill Lynch or work for herself. As discussed previously, an adviser in a wirehouse is an employee of that business and earns a payout in the range of 25 percent to 45 percent of gross revenue, depending on production. That's a good benchmark for establishing fair compensation for the owner's labor because it tracks what the market is paying for people of roughly comparable skills, revenue volume, function, and licenses. We tend to use 40 percent of revenue as a guideline for fair compensation when valuing most solo practices.

For a fee-based practice, a parallel might be the salary of a trust officer or an investment officer in a local institution. These professionals serve roughly the same role and work with similar types of clients in helping them to achieve similar outcomes. The big difference is that the trust officer is typically a salaried employee—a good benchmark. In addition, Moss Adams is now creating solid data on compensation within financial-advisory firms through our semiannual studies, and other data points are available to benchmark compensation as well.

Fair Reward for Ownership

The second factor to consider in determining whether a practice earns an adequate return involves whether the practice generates enough reward for the risk associated with ownership. Investors obviously expect a return on their investments. For a buyer, the target practice is an investment. A key item to measure is the return that the investment can generate.

Some people will invest in a business to buy a job. But buying a job in this industry is not entirely logical if the buyer is putting his capital at risk and taking responsibility for the management of the practice. Beyond adequate compensation for labor, the business must offer a demonstrable reward for ownership. The income over and above the amount the owner receives as an employee of the practice, less overhead expenses, is the reward for the risk the owner takes (see *Figure 7.1*).

Buyers of financial-advisory practices should evaluate these two components carefully. Sellers of financial-planning practices should also evaluate whether they're getting rewards for both labor and ownership and, if they're not, begin managing the business in a way that produces satisfactory results.

FIGURE 7.1   **Risk and Reward**

Revenue

– **Direct expense (reward for labor)**

= **Gross profit**

– **Overhead expense**

= **Operating profit (reward for ownership)**

A Word to the Buyer

As a buyer, you need to be vigilant in your review of the transaction. Many buyers are so eager to take over a book of business that they willingly believe whatever they're told about a target practice. Buyers always need to temper their enthusiasm and focus on economic reality.

Your judgment about whether to buy a practice should be based on a number of critical questions:

♦ If I invested the same amount of money in efforts to improve and expand my own firm, would I produce a better return with less risk?

♦ Why should I pay for the potential of a practice if that potential can be realized only through my own efforts?

♦ When the seller tells me that certain expenses will not continue with the practice when I buy it, what confidence can I have that this is true?

♦ And why didn't the seller minimize those expenses when he was running the business?

♦ If the practice has never shown the capacity to generate higher income, why pay the seller as if it had?

♦ What is a reasonable level of client attrition to assume?

♦ If I can't afford to pay cash, can I afford to amortize the loan and still make a good return on my investment?

The decision to purchase a financial-advisory practice is not purely a function of value. The cultural issues, the practice-management issues, the transitional and legal complications, and the structure of the deal all affect your future financial success. If you decide you do not have the courage or a strategy clear enough to expand through acquisition, you have not lost the opportunity to grow. If you turn your attention inward and commit your resources to yourself and your existing practice, you may be able to achieve the same level of financial return and professional satisfaction without the risk that goes with paying for somebody else's practice.

A Word to the Seller

Although there is nothing wrong with asking for a price higher than the appraised value of a practice, it's important to put the perception of value into context. Remember that all buyers require some return on their investment. If they're forced to struggle to understand how they can realize a reasonable return after purchasing your practice, they will usually decide to keep the money and focus on building their own business internally.

Like most small-business owners, a good number of financial-planning practitioners have a heightened (that is, inflated) perception of their business's value. One of the most helpful exercises you can go through is to invest in a formal valuation of your practice. That valuation will give you an informed opinion of what an outsider might think your practice is worth; it will also serve as a self-examination to assess what areas need to be enhanced to maximize value.

If your perception of value is unreasonable, you may find it difficult and frustrating to move discussions forward with potential buyers. Qualified buyers, more often than not, will be somewhat more experienced in business transactions. As discussed earlier, value is ultimately not driven by how long you've been working in the business or by your annual gross. Value is driven by:

- ♦ The cash flow of the practice
- ♦ The transferability of the business practice itself
- ♦ The sustainability of earnings of the practice
- ♦ The reasonable potential for additional growth

Short of engaging an independent valuation expert to render an opinion of the value of your practice, you can use the guidelines set forth in this book to perform your own cursory assessment. You may not want to share this valuation with the buyer, but you can use it as your guide in defining an acceptable price. A typical financial adviser is likely to realize much of the value of his or her practice in the form of current personal income. Generally, all profits generated after paying for overhead expenses are distributed to the owner. In other words, most advisers do not retain many of the profits from the business to fund growth and they do not invest much in creating a firm's identity outside of their own personal reputation. In such a case, the adviser will be able to get something for selling the business only if another practitioner or financial planner can make money with it. If the practice cannot generate an adequate return for a new owner, it has very little value to a buyer.

Timing and Process

Pursuing, courting, and negotiating a purchase or sale will try your patience. Whether you're a buyer or seller, from the moment you decide on your strategy to the moment you consummate the sale, the process can take as long as 18 months (see *Figure 7.2*). The simpler the transaction, the faster it can be completed; some sales occurring on the Web-based platforms such as Schwab Transitions or FP Transitions are resolved within two to three months.

The challenge for many people on both sides of these transactions is that they lack clarity about what they're looking for. When Samuel Johnson wrote the first English dictionary, a woman said to him,

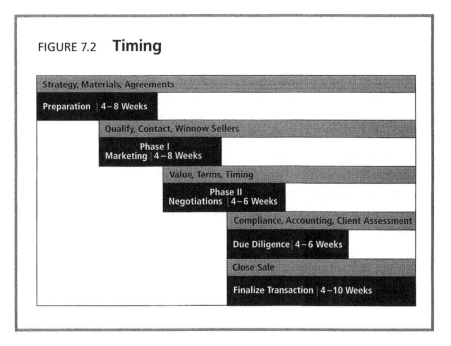

FIGURE 7.2 **Timing**

Strategy, Materials, Agreements

Preparation | 4–8 Weeks

Qualify, Contact, Winnow Sellers

Phase I
Marketing | 4–8 Weeks

Value, Terms, Timing

Phase II
Negotiations | 4–6 Weeks

Compliance, Accounting, Client Assessment

Due Diligence | 4–6 Weeks

Close Sale

Finalize Transaction | 4–10 Weeks

"Sir, this book is filled with vulgar words." He replied, "Madam, you were looking for them."

When we're clear about what we're seeking, discovery comes more quickly. That's why the process should always begin with a vision of what you want to accomplish. And that vision should include defining the characteristics of the type of firm or individual who would be the best match for your deal.

As a seller, you need to be clear about what you're trying to accomplish with the sale. Is it to maximize value? Merge to facilitate growth? Provide continuity for your clients? Get immediate liquidity?

As a buyer, you also need to be clear about what you're trying to accomplish. Add capacity to serve your clients? Add clients? Build market share?

As you define your goals, you must ask, Which type of buyer or seller would help me accomplish them? What are the characteristics of that firm? What is its typical client like and what are the firm's processes? The answers to these questions will help you to formulate your approach to the transaction. With a clear idea of what you're looking for, you can winnow the list of prospects. With a shorter list, you can begin to negotiate in earnest until you come to an understanding with the other side. Once the due-diligence process is completed and final negotiating points are set, you can consummate the deal.

The time it takes to get from the point at which you engage the target to the moment you complete the sale is almost always longer than you expected. There are bound to be hurdles from details in the legal agreements and nits that come up during due diligence. As with any project, planning tends to minimize the disruptions, but it's impossible to anticipate every hiccup in the process. Still, beginning with the end in mind will keep you focused on the objective and advance the negotiations in the direction you want the transaction to take.

8. THE SELLER'S PERSPECTIVE
Coming to Terms

ESTABLISHING GOALS AND developing a selling strategy are the essential first steps in finding a suitable buyer for an advisory firm. As the seller, your goals define what you want to accomplish through the sale; a sales strategy helps you define your firm and differentiate it for the universe of potential buyers. Unfortunately, many owners don't take these steps. The result is a seller who goes through the process of finding and negotiating with buyers, only to discover in the end that he has wasted his time and the time of the prospective buyers.

This is often the case when a seller is approached by a consolidator. In recent years, financial buyers interested in aggregating advisory firms have been approaching practitioners of all sizes with very tempting offers. Typically, the offer includes a substantial cash down payment combined with equity in the new company, with the idea that this larger enterprise will eventually go public or sell to another company at an even higher multiple. This eventuality is called *lift*, meaning the effect of combining smaller firms into a larger, more valuable entity. In any case, without considering other offers or even establishing what they're trying to accomplish with the sale, sellers will sign a confidentiality agreement and a letter of intent and find themselves a long way down the due-diligence path before they realize that they've not considered any of their other options. Ideally, potential sellers will have this epiphany before everybody's time has been wasted, but it's not easy to reject the overtures of a persuasive suitor.

First Things First

In today's market, which offers numerous potential buyers for every seller, sellers can seek the firm that will best meet their needs. But even in a seller's market, it can be difficult to find a buyer that will meet all of the seller's requirements for the transition. So sellers need to prioritize their objectives and decide which ones are nonnegotiable. A selling strategy that's well thought out and in sync with your goals will enable you to create a profile of the ideal buyer. Essentially, you are looking for a buyer that meets all your nonnegotiable objectives and as many of the other goals as possible.

Defining Your Goals

Everyone has different objectives for the sale of a firm. It's important to think in terms of what will happen to your business once it is sold. If you're like most sellers in the industry, your goals are focused on six key issues:

1. How will your clients be served after the transaction?
2. Will your staff have jobs after the deal, and if so, how will they be managed?
3. How will the business be managed?
4. What is the liquidity/timing of payment for the business?
5. Is it important that you leave a legacy in terms of brand or your own identity?
6. When do you want to physically exit from the business—at the time of sale, or sometime after?

When you clearly define success in these six critical areas, you'll be able to filter out buyers who are unable or unwilling to meet your needs. What's more, with clearly defined objectives, you'll be ready to define your sales strategy. A sales strategy consists of the following components:

1. A clear list of the nonnegotiable objectives
2. A defined range of value, including the minimum amount you will accept
3. A clearly articulated list of strengths that might justify a premium price

4. An understanding of the firm's weaknesses—with a strategic twist that will be compelling to prospective buyers

Defining the nonnegotiables. The nonnegotiables are simply the objectives for the transition on which you will not compromise. They are different for each business owner and must be defined by the individual seller. Nonnegotiables, or "deal killers," may include objectives related to caring for staff members, the level of support available for existing clients, the services offered by the new firm, and the level of noncompetition or nonsolicitation required.

Determining your firm's value. A realistic perception of the firm's value is the essential starting point for any negotiations (see chapters 1–4 on valuation). The problem we've observed as the process unfolds is that sellers set their sights at the top of the range of potential value. They give no serious consideration to the other end of the continuum because they prefer not to sell for that price. The benefit of defining a range is that it helps you as the seller to challenge your own assumptions in advance of negotiations and prepare for the consequences of getting offers below your expectations. Ultimately, if you know how much liquidity you will need, then you'll know when to commit to a deal and when to walk away.

Knowing your strengths. If you have staff, processes, knowledge, or market presence that a buyer will find desirable, you should quantify these attributes. Talking to the buyers about your strengths from the buyer's perspective will help you obtain a premium price for the business. The advantages that the seller brings to the table can get a buyer excited about the opportunities the practice affords.

Considering the following questions will help you find a way to frame these advantages:

1. What can you provide the buyer that will benefit his existing clients?
2. What opportunities for growth—made possible only by your firm's expertise, processes, et cetera—can you offer the buyer?
3. What expenses might be eliminated from the business in a transition of ownership?
4. What incentives do you already have in place to tie staff to the organization?

5. What technology do you employ that will enable a buyer to gain greater efficiency?

6. How does your existing business plan capitalize on future growth opportunities?

Knowing your weaknesses—with a twist. Knowing your firm's weaknesses is important for two reasons. First, it allows you to have a realistic understanding of what a buyer might pay and how much she may or may not benefit from the transaction. Second, it enables you to target buyers who can shore up those weaknesses. Therein lies the twist. If a buyer can shore up the seller's weaknesses, she may be willing to overlook them to some extent, which could translate into a higher selling price. Suppose a firm's weakness is in its marketing processes. If a buyer has confidence in her own firm's marketing procedures, she may overlook that weakness in the seller's firm. The seller's firm, on the other hand, may have a strong location, and the buyer may see that strength as an excellent complement to her own marketing expertise and a way to ultimately create a firm poised for growth. This combination reduces the risk of the transaction, builds a firm foundation for growth, and motivates the buyer who recognizes the untapped potential.

We have observed on a number of occasions when persuasive sellers have convinced buyers by telling them, "Under your management guidance, we're sure you can make this practice more profitable." Buyers are not impervious to flattery, especially when it becomes obvious that a few changes in the seller's business could translate into higher cash flow for the buyer. But as buyers become more sophisticated, it will be more difficult to persuade them to both pay a high value *and* invest in improvements in the business they're buying.

Sellers should consider the advice realtors give to homeowners before they put their house on the market. Do what you can to clean it up before your open house.

Profiling the Ideal Buyer

Once you've defined your objectives and created a sales strategy, you're prepared to identify the characteristics of the ideal buyer. For example, if your main objective is to maximize liquidity in the transaction, you'll look for a buyer that's growth oriented, has capital available to fund the growth, will enable you to participate in the growth, and will compensate you for your contribution to it. Of course, if you have the conflicting desire to get out of the business quickly, you'll ultimately have to decide which objective is more important and pursue a buyer that will best enable you to meet your most pressing objective. Profiling different buyers within the industry will help you further examine and target the ideal buyer.

There are three types of buyers:

1. Strategic
2. Financial
3. Individual

Strategic buyers. A strategic buyer will likely be a bank, CPA firm, or other large advisory firm that wants to either expand its business or enter the market. Strategic buyers prefer that the advisers remain with the business and help it grow as part of a larger enterprise. Banks have been particularly big buyers of advisory practices during recent years and often pay the highest multiple. Larger advisory firms and CPA firms are looking more often for mergers than for acquisitions.

A good example of this is Western Alliance Bancorporation, a holding company based in Las Vegas that acquired Phoenix-based Miller/Russell. Miller/Russell added more than $80 million of new assets in direct referrals from the bank after the merger, and the bank asked the firm to open registered investment advisory offices in each of its three locations. This merger is a good example of how such an arrangement can accelerate the growth of the advisory firm to the benefit of both parties.

Another example of an effective acquisition is Wealth Trust, a Tennessee-based consolidator that helps its acquired firms achieve efficiencies but allows the firms to retain local autonomy. Each of the firms acquired by Wealth Trust is a money manager. No deal is identical to any other because Wealth Trust recognizes that each firm brings a unique mix of clients, assets, and economic structure to the merger.

Financial buyers. Financial buyers are often referred to as roll-up firms, or consolidators. The best example of this is National Financial

Partners (NFP), which acquired more than 100 RIA, employee benefit, and insurance practices throughout the United States before going public. It used a formula valuation; paid for the purchase with a combination of cash, stock, and incentives; and by virtue of its size, leveraged up the multiple to all of the firms when it went public. A firm with a similar strategy is New York–based Focus Financial Partners, which targets midsize-to-large RIA firms that specialize in comprehensive wealth management.

Delessert Financial, a Boston-based wealth-management practice, opted to sell to NFP because the merger allowed owner Christiane Delessert to accomplish several goals. One was to get immediate liquidity, which satisfied her personal financial goals; the other was to help her young associates take over the firm and serve as her eventual successors. Although Delessert may have been able to command a higher value by pursuing a strategic buyer, the combination of considerations—including management succession, client succession, financial reward, and a degree of independence—ultimately swayed her.

Individual buyers. Individual buyers can come from either inside or outside the business. Typically, individual buyers don't pay the highest price because they have the least capital. Further, the purchase price will often constrain their cash flow for several years until they pay off their obligation. Individual buyers—especially those who've been groomed as successors—often make the best buyers, however, because they often have both continuity with the clients and a shared philosophy with the selling adviser. The big challenge for sellers is making sure these individuals have the physical capacity to handle the business they're about to buy. If they already have a full book of clients, they will need to have a solution for how they might handle the additional business. This is especially important if the practice is sold on an earnout tied to future performance.

Going to Market

You know what your practice is worth. You know which of your objectives are key and which are negotiable. You have a good sense of which buyers will be most attracted to your business. It's time to put your for-sale sign in the window.

Marketing the Business

A key step in putting your business on the auction block is letting potential buyers know it's there. Marketing materials should tell enough about a seller's practice to generate interest but not so much that they give away all his negotiating leverage and the opportunity to expand on the firm's strengths and value to prospective buyers later on.

Investment bankers often refer to the marketing materials used to generate interest in a business as "the book." The book is a combination of basic facts and descriptive literature about the business. Of course, prospective buyers need to have enough information to remain interested, but the content has to have sizzle. It has to be readable and compelling. It has to paint a picture of both future opportunity and past success.

If the practice being sold is small and listed on a site such as FP Transitions or Schwabtransition.com, it's unlikely that the owner will need to exert as much effort to package the business formally in a book. That said, the seller still will need to be organized in a way that conveys the strong points of the business and downplays its shortcomings.

Preparing for sale can be like a chess game. It's not just the move you're making now that's important but the three or four you're about to make. Anticipating the type of information the buyer will require and providing it promptly upon request gives you a degree of control over the process. The owner needs to give the appearance not only of being ready for the sale but also of having the poise and readiness to address whatever questions may arise. Although a seller need not release everything at once, you should be prepared to present appropriate materials quickly. Initially it's best to release only preliminary marketing materials that are for public use. More confidential information should be released only after the prospective buyer has signed a confidentiality agreement.

Promotional Materials

The marketing materials the seller prepares should tell a prospective buyer about the practice—clients, services, processes, marketing, and finances—and should highlight the following:

◆ **Business profile**
  —Practice focus
  —Brief history of the practice
  —Organizational chart
  —Copy of ADV form, if applicable
◆ **Client profile**
  —Average age (segment by categories if possible, for example, under 60, 61–65)
  —Client distribution by size and location (cities, states, counties, et cetera)
  —Segmentation by dollars of investable assets
  —Segmentation by types of investments and other products/services
  —Notable centers of influence for referrals
◆ **Business processes**
  —What is the nature of financial or retirement planning (if any)?
  —Who performs the work and how?
  —How do you deliver services to clients?
  —How are clients charged for each service? Are any services provided at no charge?
  —Are there any important staff members who may transfer with the sale?
  —Can the firm provide copies of client-service contracts, if applicable
◆ **Staffing and leadership**
  —Experience and credentials of the team
  —Organizational chart
  —Roles and responsibilities
  —Career path
◆ **Marketing**
  —What are the primary ways in which the firm attracts clients (referrals, seminars, and the like)?
  —Does any one source represent the majority of new business acquired?
  —What does the firm do to help ensure retention of clients?
  —Does the firm distribute literature, articles, or testimonials about the practice?

♦ **Finance**
  —In broad terms, how has the business grown in gross revenues
    over the past five years?
  —How have overhead costs changed over the past five years
    (gross numbers)?
  —How has the mix of income (commissions, trail income, fee
    income) evolved over the past five years?
  —What is a reasonable projection of future income from the
    existing book of business?
  —What justifies the expectation of value?
♦ **Compliance and safety initiative**
  —What is the firm's record in terms of client complaints?
  —What protocols are in place to minimize risks?
  —Who is the firm's legal counsel? Its compliance consultant?
  —How does the firm control the quality of service?
  —What is its commitment to continuing education?
  —What agreements with staff and with clients are in place to
    protect the firm?

Finding Potential Buyers

The process of identifying qualified buyers is a challenging one.
If you develop your selling strategy diligently, however, it should
become apparent whether the most likely buyer will be another
individual practitioner, a strategic buyer such as a bank or CPA firm,
or a financial buyer like a roll-up firm (consolidator). Armed with
a careful strategy, you can sort out the most likely candidates and
decide how best to approach them. You can also get help. You can use
one of the websites sponsored by broker-dealers, or FP Transitions
(www.fptransitions.com), an independent website that serves as kind
of an auction market for books of business. Fee-based or fee-only
advisory firms that have revenues greater than $250,000 may not
find the FP Transitions website adequate; the Schwab Transition site
(www.schwabtransition.com) may be more suitable. Fidelity's institutional services unit (FRIAG) is also offering a succession-services
platform for advisers.

To the extent your practice has become more than just a book
of business and you've achieved some size, you would be wise to

engage an experienced investment banker to assist. Apart from Moss Adams Capital, the most prominent investment bankers serving the financial-services industry are Berkshire Capital Group, Cambridge International Partners, and Putnam Lovell NBF Securities. Each of these investment bankers has a different profile for the size of firm it will represent. (For more on intermediaries, see chapter 16.)

Some sellers may not need to look outside the practice to find a buyer. Insider transactions are more seamless from the clients' standpoint and easier to facilitate, but because of the limited market and internal relationships, such transactions may not command the highest price. These dynamics are slowly changing, though, because of the higher prices outside buyers are paying.

When a seller is looking for an outside buyer, broker-dealers or custodians can often suggest the best match from among the financial advisers they serve. In many cases, the broker-dealers and custodians can use the sale of a practice as a means of recruiting unaffiliated advisers to their fold by facilitating a transaction. Keeping the business with the same broker-dealer or custodian also reduces disruption and can help prevent the sale from causing the seller's clients to change advisers. It may also be a good idea for the seller to let the product wholesalers who call on them know they are considering selling. These vendors often have a good sense of what's going on with other practices in the seller's community and may be a good source of buyer leads.

Testing the Waters

After identifying prospective buyers and preparing the marketing materials, the seller's next step should be to elicit an expression of interest from all the prospects identified. Don't try to manage this process piecemeal. If you do not want staff or clients discovering your plans to sell the firm, you should seriously consider using an intermediary who can protect the firm's identity and help you negotiate with prospects.

It's not uncommon for discussions with initial prospective buyers to break down, so it's generally a good idea to pursue the initial contacts concurrently to see which buyers emerge with serious intent.

Be careful about signing lockup agreements that prohibit you from negotiating with multiple parties at once. It's to your advantage to keep your options open as long as is reasonable.

If a prospective buyer has a genuine interest in pursuing discussions further, ask the prospect to sign a confidentiality agreement before you show any detailed information. You might even require the intermediary—if you're using one—not to disclose your firm's identity. You can then move forward and begin discussing how you think such a merger or acquisition may work. Don't discuss price or financial details until you're comfortable that the practices are compatible and about how the deal will come together.

Although difficult to enforce, confidentiality agreements represent a serious psychological commitment for most buyers. By obtaining a signed confidentiality agreement before you reveal a great deal of detail about the practice, you cover all discussions and content under the signed agreement. Buyers who are unwilling to sign the confidentiality agreement or who make numerous changes to it should be regarded with caution.

A sample confidentiality agreement is included among the worksheets offered at the back of the book, but please note that *it is important to obtain independent and qualified legal counsel to draft agreements specific to your situation.*

The First Meeting

The preliminary meeting between the seller and a prospective buyer gives the seller insight into the buyer's philosophy on running a practice and allows firsthand observations about the buyer's operational style. Come to the meeting prepared with questions about the buyer's practice, his acquisition strategy, and the planned approach to implementation. This is the forum for discovering how prepared and logical the potential buyer actually is. What he says should be in line with the strategy proposed. Watch for contradictions and press hard with questions in any areas where ideas seem to conflict. If the potential buyer is a pair or a group of partners, observe how they interact with each other. Your goal should be to gather enough information from this meeting to know whether you want to continue.

A buyer's urge to get right down to the "brass tacks" of price and terms can be overwhelming. Resist this temptation. Discussion of the pricing and terms of the deal raises the tension of the negotiations and often narrows the flow of information between both parties.

The Right Fit

An owner selling a practice has many issues to explore and questions to raise before he can decide whether a potential buyer is the right choice. One of the first, of course, has to do with price. It's clear that the industry is seeing a bubble for practice transitions. If you've been contemplating the sale of your practice, now is the time to get to market before it becomes rational again. But before you do, consider these issues:

- Make sure the buyer can afford the price. You don't want to have to take the practice back if he defaults, especially if you were counting on this money for your retirement.
- Make sure the buyer has the physical capacity to serve all the clients transferred. If he doesn't, he will likely experience attrition in the client base and the dollars you receive through the earnout will be less than you were counting on.

Other, equally important issue to explore include:
- Do we share the same values?
- Will my clients like this person?
- Will this buyer add value to the practice?
- Is the person capable of serving my clients as well or better than I have?
- Has the buyer demonstrated willingness to pay?
- Will the buyer's financial condition put our agreement at risk?
- What can I do to facilitate the transfer of client relationships?
- Is the buyer's location easily accessible to my clients?
- Will the buyer's broker-dealer affiliation (or use of a different custodian) help or hurt the sale?

Sellers are often motivated to sell because of boredom or burnout. This state of mind may make a seller impatient about the process. This transaction is important not only for the seller but also for his clients. After all, the seller has made a commitment to his clients to help them meet their financial goals. That commitment does not come to a halt at the sale of the practice. In a profession such as this, advisers create an interdependency with their clients. One of the adviser's obligations is to transition that responsibility to a competent adviser who will take over the practice.

A seller needs to ask a reasonable price, be diligent and discerning in the search, careful and thorough with the documentation, and sensitive to the cultural challenges the new owner of the practice will present. Done properly, the sale of a financial-advisory practice can be a very fulfilling experience. Done poorly, it could become one of the seller's biggest regrets.

9. THE BUYER'S PERSPECTIVE
Coming to Terms

WHEN AN OWNER contemplating the sale of an advisory practice defines his goals and develops a sales strategy, he greatly increases the odds of finding the right buyer. Purchasing an advisory firm calls for similar planning. As a prospective buyer, you need to determine what kind of firm would make the best purchase and how much you're willing and able to pay for it.

Your framework may be defined by investment return, synergy, adding capacity, growing market presence, or market share. The process is not unlike developing an investment policy statement. The idea is to create structure around the most suitable businesses to buy based on your goals, resources, and risk tolerance.

First Things First

There is more to buying a practice than acquiring a client list. Small practitioners often are interested only in the book of business. Larger firms are interested in the systems, strategy, processes, technical ability, capacity—and the clients. One of the first things you have to do is be clear about what you're seeking so that you can be more efficient and effective in the search. In our experience, the frustration experienced in a search for an acquisition is usually in proportion to the buyer's inability to define his own expectations.

To plot your approach to acquisition, it's helpful to follow the "Monopoly board" in *Figure 9.1* and think through the steps that will lead you to these goals:

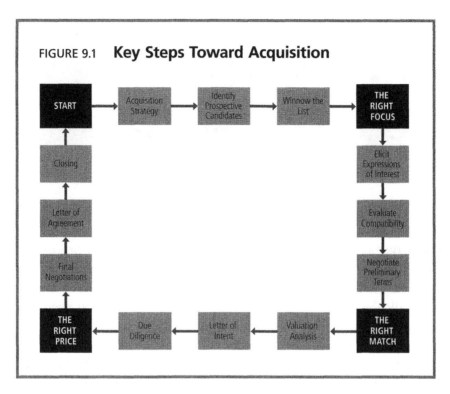

FIGURE 9.1   **Key Steps Toward Acquisition**

- ♦ The right focus
- ♦ The right match
- ♦ The right price

The Right Focus

The right focus is the development of a focused acquisition strategy. What types of businesses are you interested in acquiring and why? Where are they located? What is the makeup of their management and client base? Once you zero in on the optimal firm to enhance your own practice, the process of searching for targets becomes much clearer.

The Right Match

Here are some questions to help you define the right match:

- ♦ What type of practice would fit my current practice's culture, style, and approach?
- ♦ What client base do I want to acquire?

- Should I be using the acquisition of a practice to enhance technical expertise?
- Should I acquire a practice to diversify my business?
- Should I acquire a practice to add leverage and capacity to my existing business?
- To what geographic area should I limit my search?
- What financial parameters am I looking for in a practice?
- How do I want to structure the terms of the transaction?
- Do I want the present owner(s) to remain part of the practice? For how long?
- Do I want to acquire the practice's staff or attempt to integrate the business into the structure of my existing firm?
- Should the acquired firm be affiliated with my broker-dealer so that the transaction is seamless to the client?
- Will the client base of the firm I acquire have to be transferred into a fee-only relationship? If so, how does that need to be positioned?
- Are my consulting and asset-management fees consistent with those of the acquired firm?
- How much can I afford to pay as a down payment?
- Am I willing to borrow from a bank to finance some of the transaction? If so, how much? How large a loan would I qualify for with the bank?

The Right Price

Once, after we spoke at a broker-dealer–sponsored conference, a longtime financial adviser approached us to offer his opinion: "I have two things to say to you," he said. "First, as a seller of a practice, I think you're completely off base; second, as a buyer of practices, I think you couldn't be more right." We were pleased that we had annoyed only half of him.

Some advisers and industry observers believe that the conventional view on valuation—in which various factors are considered and analyzed to determine fair market value—has been debunked by the multiples that are being paid in today's market: hypothetical valuations are irrelevant; the market dictates the price. "What's more," they say, "It's a new economy. No matter how much buyers pay for these practices, it's still cheaper than getting clients through conventional marketing and the payoff is much quicker."

The truth is there are times when such irrational exuberance has made us reexamine our approach to practice valuation. After all, these are the prices that real buyers are paying real sellers. Indeed, this may be the most active market in the history of practice transitions. Still, we do not believe the prices indicative of this marketplace for financial-advisory firms reflect prudent business choices.

Practice at any price. What's at the heart of such recklessness? Professionals, people who've been trained to critically evaluate their clients' financial circumstances and recommend a course of action, often fail to apply the same discipline to their own practices. Like the fat, wheezing doctor or the wigged-out therapist, they forget the adage "Heal thyself." In financial-advisory firms, such quirky thinking may manifest in how the owners treat their staff, how they manage their overhead, or how they price their services. Each of these factors is critical in propelling advisers toward financial independence through better business practices, but often they are elements that fail to get the time and attention they deserve.

Similar irrationality is illustrated in the current rash of practice acquisitions. Financial advisers are paying too high a price to acquire books of business. By using rules of thumb rather than sound valuation, they assign relatively equal value to all practices regardless of the quality of the income, the potential of the client base, or the cost of doing business—factors unique to each firm.

But these days, a warning such as this is like a voice in the wilderness. Smart people in and around the advisory profession have been exhorting advisers to use an auction market like FP Transitions to sell their books of business to the highest bidders. "Forget this idea of internal succession planning," they say. "The market is filled with buyers willing to pay a high multiple of gross revenue. Why go through the pain of planning for an orderly transition, or the expense of a formal valuation, when people out there are willing to write big checks instead of building their businesses the old-fashioned way?"

Sadly, they are right. Such buyers are not hard to find. Expedience in some cases has overtaken economic logic. As with houses in hot real estate markets, many advisers are bidding up prices to get access to a client base. Who can fault sellers for maximizing value, or FP Transitions for creating an active marketplace for books of business? The problem is with the buyers who are overpaying for these assets.

According to reports published by FP Transitions, it sees a total of as many as 30 hits on a good listing. One adviser discussing a prospective purchase off this site said, "How can I not pay these high multiples? If I don't, somebody else will, and I won't get the client list." Another who used this site to purchase a practice told me, "I think I paid too much, but it was important that I buy the book so one of my competitors in town didn't get it." What these two buyers experienced was the dynamic of supply and demand. When interest is that great, sellers can command higher multiples. The question is whether the buyer can afford it. The elegance of this Web-based auction site is that it allows motivated buyers and sellers to come together, which for very small businesses is half the battle. But unfortunately, as is true with online trading, many buyers do not have the experience to make informed decisions. It's not a question of aptitude; it's a question of perspective.

These conditions are reminiscent of tulip mania and the more recent dot-com boom. Similar trends have surfaced in other industries that have attempted to consolidate over the past couple of decades, including medical practices, funeral homes, real estate brokerages, and CPA firms. In the latter case, buyers were offering 2.5 times annual fees to acquire accounting practices, although buyers and sellers in 2004 report the multiple was closer to 1. In the other professional-service industries, the markets are now virtually nonexistent because of the lack of acquisition opportunities. An even more disconcerting development is that roll-ups of service businesses often don't mitigate the distressing economic conditions that led to the sale in the first place; the conditions are merely transferred to their buyers.

Irrational exuberance aside, please be clear about two things:

♦ If a seller can maximize its return by selling the practice, it's logical to consider doing so. No one should sell a business below market as long as people are willing and able to pay the market price.

♦ Expansion through acquisition is a legitimate and prudent approach to growing a financial-advisory firm. In fact, most advisory firm owners need to think objectively about what their critical mass is

and get to that point fairly quickly if they want to optimize the effectiveness of their firms. Having a clear strategy that incorporates the
needs of your optimal client and using mergers as well as traditional
business-building methods to add those clients are effective ways of
getting the job done.

Know what you're buying. But make sure the purchase is achieving the goal intended. Advisers are paying large multiples for books
of businesses, even when many of the clients they're purchasing are
not in their sweet spot. What's more, through their bidding, they are
driving up the cost of practices to premiums that defy economic logic.
Sophisticated buyers know this; volume-driven "producers" do not.

Let's consider the example in *Figure 9.2* to demonstrate this
phenomenon and offer dimension to the discussion of valuation.
First, the assumptions: Suppose a practice generates $500,000 of
recurring gross revenue. According to our studies of thousands of
advisory practices during the past 10 years, the typical practice at
this level spends more than 40 percent of its revenues on overhead,
such as rent, utilities, administrative staff, and other general and
administrative expenses. Studies also find that when establishing fair
market compensation for professional staff, such as financial planners,
portfolio managers, financial advisers and so on, the typical practice
pays out about 40 percent of its revenues in professional compensation—called a direct expense. The owner's base compensation is
included in direct expense. If advisers manage their practices well,
they typically get an additional distribution from any profits left over.
In this example, 20 percent, or $100,000, would be the pretax profit
on this business.

Some pundits in the profession vehemently disagree with this
notion of recognizing compensation for the owner of a solo practice.
They argue that owners get paid out of what's left over and that is
what real cash flow is. Although that is true, it's not appropriate or
relevant in terms of valuation. A practice is not a passive investment; it
requires the labor (and wisdom and experience) of the owner-adviser
to produce the revenue. A direct cost is attached to this. For example,
if an adviser worked for a brokerage house, the brokerage house
would pay about 40 percent of the gross to produce this revenue.

That 40 percent is a good benchmark for measuring fair compensation for the owner of a practice and for other professionals generating the revenue in an advisory firm.

What's more, following protocols for valuation as defined by organizations that set these standards, some recognition for the cost of professional labor needs to be considered. That's because the numerator in all business valuations is free cash flow—the amount left after all expenses including fair compensation to the owner are paid. And as a practice becomes larger, there comes a time when the owner cannot physically serve all the clients he acquires; he will need to hire other advisers at a cost. This is the ultimate logic in quantifying compensation as a deduction before defining free cash flow.

But regardless of which approach you believe is right, it's important to know how current practice pricing compares to the required rate of return for alternative investments, especially publicly traded common stocks (every investor has choices: buy a practice, buy mutual funds, buy hedge funds, buy individual stocks and bonds, et cetera). So for the purpose of this exercise, let's start with the same foundation, by deducting fair professional labor costs and all overhead to get to a net profit number. And to make this analysis truly comparable with alternative investment vehicles, let's also apply a C corporation's tax rate (see Figure 9.2).

Applying the multiple for fee-only businesses that many say is the current rule of thumb for these firms—2.3 times revenue—the value reaches $1,150,000. Dividing $1,150,000 by net profit of $70,000 results in a price-to-earnings multiple of 16.43. Divide that multiple into 1, and the result is a required rate of return of 6.09 percent.

By comparison, large multimillion-dollar, well-capitalized, well-managed investment-advisory firms in the public market have current P/E ratios (with earnings defined the same way) in the same range. So here's the question: how can one rationalize a rate of return equivalent to an investment in the equity markets for a book of business completely dependent on the owner, with no systematic marketing and an aging client base that eventually will be depleted? Is it because of the growth potential that the seller could not realize? Is it because this way of procuring clients is cheaper than traditional marketing?

FIGURE 9.2   **Simple Financial Statement**

Revenue	100%	$500,000
Direct expense	40%	200,000
Gross profit	60%	300,000
Overhead	40%	200,000
Operating profit	20%	100,000
Estimated tax		(30,000)
Net profit after tax		$70,000

Affordability. Does it not seem shocking that at a capitalization rate of 6.09, the rate of return isn't much greater than a relatively risk-free investment like a long-term Treasury bond? Buyers would do well to think in financial terms—as investors do—when making these decisions. Ramping up takes money, and it's reasonable to pay a strategic premium if the goal is to amass a lot of assets and a lot of clients to build a market presence. But enthusiasm for this growth strategy must be tempered with some common sense on practice pricing.

Even though almost every one of these deals is structured with an earnout in which the buyer pays the seller a percentage of the gross for a defined period of time, an agreed-on valuation sets the foundation for the net payments to the seller. Should the buyer agree to a high value as the foundation, he could find himself working a lot longer before he realizes any meaningful income from the practice. Two mitigating factors would be a faster-than-normal growth in assets to manage from existing clients or synergy in the acquisition that propels the combined firms together at a faster-than-anticipated clip.

Many will argue that such a premium can be defended when the buyer is not paying any additional salaries, as long as he will be serving the new clients himself and not hiring additional advisers to do so. But once a buyer has to add professional staff to service the portfolio of clients acquired, he'll need to apply sound economic logic to the valuation model—including defining the direct expenses (professional staff compensation)—to determine net return. And the amount the buyer sacrifices in current compensation could be viewed as an equity investment in the business. Then the question becomes "All things considered, what is your return on equity?" At what point does the premium become unaffordable for the buyer?

If a client asked you whether he should pay a premium over the market price to invest in equities, what would be your advice? If you were the client, what advice would you expect to hear? Or does irrational exuberance not apply to you?

The final caution on price must be "Buyer beware." There has never been a more active marketplace for the purchase and sale of practices, which makes buyers vulnerable, especially if they've never acquired a practice before.

Finding Potential Sellers

Finding sellers takes work, planning, research, and a lot of phone calls. Sellers of practices are consumed with secrecy about their plans, and for obvious reasons. Like many buyers, you may find it's best to use an intermediary to search for possible acquisitions so you can remain focused on maintaining and building your core business.

Tapping industry professionals is usually the best method—for both buyers and sellers—for finding prospective acquisition candidates. Some good sources are listed in *Figure 9.3*.

Don't assume that one contact with a referral source will be sufficient. If you're serious about acquisition, you'd be wise to keep in touch with the sources of referral, if only by dropping them an occasional note reminding them of your continued interest. Persistent phone or personal contact can be agitating, but small reminders in the mail are harmless and useful and show serious intent.

There are other options of course, although they tend to be less effective. If you plan to advertise, you need to be very specific about what you're looking for and provide a discreet means by which the

FIGURE 9.3   **Industry Sources**

Broker-Dealers and Custodians

Start by asking your broker-dealer or custodian for information about potential sellers. The firm has a vested interest in keeping your business within its system and may also serve as a matchmaker for individuals contemplating retirement or expansion. Many maintain a database of potential sellers and interested buyers within the firm, a valuable resource to tap.

Professional Associations

The Financial Planning Association (FPA), the National Association of Personal Financial Advisors (NAPFA), the Personal Financial Planning sections of the American Institute of Certified Public Accountants (AICPA), or some other relevant group are obvious choices. Although they do not have offerings specific to mergers and acquisitions, each of these groups provides access to like-minded advisers who may be at the stage of contemplating a sale. Participation in their industry conferences will also give you exposure.

Local Community

Practitioners may not be active in the buyer's professional association, but they may still be visible and credible financial advisers in their communities. The easiest transactions are those that occur where you live, because they provide a much greater opportunity for you to bond with the new clients. A change in ownership also creates risk in client relationships, so it's important to find ways to minimize this risk.

Industry-Specific Websites

Several websites list and match buyers and sellers of financial-advisory practices, including www.schwabtransition.com, http://ria.fidelity.com, and www.fptransitions.com. Websites that list these types of practices appeal to both buyers and sellers because they're private and anonymous. The website listings are generally paid for by the buyer or the seller and run roughly from 10 basis points on the assets sold to 7 percent of the total transaction value when a deal goes through.

Other Buyers

If you're an adviser looking to purchase another firm, it's important to learn who else is hunting. Other potential buyers will not be interested in every practice that comes to their attention. Hence, it's a good idea to ask those buyers to refer you to any practices that don't fit the bill. One of them may be just right for you.

Advisers, Wholesalers, and Other Resources to the Industry

Approach the people who are exhibiting at conferences and others who serve as resources to the financial-advisory community. Although some of what you hear may be rumor, those who deal with practitioners regularly know more about the comings and goings of people in this industry than others might. A buyer's list of contacts might include software vendors, product wholesalers, trust company officers, attorneys, and consultants.

Investment Bankers

Once a firm's value reaches $5 million to $10 million, it's prudent for the owner to engage an investment banker rather than perform the search and negotiations on his own. The challenge is finding a banker who will represent such firms. The most prominent investment banks specializing in the financial-services industry—Berkshire Capital Securities, Cambridge International Partners, and Putnam Lovell—are outstanding in their field and, as a result, tend to focus on much larger enterprises. Moss Adams Capital is filling this void by focusing on RIAs of $5 million to $20 million in value.

prospective seller can respond. You may, for example, have the response directed to an independent individual or firm so the third party can screen prospects without prematurely revealing who they are.

You might also do a canvassing search, sending letters to practices in targeted cities within a geographical area. Such contact is certainly the most direct route, but it takes the most time and exposes your identity unless you hire an independent consulting firm. In this type of search, you might enclose a signed confidentiality agreement and criteria checklist with the initial letter of introduction. This step speeds the process and gives the potential seller the comfort of knowing the identity of the firm that's interested in his practice. The candidate would sign the confidentiality agreement, fill out the checklist of primary and secondary criteria, and send them both back to you or your intermediary, who would then evaluate the checklist to determine if a phone interview should be set up.

Buying outside your network. Buying a practice that's affiliated with a broker-dealer different from yours involves two significant transitions: moving clients to a new broker-dealer and the transition involved in the actual sale of the firm. The two combined can give clients a reason to change to another advisory firm altogether. To prevent that from happening and to facilitate the smooth transition of the business, we recommend the first step be for the acquisition target to affiliate with your broker-dealer. The purchase transaction may then commence once the accounts have been transferred.

Buying from a family member. The transfer of practices between family members—usually from one generation to the next—is not uncommon. A parent or other family member may make a suitable seller if he has a business that you can assimilate and improve. Special issues must be considered in such transactions however.

♦ *Commitment:* First of all, it's important that the buyer confirm that your business is in fact the business that he wants to be in. There also needs to be a commitment from the seller that he will actually transfer the business. In some cases, for example, the parent intends to transition the practice to the children but never actually leaves the firm and cannot give up control. For the transfer to be successful for both parties, their hopes and plans need to coincide to some degree. Too many family business transfers result in resentment and family disharmony instead of the legacy they're intended to establish.

♦ *Assessment:* If the buyer decides to proceed, it's important that he assess the purchase of a family member's practice just as thoroughly as he would any other. It's critical for the buyer to evaluate whether the purchase of this particular practice is a good business decision and for the seller to evaluate *objectively* whether this buyer is the right choice. Third-party experts can be most helpful in such an evaluation.

♦ *Clients:* It's most important that the firm's clients see the second generation as a suitable successor. The trust and respect the parents earned are not automatically transferred to the children. The transition and introduction of the new owner need to be handled as delicately as—if not more so than—they would with any buyer.

♦ *Valuation:* Another issue that requires special care in the sale/purchase of a practice between family members is the valuation and sale price. If the practice is sold for anything less than fair market value, the sale could have gift tax implications. It's generally prudent to obtain an independent opinion of fair market value to document intrafamily transactions.

Buying a practice with multiple advisers or reps. A target practice that has multiple advisers comes with problems as well as opportunities. Most buyers like the idea of a practice that's integrated and has several practitioners to help build a business. But multiple advisers with different agendas, serving different markets in different ways, can make the sale discussions tedious and unworkable.

Although meetings should include all principals, you should insist on negotiating with only one party who has the authority to negotiate on behalf of his or her partners. This is a good test for uncovering how harmonious and integrated their relationship is; it's also a good indicator of what your future relationship with them might be like. The process also helps you to identify the true center of influence in the firm.

Evaluating Candidates

Compatibility

The purchase of a financial-advisory practice is not purely a function of value. Cultural issues and practice-management issues will also affect the likelihood of success. The process of valuation is essential for evaluating a practice's financial health and potential. As important as these economic considerations are, an equally critical step in evaluating a candidate's suitability is determining how well the buyer's and seller's values, philosophies, and business cultures will fit together. Hooking up with a firm that has strengths that yours lacks can be a smart business decision, but the cultures and philosophies that foster the strengths of both firms must be assessed to determine whether the merged practice will be solid enough to stand after the merger.

For many, the art of the deal making is what's most appealing. But compatibility issues relating to culture and philosophy are critical to success and you must address them up front. When deals unravel, it's often because of unanswered questions. As a buyer, the sooner you can resolve the compatibility questions, the less time you'll spend chasing after deals that ultimately will not work.

The following questions are all key to uncovering how suitable the target practice is for you as a buyer.

♦ Do we share the same values?
♦ If the seller stays in the organization, will he fit in my organization?
♦ Will my clients like the seller? Will my staff?
♦ Are the seller's personality differences and trust issues surmountable?
♦ Will the seller's clients be geographically accessible to me?
♦ What will the seller do to facilitate the transfer of client relationships?
♦ Will the seller's broker-dealer affiliation help or hurt the sale?

Approaching the Prospects

Contrary to what you might assume as a buyer, sellers are not the only ones that need to market themselves in these transactions. Buyers also need to be prepared to share information about their firm and its strategy. You should approach each meeting with a prospective seller armed with everything required. An unprepared buyer who can't articulate his strategy, its merits, and its value for the seller signals a lack of organization at best and incompetence at worst.

You need to be prepared to disclose the broad aspects of your strategy and the fundamentals of your current business in order to elicit meaningful comments and observations from the owner of the target practice. Have a standard, consistent description of your practice and be ready to articulate your plan at each initial meeting. This approach of opening up to the seller before you start asking him to share pertinent information about his own practice can help build trust and assist you in obtaining useful insights. Remember, although you might not buy this particular practice, the information you gather is of tremendous value to you in the decisions you'll make as you continue your search.

The list of marketing materials—called "Sample 1: Document Request List" in the appendix—outlines the information you'll need to request from the seller. You should be prepared to share similar types of information about your own practice with the prospective seller or any other parties that may be involved in the transaction. For instance, if you anticipate asking a bank or other lender to finance the acquisition, this is the time to make sure your house is in order. Chapter 10 discusses the expectations and requirements of financial institutions in more detail, but most lenders will expect to see three to five years of your financial statements and tax returns and may be interested in information on your revenue sources, client base, et cetera. Such information can take time to gather and organize, and that should be done in advance so that the negotiating process will not lose momentum.

The Initial Meeting

If your review of the marketing materials and the preliminary information the seller shares is encouraging, it's time to put the prospect to a "smell test" and begin the preliminary discussions. Hold all meetings, including the initial one, with the key decision makers from both sides present. If there are three principals who have to concur on a decision to sell, then your best plan is to have all three present at all meetings. As mentioned earlier, this is a good test to see how harmonious and integrated the partners' relationships are. If they can't agree among themselves early on, it may be best to walk away.

Both sides should be prepared with what they regard as their deal killers, so that these issues are not brought up too late in the process. Neither party wants to waste time, and unless important issues have been clarified up front, you run the risk of aggravating everyone, including yourself, in these discussions.

Gaining an understanding of the seller's issues while remaining focused on your strategy will afford you the best path to a rewarding deal for both sides. Not everyone will be happy with every part of the arrangement, but everyone should be satisfied with the overall outcome. Above all, both you and the seller should always be prepared to walk away from any proposed deal if the outcome does not support either party's overall strategy. Use the initial meeting to learn enough to determine if there is merit to continuing the negotiation process.

The agenda. Have a uniform agenda for the first meeting. Keep your strategy in focus at all times: that's why you're there. Remember the target practice criteria you've established to screen the candidates.

Getting to know each other at the outset is typically the start of any first meeting. It's ideal if you can do that in a manner that yields information and insight about the seller yet keeps you both at ease. Be ready to reciprocate actively with the seller. Many of the philosophical and emotional issues that need to be discussed and analyzed can be explored at this stage. Trust issues will come out almost immediately in this part of the discussion, signaled by how open the seller is with you and how open you are in turn.

Staying focused will help you maintain control of the process. If the seller is unprepared, he will usually attempt to gain quick control of the meeting and start making statements about what is or is not acceptable in a deal. These comments are not necessarily well-thought-out positions on the seller's part.

It's important to understand the psychology in play in the initial meeting. If the potential seller controls the discussion, he will assume you understand and agree with most of the statements made unless you disagree with or dispute the seller's position. That risk is part of any first meeting when you're interested in the target practice and want to avoid contradicting, arguing, or saying no to the prospective seller at such an early stage, a move that could undermine any future negotiations and ultimately block the purchase. Nevertheless, positive posturing toward the seller will make it appear as if you agree and approve of his statements and comments. For now you are at a disadvantage, and from this point on you'll have to work uphill to get back to even in presenting the terms and conditions of your proposal.

Throughout the interview, stay connected, cordial, and cooperative. If the deal is to be truly successful, both parties will want to feel that they've satisfied a majority of their conditions. Adopt a win-win attitude in describing your strategy and what's in it for the seller. Buyers who come across as aloof and arrogant set the stage for a difficult negotiation process—if it even gets that far. Discussions need to last at least long enough for you to determine if the target practice merits further consideration.

No deal. By the time you schedule the first meeting with a prospective seller, you will have expended a considerable amount of energy, time, and money in preparation. A target practice is just that. Throughout the process of approaching target practices, bear in mind what good salespeople know: a firm "no" is just as important to get as a "yes." Knowing where you stand at the end of the first meeting is essential, so that you can determine whether to spend more time with that target practice or move on to another. There will be many candidate firms with which you will not want to continue a dialogue after the first meeting. That's okay. It's to be expected. In fact, a majority of the target practices will fall out of the running for some common reasons:

- ◆ The target practice may lack a genuine interest in selling.
- ◆ The target practice may not "click" with your firm, or the practice may not fit into your strategy.
- ◆ You may discover the target practice does not meet enough of your target practice criteria.

- ♦ The target practice may place too much emphasis on its own strengths and underestimate its shortcomings.
- ♦ The seller may want too much money from the outset.
- ♦ The prospective seller may get cold feet about losing his independence.
- ♦ The principal of the firm being sold may see that his personal objectives cannot be achieved through sale.

The Buyer's Goals

In the first face-to-face meeting, you have a number of goals to accomplish as the buyer. You need to communicate your strategy and find out how well the target practice fits into it. You'll want the potential seller to be as positively engaged in this process as possible. In the final analysis, after this first interview, the two parties will either part ways or continue the process toward a successful deal. Both outcomes are valuable. If the target practice does not end up fitting your strategy, don't view the process as a waste of time. Remember, the whole process of the search is gathering valuable and useful information from various practices.

The following questions, which echo the items discussed under "Compatibility" (page 134), cover the most important ones you'll want answered or at least discussed by the end of the first meeting with a potential seller:

- ♦ Do the seller's business values and operational philosophy seem to fit with mine?
- ♦ Is the seller committed to selling?
- ♦ Is the seller interested in becoming part of another organization?
- ♦ Is the seller's timetable the same as mine?
- ♦ Will the seller stay for the required period for the transition of his business?
- ♦ Are the seller's personality differences or trust issues insurmountable?
- ♦ Does the seller's notion of practice value fit within my parameters?
- ♦ Can the seller forgo independence if that will be required in the acquisition?

♦ How closely does the practice align with my other target practice criteria?

Whether you're acquiring a book of business or an enterprise with systems, people, processes, and substantial revenues, the opportunity is both exciting and daunting. The exciting part is that the market is dictating the need to get to some level of critical mass. Costs, on average, are rising faster than revenues for most advisers; more pressure on compliance is distracting the smaller advisers from client service and revenue generation; competition is making it harder to differentiate; new hires are wary of small firms. Through acquisition, you can build a practice into an enterprise that is the optimal choice for both clients and talent.

The daunting part of the endeavor is that when you acquire a professional-services firm, you're relying on the behavior of people—both clients and staff. Unlike a manufacturing and distribution company, for which the product or the process or the brand is the driving force, an advisory business can be whipsawed by the whims of individuals. Further, service businesses are, by definition, labor intensive. Although there are opportunities to gain leverage and improve your financial returns, it's easy to disrupt the economics of your business should a key client or key staff person leave. As a result, the period between executing your acquisition strategy and getting to critical mass is a high-risk, highly stressful time when you must stay focused on managing the practice and pushing for integration as quickly as possible.

In this chapter, we looked at a lot of the risk factors and crazy decisions that buyers make. That does not mean that acquiring a practice—or even a book of business—is a bad decision. Approached prudently and patiently, such acquisitions have tremendous potential to help you achieve your overall business goals.

10. GETTING ALL THE WAY TO YES
Coming to Terms

IN STRUCTURING THE sale or purchase of a practice, a number of critical issues must be considered and satisfactorily negotiated. Because selling a business is usually an emotional experience, it's best to involve a trusted professional in this process. Rational, logical decisions don't come easily from either side of the transaction if the atmosphere is emotionally charged. Frequently, someone says something that's better left unsaid, and it's difficult to get the process back on track once such misunderstandings arise.

The Deal Structure

Many practitioners go through the process of identifying buyers and even negotiating the purchase price but fail to consummate the transaction because of an inability to agree to terms.

Issues to Negotiate

Critical issues that have to be negotiated, apart from the purchase price, include:

- Stock sale or asset sale
- Asset sale or consulting agreement
- Noncompete agreement
- Buyback provision
- Representations and warranties
- Indemnification and hold-harmless clauses
- Performance of duties
- Protections
- Continuing commissions
- Security or collateral
- Payment terms
- Earnout
- Installment sales
- Down payment
- Resolution of conflicts

Stock sale or asset sale. When the business involved is a corporation, as opposed to a limited liability company (LLC) or partnership (PS), tax implications can be especially tricky for both the buyer and the seller, depending on the structure of the transaction. Most practices are purchased based on the assets of the business. Because of liability and tax treatments for the buyers, they rarely purchase the stock in an entity. *Figure 10.1* summarizes the tax ramifications for both buyers and sellers in the case of a stock sale involving a C corporation, which represents about one-third of all advisory firms, according to random studies we've done of the industry. The asset sale "problems" are eliminated with the S corporation election.

If a buyer purchases the *assets*—that is, the book of business and other fixed assets—the seller generally will treat the transaction as a capital gain for tax purposes. Please note that in a C corporation, the capital gain doesn't matter since it is taxed at the same rate as ordinary income. This consideration applies if an S corporation or another pass-through entity such as an LLC is involved. However, the buyer may not expense the purchase price in the year of the purchase; rather he will have to depreciate fixed assets over their useful lives and amortize intangible assets over 15 years, as summarized in *Figure 10.2.*

If the price is paid over time, each payment of principal will create a taxable event for the seller (a so-called installment sale). The buyer, on the other hand, may immediately begin depreciating the full cost of the asset. An appropriate interest rate should be assigned to the sale of assets if it is done over time. If the parties don't assign an interest rate, the IRS will do it for them by treating a portion of each payment as interest.

If the price is paid with a *forgivable loan,* then each time a portion of the loan is forgiven the seller will have to pay ordinary income tax on that portion. A forgivable loan is common under circumstances in which an adviser with a large book of business comes over to another firm and receives a large up-front payment—the buyers use these as a hedge against attrition in the book of business and against the adviser's leaving the firm early. The sale of assets is the only option available to practices that function as sole proprietorships and therefore have no ownership shares they can transfer.

FIGURE 10.1 **Tax Ramifications of a Stock Sale**

	Buyer	**Seller**
Tax Treatment	The buyer records all assets (tangible and intangible) and liabilities of the practice without adjustment on the books. As a result, depreciation deductions will generally be lower compared with a purchase of assets. (If the agreement allows for a Section 338 election, the buyer will get a step-up in basis on a stock sale, and the seller treats the transaction as an asset sale.)	The seller generally owes capital gains tax on the difference between his basis in the shares and the stated sale price. In some circumstances, there may be ordinary income tax treatment.
Liability	The buyer generally assumes all liabilities arising from the purchased practice unless the purchase agreement sets other provisions.	The seller is generally relieved of all liabilities.

Sellers should work with their tax advisers on ways to minimize the consequences of an asset sale, especially if the entity is a C corporation. The double taxation of asset sales by C corporations is onerous. In most circumstances, it appears that it's best if the advisory firm elects S corporation status over a C corporation, or to set up from the start as an LLC. The good news is most financial advisers may be able to allocate a portion of the purchase price to personal

FIGURE 10.2 **Tax Ramifications of an Asset Sale**

	Buyer	**Seller**
Tax Treatment	The buyer *may not* expense the purchase price in the period of the transaction. Instead, the assets will be depreciated over their useful life. Intangible assets are amortized over 15 years.	Generally, the seller (the corporation in this case) recognizes a capital gains tax on the difference between its basis in the assets and the stated sale price. The amount of tax to be paid depends on the corporation classification (C versus S corporation).
Liability	The buyer assumes no liabilities arising from the purchased practice unless specified separately in the purchase agreement.	The seller remains liable for all liabilities of the practice before the transaction.

goodwill instead of to the business. Sale of personal goodwill would incur capital gains tax instead of double taxation through the C corporation because it would be attributed to value created by the owner personally, as opposed to value owned by the corporation. This is especially viable with smaller firms, in which the value of the firm is closely tied to the owner personally. What's more, securities commissions can be paid only to licensed individuals, not to business entities, so the value of the insurance business is very closely tied to the individual.

Asset sale or consulting agreement. If the value of the purchase is allocated to a consulting agreement, the buyer may generally expense the payments on consulting agreements when they are paid, but the seller will have to record the proceeds as ordinary income for tax purposes. This will affect the seller's Social Security income and the amount he pays in tax. Specifically, the seller will not get capital gains treatment on the receipt of consulting payments, which can significantly increase his total tax. So, if justified, a portion of the purchase price may relate to continuing services provided by the seller, and this should be a consideration in your negotiations.

To avoid any unpleasant surprises from the IRS, it's essential that both parties agree to the specific structure and be consistent in how they classify the terms in their tax returns. It's also important that the parties in this transaction get advice from tax accountants experienced in business transactions because of the nuances in deal structures (see *Figure 10.3*).

Noncompete agreement. It may appear obvious that a seller is planning to get out of the business if he transfers ownership of his practice, but it's prudent to get that intention in writing to ensure the seller does not recruit the best clients away from the practice after leaving.

A noncompete agreement has to be reasonable and enforceable and should have a limited duration, a well-defined geographic scope, and a definition of what business activity is strictly prohibited. There should also be a meaningful penalty for breach of the noncompete agreement, such as forfeiture of the remaining payments due or the requirement to share the income earned from the clients procured during the noncompetition period. Each state has its own interpretation of what is enforceable. It is necessary to hire local counsel familiar with these laws to draft any agreements.

FIGURE 10.3 **Treatment of Consulting Agreement**

	Buyer	**Seller**
Tax Treatment	The buyer is able to expense the entire purchase payment in the year incurred.	The seller records the proceeds as ordinary income for tax purposes and must pay ordinary income tax and FICA.

Note: Neither party benefits much from allocating part of the sale price to a noncompete agreement. The buyer will have to amortize the value of the noncompete over 15 years and the seller treats the value as ordinary income for tax purposes. In some jurisdictions, however, the power of the noncompete is determined by the amount paid for it. Again, a good adviser can help protect you.

Buyback provision. When a practitioner sells his practice, he usually has no interest in taking it back. But there are protections a buyer may want to put in place—called buyback provisions—in the event that the seller becomes dissatisfied with how the buyer is handling the book of business. For example, the buyer may just be servicing the top 20 percent of the clients and ignoring the rest, which could affect the payment terms. If a buyback provision is structured into the deal, the contract must spell out the terms and conditions of such a transaction as well as the circumstances that might trigger the provision. These types of provisions could have unfortunate tax results for the seller. In effect, the seller may end up paying tax on assets he bought back, which he then depreciates.

Representations and warranties. Although representations and warranties appear standard, often the nuances to the language in these sections are designed to disclose what each party is representing to the other about the business and the transaction. The warranty portion is an assurance to the other party that what is being represented is true. Both parties to the agreement will want to consider the terminology on representations and warranties very carefully to ensure they understand what the other is representing in the agreement. For example, one would typically spell out these terms:

♦ Both the buyer and seller have the authority to make the transaction.

♦ There are no pending surprises, such as customer complaints, investigations, or lawsuits, that they are aware of.

♦ The information that has been supplied by either party in the course of the negotiation is accurate and complete.

♦ The agreement does not breach any other agreements the parties may have with others.

An example of language that represents each is in good standing might read as follows:

Good standing. Buyer and Seller hereby warrant and represent that each is a registered investment adviser in good standing, that their respective regulatory filings are current and accurately reflect their advisory operations, and that each is in compliance with applicable state and federal rules and regulations pertaining to registered investment advisers. In addition, Buyer and Seller warrant and represent that neither is (nor are any of their respective principals and/or associated persons) subject to any statutory disqualification set forth in Sections 203(e) and 203(f) of the Investment Advisers Act of 1940 (or any successor statutory sections or rules), nor is either one (nor are any of their respective principals and/or associated persons) currently the subject of any investigation or proceeding that could result in statutory disqualification. Buyer and Seller acknowledge their obligation to advise each other with respect to these representations shall be continuing and ongoing, and should any representation change for any reason, buyer and seller warrant to advise the other immediately, together with providing the corresponding pertinent facts and circumstances.

There are numerous additional possible representations and warranties, which your attorney can help you to identify.

Indemnification and hold-harmless clauses. Risk can largely be transferred through the language in the indemnification section of any agreement. The seller and buyer must agree on which party bears the risk, and hence the cost, if any material feature of the business or any disclosure or representation of the seller proves to be wrong. In such cases, the buyer sometimes forces the seller to carry the burden of risk in the indemnification section.

A seller should make sure there is a time and dollar limit on any indemnification offered to a buyer. The nature of this business is that everybody is vulnerable to lawsuits. Each party should spell out what he is and is not willing to be responsible for. Typically, both parties hold each other harmless and indemnify the other party for any claims, liabilities, or damages arising out of any act, error, omission, or defalcation that may have occurred or could occur before or after the sale. Some thought may be given to how parties will handle issues that occur or are aggravated over a period of time that includes both periods of ownership. Such issues might include employee theft that may have begun before the sale and continued during and after it.

Performance of duties. Typically, when a practice changes hands, the buyer expects that the seller will help in the transition. It's important to spell out those expectations in the agreement, clarifying how long the transition period will be, what the specific duties of the seller will be in the transition, and even how many hours per week the seller will be called on to work.

For example, you might state that the seller (1) will remain part of the practice for one year, (2) will work no less than 30 hours per week, and (3) must agree to have meaningful contact with and provide an introduction to the top 100 clients. Again, failure to perform the duties may result in some penalty such as a reduction in the purchase price or in the payments under a consulting agreement.

Following is an example of language related to performance:

> **Buyer's inability to perform.** Following the first 12 months subsequent to closing, neither party shall be able to terminate this contract except as may be mutually agreed. This restriction shall not apply to termination by Seller if (1) Buyer is unable to fulfill its payment obligations under this agreement, and Seller has provided Buyer with thirty (30) days' prior written notice of its intention to terminate, with an opportunity to cure such payment delinquency(ies), deficiency(ies), and/or provide security to the reasonable satisfaction of the seller within the thirty- (30-) day notice period, or upon such other reasonable terms as approved by Seller; or (2) Buyer becomes subject to a reportable event pursuant to paragraph x.ox of this agreement, which cannot be cured by Buyer within thirty (30) days from the date thereof, or upon such other terms as reasonably provided by Seller.

Resolution of conflicts. When the buyer and the seller are in different locations, the agreement should state the jurisdiction for any resolution of conflicts, which will minimize the expenses incurred in defending or prosecuting a position. Ideally, the document will provide some means of resolving conflicts early and at less expense than litigation, such as some form of mediation or arbitration. To the extent possible, the agreement should be specific with respect to the guidelines the mediator should follow as to the standard of value, and it should specify who would be responsible for what costs.

Protections. No one can fully anticipate what might happen to the individuals during the term of the agreement in such a transaction, but there are protections that should be considered for both sides.

If you're a buyer, you're likely to be concerned about what happens if the seller dies or becomes disabled early in the transition of the practice. This is a business risk you can best protect against by having the seller provide for death or disability protection (insurance) during the term of the transaction. In the realm of the deal, the cost of such protection is not usually onerous and should not warrant becoming a major sticking point in negotiations. Both parties can agree, instead, that in the event of some catastrophe, the buyer will complete the obligations under the agreement by paying the estate or a designated beneficiary.

If you're a seller, it's reasonable for you to request some protection too, likely in the form of insurance that compensates the seller in the event the buyer cannot fulfill his or her obligations under the agreement due to death or disability. If one party or the other is uninsurable, then the parties to the transaction can negotiate funding either of these possibilities with some other type of security or collateral.

Continuing commissions. The National Association of Securities Dealers' continuing-commissions policy (NASD Rule IM-2420-2) prohibits the receipt of commissions by anyone who is not licensed as a registered rep *unless the parties have a bona fide contract*. The policy allows for continuing commissions on existing accounts to be paid to a representative, a surviving spouse, or beneficiaries, after the representative's employment with a registered firm ends because of death, disability, or retirement *provided bona fide contracts call for such payment*. The policy does not permit the solicitation of new business or the sharing of commissions on business from new accounts with persons who are not registered.

Security or collateral. Most attorneys encourage their clients to obtain some security, guaranty, or collateral from the buyer to ensure full and complete payments are made on a timely basis. This is a negotiable area for both parties and should be entered into very carefully. In most transactions structured as an earnout in which the buyer agrees to pay the seller a percentage of the gross, there is no guarantee of the payment amount, only an expressed percentage. Earnouts may also be structured so that the parties agree to a fixed price and the payments are made out of the earnings of the practice. In either case, there should be some recourse for the seller should the buyer default.

Payment terms. It's important to be specific about the length and amount of payment, and about the basis of payment. For example, if the transaction is structured as an earnout in which the buyer pays the seller a percentage of the revenue generated for a period of time, the agreement should be specific as to the business on which the revenue is based and the clients to which the revenue relates. The parties should be sure to include an exhibit that identifies the specific clients being transferred. An earnout may also refer to the terms of the agreement in which the seller essentially finances the transaction by allowing the buyer to purchase the practice at an agreed-on price out of the earnings of the practice. In either case, the agreement should also state the frequency of payments (monthly should be the minimum) and how the payments will be made (for example, a commission split generated through the broker-dealer). As with all terms and conditions, the agreement should spell out the penalty for violating the payment terms.

Earnout. Few financial-advisory practices and investment-management firms actually exchange hands on the basis of cash on the barrelhead or on the value alone. Even when they do, the practice is usually paid for over time, with the buyer paying the seller out of the earnings of the practice, which is one definition of earnout. More typically, the earnout is structured so that the buyer pays the seller a percentage of the gross revenues that are generated from the book of business for a defined period of time.

Although there is nothing inherently wrong in agreeing to a fixed price at which the practice changes hands, the reason the earnouts are typically structured as a percentage earnout over time is because of the uncertainty about the book of business transferring in total.

The buyer is perceived to assume most of the risk in a fixed-price transaction, with the greater burden of risk transferring to the seller in an earnout based on future revenues. Remember, in negotiations, whoever assumes the most risk should get the most benefit. In an earnout, the parties could agree to a higher initial valuation to compensate the seller for the risk.

Calculating an earnout includes the following steps:

Step 1: Divide the agreed-on value by the first year's adjusted cash flow. The result tells you the length of time (or earnout period) it will take for the practice to generate enough cash flow to pay the value, assuming it's able to sustain the projected level of earnings.

Step 2: Divide adjusted cash flow by projected revenue. The result is the return on ownership, expressed as a percentage of sales. This percentage is the amount the buyer pays the seller on the gross revenues of the practice for the life of the earnout agreement determined in step 1. For the buyer to pay a higher percentage than the practice can apparently generate in cash flow would mean cutting into her own reward for labor. The buyer may agree to this as a cost of acquisition (in lieu of labor spent on other marketing activities), but it should be recognized and evaluated as such.

For example, if the practice generated annual revenues of $350,000 and an adjusted cash flow of $75,000, the return on ownership would be 21.43 percent of sales (75,000 / 350,000 = 21.43 percent). In this case, the buyer would offer to pay the seller no more than 21.43 percent of the gross revenues generated by that book of business for a defined period of time. These discussions may truly test the negotiating skills of both buyer and seller.

The seller should set some thresholds of performance to protect against the buyer skimming the cream of the business. For example, the agreement may state that the buyer agrees to produce at least 50 percent of the historical annual income for the term of the earnout agreement. Should the buyer fall short of this threshold, he would still have to pay a sizable amount to the seller. This provision protects the seller and motivates the buyer.

Note: Earnouts apply to all income generated during the term of the agreement by the book of business transferred, including trails, service commissions, and retainers. To the extent the adviser has built a practice that generates more predictable income, such as retainers or fee income, then that adviser has enhanced the value of the practice or at least enhanced the transferability of the book of business. The operating leverage gained from this style of practice should result in greater earnings and profitability. This style also minimizes the risk, therefore enhancing the value.

Another approach to calculating the earnout is to define the term of the earnout first, then work backward. For example, let's assume the parties agree to structure the earnout over three years. If the business is valued at $725,000, this means the buyer expects to receive $242,000 per year: dividing $242,000 by the annual gross revenues of $560,000 tells us the expected annual payout on a three-year deal is slightly more than 43 percent of the annual gross ($242,000 / $560,000). Put another way, assuming the gross revenue holds firm at $560,000 per year, the buyer would pay the seller 43 percent of the annual gross to reach the $242,000 annual payout. Of course, if the gross declines, the buyer will pay the seller less in dollars, since the earnout is tied to 43 percent of future gross.

In any transaction, the tax perspective has many nuances. Many complexities of an earnout can't be adequately addressed here; you should consult with a qualified CPA familiar with the tax impact of such transactions before agreeing to the terms.

Installment sales. When selling a book of business, a practitioner typically incurs capital gains tax on the transaction. A new tax bill was signed in December 1999 prohibiting accrual taxpayers from using the installment method to extend the period over which capital gains taxes are paid. Because earnout payments are considered installment-type sales, this escalates the point at which the accrual-basis taxpayer must make the tax payment. Although this will not affect most sole practitioners who practice cash-basis accounting, it will have a significant impact on practices (primarily corporations) that use accrual-based accounting.

Down payment. Although rarely requested and certainly not required, a down payment is another form of security and helps to weed out the tire kickers or those just looking to skim off the best clients. The seller can approach the down payment in a number of ways. He could make the down payment equal to the market value of the tangible assets being sold or make the down payment equal to the estimated final payments (perhaps the last two to three months) in their earnout agreement. The balance due or any other adjustments can be reconciled at the end of the term of the agreement. Many prospective buyers have a difficult time accepting this idea and are unwilling to make a down payment. In some transactions, requiring a down payment may scare away good potential buyers who would otherwise consider their time, effort, and expense a clear indication of their sincere interest to potentially make an offer.

Financing

Most ownership transitions between independent financial advisers—at least at the small end of the market—tend to include earnouts wherein the buyer pays the seller a percentage of the future revenue for a defined period of time, as discussed previously. In some instances, the parties to the sale agree to a specific price that is earned out over time.

Earnouts, by definition, mean the seller is financing the sale. So not only is he at risk for transferring the book of business to someone who may not serve the clients well, he is also at risk as the banker in the transaction.

In addition to seller financing, bank financing may be a possibility in some transactions. A bank typically will want to confirm that (1) the valuation is supportable and documented by a qualified professional appraiser who is knowledgeable about the industry and (2) the acquired business can generate sufficient cash flow to support the practice as well as the loan on the purchase. Even with these conditions in place, it's unlikely the bank will finance 100 percent of the purchase price unless the buyer is willing to pledge other assets.

The bank's relationship will be with *the buyer*, and the bank will generally require the following information:

♦ Five years of financial statements and tax returns from the buyer
♦ Positive operating-adjusted free cash flow for the last four consecutive years
♦ Evidence that a dedicated staff will likely stay with the practice
♦ A clean credit report on the buyer, both personal and business

♦ Consistent annual revenue growth, in the range of 10 percent over the last five years

In addition, the bank will usually require a personal guarantee from the buyer, and it will require that his personal verifiable net worth, exclusive of the business, be at least two times the proposed borrowing, that his credit report be satisfactory, and that his regulatory record show compliance with industry and firm regulations.

Now banks use credit-scoring tools for most small-business loans, which capture many of these same elements but in more quantitative terms. In other words, not only are they evaluating the borrower's ability to repay but they assess that willingness based on past credit history. Historically, lenders have analyzed financing requests based on the "five Cs," which in a way are still relevant today:

1. Character
2. Capacity
3. Collateral
4. Capital
5. Conditions

1. Character. Various degrees of investigation are done regarding the principals in the transaction, evaluating an established record of success, including but not limited to their financial status and experience in the related field.

2. Capacity. Because of a propensity of buyers to overpay for a business, the bank will want an independent review of the business to evaluate whether the purchase makes economic sense. The review can include these elements:

♦ Future cash flow tests with various assumptions
♦ Cash flow analysis and debt-service coverage using personal financial statements
♦ Two years' tax returns
♦ Credit report and contingent liabilities
♦ Assessment of ability to manage floating pricing and balloon terms
♦ Continuance of cash flow based on the necessity of the seller's involvement to retain business
♦ Collateral and signature support from the seller

- Partial or full guarantees to the financing source
- Secondary cash flow or hard collateral for risk mitigation
- The long-term intent of the purchaser—will he be able to obtain financing to implement the next stage?
- The remainder after debt service

Debt amortization should never exceed five years; three years is recommended since the cash flow may not last that long, given risks of client satisfaction, death, et cetera. The most serious risk is diminished interest on the part of the buyer, that is, no economic motive to continue the transaction (service the debt) if cash flow does not cover the financing cost, debt repayment, and opportunity. In making the loan, the bank will consider the potential for a decrease in the cash flow assuming business interruptions, competitive barriers, and proprietary product restrictions.

3. Collateral. Valuation/stock in the corporation may be severely restricted and have no effective liquid market value. The bank will expect controllable ownership, ability to pay the maximum initial advance, and the ability to maintain payments. Because there may be no way to "perfect" commissions as collateral, the bank views commissions only as a source of repayment. The bank also considers unrelated collateral.

4. Capital. Agreements based on seller buybacks are unusual because the seller generally has no interest in getting back into the business. The bank financing does not include underwriting the equity portion of the sale, as banks expect the equity to come from the buyer or be financed by the seller.

5. Conditions. These may include economic, market, regulatory, and legal conditions. Will the structure of the purchasing entity (that is, LLC, S corp, partnership) be acceptable to the bank?

Closing the Deal

After the parties have spent a significant amount of time and energy on negotiating and finalizing their terms, it's time to close the deal. If all the conditions specified in the purchase agreement are met, the buyer and seller will exchange the documents described in the agreement and shake hands.

The documents exchanged typically include:

♦ Escrow agreement, if escrow is used

♦ Settlement sheet, with the expenses related to the transaction
that the buyer or seller has agreed to cover, including the fees of
outside advisers who work on a success-fee basis

♦ Transfer documents, such as bill of sale and titles

♦ Any debt notes used as part of the payment

♦ Covenants not to compete, consulting agreement, employment
agreement, et cetera

Now the buyer and seller can move on to the most important part
of the agreement—making it work.

The Successful Agreement

As you prepare for the process of finalizing the agreement, you may
find these guiding principles will keep you on track:

♦ Don't let the lawyers negotiate the economics of the deal. Their
job is to make sure the terms are legal. If you need financial advice,
seek out a qualified investment banker, valuation consultant, or
accountant with experience in business transactions.

♦ Recognize that a letter of intent is not a binding agreement to
buy or sell. It generally contains an exclusivity period, and you must
be prepared that it may not come to completion.

♦ Once you fall in love with getting acquired, you run the risk of
falling out of love with running your business. Don't get distracted
from the fundamentals. It's a long and tedious process, as you will
see once all the terms are identified.

♦ When you engage legal counsel for the document drafting and
elements in the due-diligence process, be sure to retain a lawyer
who understands the full impact of the Investment Advisers Act,
not just the corporate impact. There are many nuances involved in
the purchase and sale of a financial-advisory firm that escape those
not familiar with the act's myriad regulations.

♦ Don't shy away from doing background checks. The financial-
advisory industry allows for full disclosure, so be sure to find out all
you can.

♦ When you enter into the negotiations, be sure to discuss what the compensation of the seller will be in addition to the purchase price. This consideration is frequently ignored in the valuation and postmerger integration, and the oversight frequently leads to deals blowing up a short time later.

♦ Be sure any investment banker or broker of any type you engage to assist you with the transaction is properly licensed. The minimum requirement in many states is a real estate broker's license (weird but true), but you're generally better advised to engage someone who has the appropriate NASD licenses to sell securities, which in many cases is what's occurring when the business is sold.

IV

Ounces of Prevention

11. ESSENTIALS OF DUE DILIGENCE
Ounces of Prevention

DUE DILIGENCE IS the process by which a prospective buyer investigates, reviews, and analyzes a target business; often a seller initiates a similar review of the buyer's business. The bulk of the work is done through document review, on-site inspection, and interviews.

The Buy Side

A buyer's primary goal in the due-diligence process is to verify the facts of the transaction, good or bad, as originally presented. During the process, a buyer may or may not discover undisclosed facts. What a buyer will inevitably discover is how consistently the original seller's portrayal of the business compares with the due-diligence outcome. Discoveries made during due diligence may affect the deal, both its price and its terms. Areas of focus vary, depending on the unique circumstances of each transaction, but generally include gathering the following information regarding the target:

- ♦ Organizational structure
- ♦ Accounting practices
- ♦ Information systems
- ♦ Shareholder/capitalization issues
- ♦ Material contracts and significant customers
- ♦ Contingent liabilities
- ♦ Compliance records

Both the timing and the organization of the due-diligence process are important. The beginning of the process should coincide as closely as possible to the signing of a letter of intent. Communication and coordination should take place with a primary contact at the target company.

A detailed checklist of documents and information generally requested from the seller for review during the due-diligence process is included as Sample 2 in the appendix. This checklist offers a skeleton of the due-diligence document list; it should be revised based on what is learned about the target practice during preliminary negotiations as well as on input provided by attorneys and accountants. Given the complexity of legal, regulatory, accounting, and tax rules regarding business combinations, the buyer should always consider retaining outside specialists to help design or execute the structure of the purchase agreement and examine the seller's processes, files, and records.

The Sell Side

The seller's primary due-diligence concerns generally include seeking assurance that the purchase price is appropriate and will be collected and understanding the tax consequences of the sale. There may also be cultural or personnel issues to consider. After successful preliminary discussions and before the due-diligence process begins, it's appropriate to disclose the pending business deal to key staff or to all employees. Communicating the news to staff is important and should be planned carefully. Consider obtaining advice from a human resources consultant. Given the complexity of legal, regulatory, accounting, and tax rules regarding business combinations, the seller should always consider retaining outside specialists to help structure the purchase agreement.

Due diligence is the most invasive part of a transaction. The buyer will want to review many documents during the due-diligence process (see the checklist in the appendix). These documents should be made ready before the start of preliminary negotiations to avoid delay or loss of potential agreements. Early preparation for the due-diligence process also allows the seller to clear up any problems that may cause a prospective buyer to lower his offer or walk away entirely.

The buyer wants to feel confident in the quality of information provided during the evaluation process. Problems occur when profits are minimized in a business or when certain personal expenses are camouflaged as business expenses. A seller may claim, "The new owner won't have the same expenses, so they should assume their own costs when they value my practice." But most buyers intuitively understand they should not have to pay for their own efforts to make the practice more profitable than it was under the previous ownership. Buyers will look closely at the practice as it stands under current ownership before negotiating a purchase price. Sellers need to be prepared.

Seller's Due-Diligence Preparation

The following checklist will help manage and report finances in a way that helps both the seller and a potential buyer have confidence in the numbers provided.

- ♦ Engage a reputable accounting firm to conduct annual financial statement audits and prepare federal and state tax returns.
- ♦ Prepare written documentation regarding the design of the internal control structure and document the performance of testing that ensures those controls are operating as designed.
- ♦ Routinely prepare and maintain accurate internal financial statements and management reports.
- ♦ Account for revenues and expenses consistently.
- ♦ Recognize revenues by category so those that are transferable are easily identified.
- ♦ Justify each expense in the business before making it.
- ♦ Properly account for true business expenses. Do not manipulate expenses to minimize taxes.
- ♦ Prepare internal financial statements on either an accrual basis or a cash basis of accounting. (Moss Adams strongly recommends accrual as a better measure of economic reality, especially as more practices move toward fee-oriented or fee-only practices.)
- ♦ If certain expenses will not be transferred to the buyer, begin managing the practice as would a potential buyer to demonstrate the earnings capacity of the practice with confidence.
- ♦ Do not defer necessary expenses or improvements in the practice in hopes of bettering the profit picture. The sale of a practice

may take a long time. By deferring needs, income and the potential value of the practice are jeopardized.

♦ Perform a common-size analysis of the income statement from
  year to year. To do this, divide each individual expense category
  by total revenue. Percentage changes in any category can identify
  creeper costs in the business. (For more on common sizing, see
  chapter 2.)

♦ Use benchmarks, such as the *FPA Financial Performance Study
  of Financial Advisory Practices* produced by Moss Adams, to
  compare operating performance statistics.

Getting Down to Business

In the process of acquiring a financial-advisory business, we find
that real due diligence does not happen until after the letter of intent
is signed. Before the letter of intent, the buyers and sellers do their
ritual sniffing and try to look their best for the other side. It's not
uncommon for sellers to tart up their business to seduce the buyer;
and it's typical for sellers to try to persuade buyers that they'd be
foolish to consider anybody else.

Although the due-diligence process is generally the purview of
the buying company, we recommend that the seller investigate the
licensing, compliance history, financial commitments, and legal issues
in the buyer's background as well. We've encountered situations in
which the buyers did not have the financial wherewithal or demonstrate the ethics in past deals that they may have represented. Being
unaware of such a history would be a bad way to start a marriage.

In the case of the sellers, most of the surprises occur in what's
represented in the financial information (how revenues and expenses
were accounted for), what assets are being transferred, what restrictive agreements might encumber the seller's ability to transfer an
asset, and in some rare cases, the firm's legal and regulatory history.
Many advisory firms, for example, have referral agreements with
outside providers such as a CPA firm, which commits the practice to
paying a substantial portion of the fees generated in perpetuity. It's
helpful to know whether such obligations might transfer to the new
buyer.

Not long ago, we worked with a buyer who thought she was acquiring a much larger practice than her own. Upon further examination of the financials, we found that the seller was counting the next 12 months trailing income as current revenue. The surprise for the buyer would be in having less cash flow than she originally thought she was acquiring.

For due diligence to truly get under way, a significant amount of information and a number of documents need to be available for the buyer. This is potentially a tedious process and a point when tensions get especially high between the parties. Once the documents are received and reviewed, it's important for the buyer to determine how the findings from the review might affect the ultimate purchase price or terms. When buyers are surprised as a result of this process, they tend to want to alter the agreement to reflect their new uncertainty. This is another reason why sellers should conduct their own internal due-diligence review before going to market.

The checklists for both compliance and operations in the appendix can help you prepare for this stage of the deal.

12. ANTIDOTE TO THE POSTMERGER MELTDOWN
Ounces of Prevention

M ANY TRANSACTIONS BETWEEN advisory firms are outright sales, especially when a book of business is purchased. In such cases, the integration required afterward is relatively easy, although there are still concerns regarding whether all the clients will transfer and whether all of the clients are, in fact, desirable to the buyer.

With the sale of larger practices, the transaction is more complicated and is often much like a merger even though it may be characterized as an acquisition. Whatever the new entity chooses to call itself, both organizations need to integrate strategy, organizational structure, operations, career paths, compensation, financial management, and accountability. Ultimately, the culture of the combined organizations must be defined.

Generally, it takes three years for integration to take firm root. The first year involves ritual sniffing: as both parties attempt to get a sense of what their new partner is about, they typically work hard to avoid conflicts. The second year is a shakeout period, during which those who like the deal work to make it stick and those who've been chafing under the new model begin to leave (or, in some cases, resign themselves to being unhappy). During the third year, the acquired firm typically adapts to the parent culture, although we've seen cases in which the acquired firm changes the culture of the parent firm. When that happens, it's a consequence of stronger leadership in the acquired firm or because that firm is in a more advanced stage of development.

In preparing for the transition, we recommend that as the likelihood of the acquisition becomes apparent, the parties work diligently toward creating a strategic plan that accommodates the values, cultures, and business focus of both firms. This final vetting process, although time-consuming, is an effective way to ensure that critical issues affecting integration are addressed. Just as important, a thorough planning process exposes gaps in the combined vision of the two firms and identifies steps that must be taken to close those gaps. In rare circumstances, the process may also expose warts in one party large enough to cause the other to back away from the agreement. Although disappointing, such an about-face is in itself not a bad thing. As with marriages, a better future is in store if the parties join together for the right reasons and with the right emotions.

Developing the Strategy

During the courtship, both parties should thoroughly explore client compatibility, service offerings, technology, and positioning. It's quite possible that even advisers serving essentially the same market may have profoundly different strategies and approaches.

One newly formed organization we helped through a premerger phase encountered such a gap. Both firms were of roughly equal size. One had a strong estate-planning focus; the other had a strong financial-planning and investment-management orientation. On paper, the complementary service offerings and the client compatibility made this merger appear readily achievable. But in their client strategies, one party put greater emphasis on risk protection and insurance, whereas the other stressed buying term insurance and investing the rest. The driving force of this merger was the estate-planning firm's desire to round out its wealth-management offering, especially on the investment side; for the investment-oriented firm, the key goal was to enhance its estate-planning capability. The exploration process exposed serious differences in how they generated, sold, priced, and delivered their services. Even more problematic was the misalignment in their approaches to staff compensation, which had to be reconciled to reflect the vision the new business was trying to foster.

A strategic plan focuses on strategy—ways to capitalize on the strengths and qualities that differentiate your firm from others—and on vision, the level of success and expertise you want your business to achieve. The operational plan focuses on the steps required to implement the strategy and achieve the vision. Many firms that merge leap right into implementation before they've defined their strategy and vision, and such shortcuts lead to a lot of wasted motion. In fact, without a plan, it's very difficult for the combined firms to flourish quickly.

As you plan the merger, begin to think of the strategic answers to the following questions:

♦ Which clients will you serve and why?
♦ Which products and services should you offer to this market?
♦ Where should you focus the business geographically?
♦ How will you charge for your services?
♦ How will the firm differentiate itself from others already in this market?
♦ How will the firm define its brand and identity in the market?
♦ How will the firm define success for the merger?

Organizational Structure

Strategy and vision help define what structure to adopt for the business. If you choose to focus on the 401(k) market, for example, you will have a clear idea of what your processes are for taking deposits, how you'll communicate with plan participants, which investment choices you'll make available, and how you'll report results. If you focus on high-net-worth clients, however, the people, processes, technology, and client-service experience your firm provides likely will be quite different.

This concept is illustrated in *Figure 12.1*. When you are clear about what business you're in, you will know what your organizational structure and staffing model should look like. Without a clear vision, chances are the business will be adrift. It's a little like building a house without a blueprint. You can put the walls up, install the plumbing and electricity, and lay a roof over the top, but without a clear idea of what this house is supposed to look like when it's done, the toilet could end up in the kitchen and the kitchen in the front yard. When you align strategy, structure, staffing, and systems, you create a high-performance business. You'll also be able to identify gaps in the organization that could be filled through a merger or acquisition.

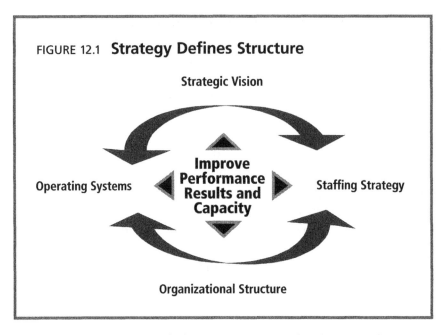

FIGURE 12.1 **Strategy Defines Structure**

Strategic Vision

Operating Systems   **Improve Performance Results and Capacity**   Staffing Strategy

Organizational Structure

One of the toughest challenges to setting the direction for a new firm is determining which staff from the combined entity will flourish in the new organization and step up to accept leadership responsibility. In a white paper Moss Adams developed for Pershing in 2005,[1] we found that the optimal operations structure was less dependent on technology than on the ability and leadership of key staff. More than likely, the back-office support of each of two small merging firms was managed by generic administrative people rather than by highly experienced and trained operations people. With the combination of the two firms comes a demand for greater sophistication in business operations. The new organization's vision and strategy should provide a framework for what those capabilities need to be.

The strategic value of operations for an advisory firm is not in expanding its capabilities but rather in the effective and efficient execution of such capabilities. Ultimately, all firms have access to the same systems and could execute the same tasks if they had to. The advantage of expanded operations is that they create the ability to execute more highly skilled tasks at an efficient cost, thereby allowing the firm to capitalize on this exceptional capability as part of its client offering. For example, every firm is able to generate custom performance reports for its clients and every firm can consolidate all assets (including nonmanaged) into one report. A firm can do this manually if required. The question is whether a firm is able to create a solution that allows it to offer the same level of service to all clients and still keep its prices competitive without overwhelming its staff or taking a significant profitability hit. Operations define what a firm can do, and this definition can be constricting if operations are inefficient or lack quality.

Traditionally, firms have split their organizational chart into a back office and a front office. The front office deals with clients, and the back office deals with data. The back office is generally hidden from the client and receives little attention from management unless something goes wrong. In such structures, people working in the back office have significantly fewer career opportunities unless they move to the front office. The separation creates a caste system that certainly affects culture, compensation, human resource decisions, and careers (see *Figure 12.2*).[2]

This dichotomy results in high turnover within operations departments, operating inefficiencies, and insufficient capabilities. The largest and most successful firms in the industry are finding that they have to dramatically change this model to ensure future success. These firms are bringing all of their people together as a team, putting them in front of the client, and assigning priorities to various operations.

As part of the postmerger integration process, both parties to a merger need to be clear regarding its protocol and processes for back- and front-office operations; how each will be handled; and how the organization might be structured for optimal success. When these details are left to chance, we've found that progress toward successful merger integration slows considerably.

Compensating Key Employees

Once a larger business has been created, the leaders of the practice need to resolve issues related to staff, such as career paths, roles, responsibilities, and compensation. What's more, it will likely become important to address the question of partnership. You'll find more on creating a career path to partnership in chapter 14.

FIGURE 12.2 **Separate Terrains**

Back Office	Front Office
• Does not interact with clients	• Deals with clients
• Receives no attention other than troubleshooting	• Is heavily recruited and well retained
• Lacks a career track	• Has greater compensation and career opportunities

As we note in chapter 14, we've found in our semiannual studies on compensation and staffing for the FPA[3] that staff roles within advisory firms are becoming clearer and, consequently, so are the staffs' expectations. This is helpful to know as you begin to cobble together an even larger firm.

Because each of the key positions in an advisory firm carries different responsibilities and expectations, it's necessary to align compensation with the strategy of the new business and with the performance expected from individuals serving in these roles. Reward structures for both owners and staff are quite divergent among advisory firms, and the differences may create the thorniest source of tension for firms contemplating a merger. In the case of owners, for example, while operating solo, they may have simply taken their compensation from the year-end leftovers. More than likely, they also ran a number of personal expenses through the business. In contemplating a merger, owners must put a more formal compensation structure in place to minimize conflicts down the road and to reinforce desired behavior going forward. After a merger, advisers often choose to pay each other in proportion to their share of ownership in the firm. Eventually, this structure results in resentment, however, because one of the owners invariably contributes far more to the success of the combined enterprise than the other.

As a result, we generally recommend that owners apply the same compensation philosophy to themselves as they would to their staff, by introducing a combination of base and incentives. It's important in this structure to value the role of management. One owner may be more proficient as an operational manager and another more adept at business development. Because both functions are key, it's important that more than just rainmaking be counted in a review of compensation. A combined firm has a lot of moving parts that need attention, and when management of an enterprise is undervalued in terms of compensation, management tasks usually wind up neglected.

For more on compensation and organizational structure, see *Practice Made Perfect: The Discipline of Business Management for Financial Advisers* (Bloomberg Press, 2005).

Pricing

The successful integration of newly joined firms requires consideration of how services will be priced. In our studies of financial-advisory practices, we've found the range of both pricing strategies and pricing philosophies so wide that it would be quite difficult to find two practices that approach things quite the same way. When merging firms have sharply divergent pricing platforms, however, it presents some obvious risks.

The most obvious difference, of course, is the case of a fee practice acquiring a practice that's primarily commission-based, with the hope of converting the clients to a fee program. Fidelity Investments observed in a study of practice transitions that the attrition rate in the client base after the sale of a practice runs as high as 40 percent.[4] Imagine what that rate might be if you changed your whole approach to serving clients, including how you charge them. For many clients, the move from commission and trails—a mostly transparent cost to the client—to some form of fee can be a traumatic change and one they perceive as expensive.

But even fee-based and fee-only firms have pricing structures that vary widely. Some RIA practices charge a retainer; others charge by project or by the hour; and others charge a percentage of assets under management. Using $1 million of AUM as a baseline, we found the spread of fees to be quite broad (see *Figure 12.3*). Starting at 150

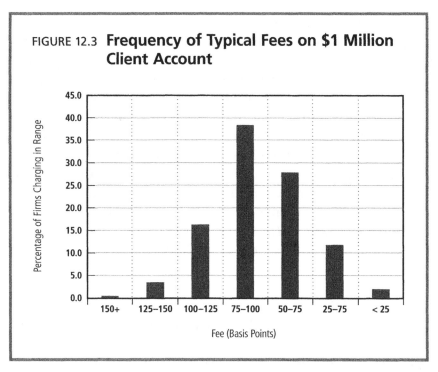

FIGURE 12.3 **Frequency of Typical Fees on $1 Million Client Account**

basis points on the high end, the range fanned to under 25 basis points at the low end, with no single fee being applied a majority of the time. (We should mention for an advisory firm's valuation, the implications of such disparity in the industry are interesting. You might wonder if you're acquiring a business that's as profitable as it can be, or if there's an opportunity to squeeze more value out of that business after the acquisition.)

In mid-2005, Moss Adams was engaged by Schwab Institutional to conduct a pricing study for one of its Market Knowledge Tool reports.[5] Having evaluated literally thousands of advisory practices before doing this study for Schwab, we found some common themes in pricing but also some not-so-common responses. By digging deeper into these research findings, we identified three core reasons (see *Figure 12.4*) for the divergent pricing practices in the advisory business:

1. The cost basis for the services that advisers offer
2. Market pricing
3. Value proposition

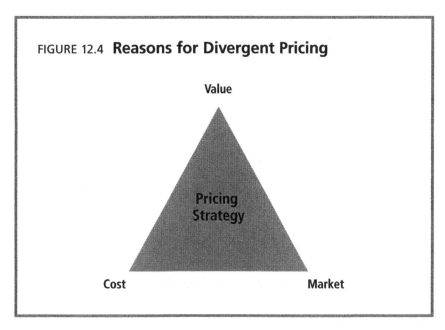

FIGURE 12.4 **Reasons for Divergent Pricing**

We've also found that when advisers use these three elements as the cornerstone of their own pricing strategies, they're able to develop a more coherent approach to managing profitability. This principle is true for solo advisers as well as for ensemble firms, but it's obviously more relevant to advisers with fee-only or fee-based practices.

Ultimately, advisers need to align their pricing with their valuation proposition. If the merged firms are primarily investment managers, this process becomes easier because traditionally the pricing is tied to assets and increases and decreases depend on market performance and total assets managed. But one of the interesting challenges for advisers is justifying why a $2 million client should be paying more for what he's getting than a $1 million client, when the service offerings and the attention demanded of the adviser are virtually identical. This, clearly, is one of the quirks of the advisory profession's value proposition.

Wealth managers may be able to defend the fee differential a bit more convincingly because they can often add more services or enhance the client-service experience to justify the increasing fees. They can also staff the client management with technical specialists or people experienced in the specific challenges of these types of clients. That said, one of the great ironies of the wealth-management business is that its practitioners attempt to position themselves as something other than investment managers yet use a pricing scheme that defines their contribution in terms of investment performance. That's one reason so many are moving toward using retainers for a portion or all of the client relationship; in some cases, they're introducing a project fee for special issues outside of investment allocation and execution.

Justifying your prices. Five useful questions come to mind when developing justification for your pricing:

- How comprehensive is your deliverable?
- Who are you serving?
- How is this different from other firms in your market?
- What typical implementation vehicles do you use (index funds, private equity ETFs, stocks and bonds)?
- What do your clients value?

The first and second questions are obviously linked. For example, if you're not serving wealthy people, it would not be appropriate to characterize your business as a wealth-management firm. You may more likely be a financial-planning firm that provides investment-management and risk-management solutions. On the other hand, if you're serving individuals with more complex needs and more assets at risk, you may delve deeper into special issues, trusts, business succession, estate planning, tax planning, and alternative investments. To a great extent, client profile and the scale of the service offering influence value. What's more, the sophistication of your offering and of your clients may dictate how much confidence you have in the fees you charge.

The advisory profession continues to change dramatically in terms of relationships with clients and how advice is paid for. The evolution from commissions to asset-management fees to project and hourly fees to retainers reflects the evolution of the profession. At each stage in the process, the adviser moves closer to becoming an advocate for the client. That's the good news, but each step in this transition requires more disclosure and more transparency.

With commissions or even asset-management fees, it's somewhat easier to bury the costs to the client because they're charged to their investment portfolio. But with project, hourly, and especially retainer fees, advisers must be consistent and clear in how they demonstrate their value, because these charges need to be negotiated and agreed on each year.

Culture and Accountability

When two financial-services organizations finally merge, the cultural wars begin. Sometimes the challenges are tangled in what a firm perceives as its "values," but often the differing mind-sets between entrepreneurs creates clashes on a Roman scale. The gap is not so much a matter of right and wrong as it is the difference between being the lion or the Christian. Both are fighting for survival, and both are fighting from their strengths. The final result could mean that only one side comes out a winner.

When a merger is first contemplated, a focus on the cultural issues should be part of the mating ritual. It's important to be clear on what the firms have in common and how their philosophies differ in terms of dealing with clients, staff, money, and mission. How does the other party define success? What does the firm value? What is the owner's ambition? What is the owner's tolerance for risk?

Parties to a merger or acquisition should not leave roles and responsibilities loosely defined. Without clear accountability, it's difficult to measure success or fulfill the other's expectations. Often, instinctive efforts to appease by not asking for accountability causes conflicts down the road. In the most successful mergers we've observed, each person from owner down to receptionist knows what his role will be, how she will be evaluated, and how each is expected to perform.

Throughout the preliminary courtship, the idea of having a bigger, better, and stronger practice often seduces advisers into closing a deal without properly considering the painful process of building a new organization. But that, in fact, is what it is. Combining enterprises—especially the small businesses most advisers own—can be very compelling and exciting. But success eludes those who do not think strategically, accept accountability, and remain focused on the endgame.

Chapter Notes

1. Pershing Advisor Solutions and Moss Adams, *Mission Possible: Finding the Optimal Operations Model for Your Advisory Practice*, October 2005.

2. Ibid., p. 4.

3. Moss Adams, *2005 FPA Compensation and Staffing Study*, sponsored by SEI Investments, September 2005.

4. Press release, "Transition Fallout: Up to 40% of Assets." *Investment News*, June 13, 2005. http://content.members.fidelity.com/Inside_Fidelity/full Story/1,5205,00.html.

5. Moss Adams and Market Knowledge Tools, *Pricing Strategies for Maximum Success*, Charles Schwab Institutional, October 2005.

13. MAKING IT LEGAL: A SEQUENCE OF STEPS
Ounces of Prevention

WHEN IT COMES time to authoring an agreement that establishes both parties' understanding of the deal, a multitude of legal details arise. For both buyers and sellers, the legal steps toward finalizing a mutually agreed-on deal involve a number of components and strategies. There is a default sequence of legal events that unfolds as a transaction approaches the final agreement. It begins with letters of confidentiality. Once an understanding is reached, the parties move to a letter of intent, followed by imposition of a "no-shop clause," then on to due diligence, and finally the purchase agreement.

Step 1: Letter of Intent

The parameters of a deal are articulated in the letter of intent. The document's goal is to establish the material terms of a transaction—that is, terms that would cause undue surprise or harm to the other party, such as price. The material terms of a transaction refer to any specifications or conditions on which the transaction is wholly dependent and cannot be excluded. The letter also serves as a commitment of the parties to enter into the negotiations of a transaction in good faith—in other words, both sides will make a reasonable effort to make sure the transaction goes through. Although the letter of intent is not a legally binding document, it does establish the intentions of the parties, a due-diligence period, and a prospective schedule to close the proposed transaction.

There are times when a letter of intent is unnecessary, such as with an internal transaction or if the deal is very small. We still recommend having a confidentiality agreement, however, before providing any material documentation to the other party. (A sample letter of intent is included in the appendix.)

Essentials

A standard letter of intent typically sets out a confirmation of understanding between the parties with respect to the principal terms and conditions of the deal in the opening paragraph. That paragraph will also describe the structure of the transaction, such as the acquisition of all outstanding capital stock of the company and assumption of all assets and certain liabilities by the purchaser.

In addition to defining the parties and structure of the transaction, the letter of intent should contain a very important clause. This clause will clearly state that the terms and conditions in the letter of intent are not exhaustive and that the document does not contain or address all matters necessary for the successful completion of the deal. All standard letters of intent should contain this clause. The letter of intent can be as thorough or as general as the parties desire. Typically, letters of intent strike a balance between the two extremes: they provide sufficient detail to give form to the primary understandings of the parties yet remain general enough for both parties to retain room to negotiate. The major categories of terms and conditions included in a letter of intent tend to be:

♦ **Basic terms of the transaction:** The letter describes the acquisition target, structure of the transaction, assets and liabilities under the deal, purchase price or valuation method, and form of the transaction.

♦ **Respective parties' obligation:** Each side will want to achieve as much clarity as possible regarding what it's responsible for in order for the deal to proceed.

♦ **Imposition of obligations:** This term refers to either side imposing an obligation on the other for the deal to proceed. The most common imposition of obligation is the no-shop clause, also known as the *lock-up* term. Serious buyers often insist on this clause because it enables the buyer to prevent the seller from attempting to obtain a higher bid from any other party during a specified period, usually 60 to 90 days. In terms of tactical advantage, the buyer has restricted access to the seller.

♦ **Identification of transaction-associated expenses:** Depending on the complexity of the transaction, the parties to the transaction may enumerate how expenses will be allocated.

Setting Parameters

If you're planning on using an attorney to draft the letter of intent, be as clear and comprehensive as possible in your communications with the attorney. Clarify and define the key terms to be used throughout the document, and ensure that your responsibilities are strictly articulated.

The parties must also determine at the outset whether the letter of intent is meant to be a legally enforceable document. According to Tom Giachetti, chairman of the securities practice at Stark & Stark, a law firm with offices in Princeton, New York, and Philadelphia, in the event of a dispute, courts will examine the language, the conduct of the parties, and other relevant circumstances to ascertain whether the letter of intent is in whole or in part legally enforceable. Although courts are very reluctant to force consummation of the transaction, certain portions of the letter of intent should be legally binding (assuming they're properly drafted) including confidentiality provisions, return of documentation, and costs and actual damages incurred by the nonterminating party in the event of a material breach or bad faith by the terminating party.

As the contents of the letter of intent are enumerated, it's important to deliberately think through the positive and negative implications of each material term. For instance, the no-shop clause typically works to the buyer's advantage. However, if the seller is confident of a demand for the business, the no-shop clause can be capped at a period of 30 days, as opposed to 90 days. Essentially, the seller can make a counteroffer with a no-shop clause for those 30 days and possibly impose a premium if the buyer wants to extend the period for an additional 30 or 60 days.

If there is too much uncertainty, neither party should feel pressured to proceed any further with a letter of intent, or any other

FIGURE 13.1 **Commitments of a Letter of Intent**

Binding Provisions	Nonbinding Provisions
Buyer due diligence (or "right to investigate")	Type of transaction
No-shop clause	Purchase price (or calculation methodology)
Termination clause	List of definitive agreements
Confidentiality agreement	Conditions to consummation of the acquisition
Expenses	
Public announcements (or preclosing covenants)	
Miscellaneous (contains references to specific clauses in the letter of intent that apply in the event of a dispute)	

agreement. All issues must be satisfactorily resolved. Whether buyer or seller, maintain your focus on your objectives, respond to reasonable concerns in a professional way, and attempt to obtain some benefit in exchange for every concession you make. As in an auction, you need the self-discipline to walk away from the transaction if it's outside your realm of financial, emotional, or strategic comfort. Again, be sure to involve your CPA and lawyer in identifying all the critical issues before you sign, because you want to make sure that what you net (as a buyer or a seller) is what you intended.

Clearly, the letter of intent involves a lot of effort, money, and time. So why would anyone bother going through such an exhaustive process? For both the buyer and the seller, the letter of intent symbolizes the gravity of the commitment to the transaction. It contains both binding and nonbinding commitments from both parties and, moreover, serves as the template for all future agreements (see *Figure 13.1*).

Best Practices

There are some best practices that are wise to observe when contemplating a letter of intent. Some general guidelines include:

1. **Due diligence:** Serious and substantial due diligence helps the buyer to understand the business. From a buyer's perspective, it's like having the house inspected for termites and dry rot before making a commitment to buy. Sellers often benefit from the buyer's due diligence, but they will need to perform their own due diligence as well, especially if they are financing the deal (that is, if a portion of the purchase price is contingent on certain events, is deferred, or is to be paid over time via a promissory note).

2. **No-shop clause:** This protective clause affords the buyer a period of exclusivity to pursue due diligence and assures the seller that the buyer is a serious candidate for purchase. It is important to pay attention to the duration of the no-shop clause.

3. **Material terms:** To ensure a smooth transaction, it is extremely helpful to address the material terms in the letter of intent. Examples of material terms are indemnity obligations, noncompete and employee-retention requirements, and closing conditions.

4. **Agreement to agree:** This component in the letter of intent confirms the good-faith obligation of both parties to pursue the transaction. In some cases, the letter of intent leaves open terms and conditions, and the agreement-to-agree clause holds both parties to negotiate those terms and conditions to resolution.

According to Giachetti, who specializes in serving securities and insurance firms, the types of documents and information that flow from the letter of intent include:

♦ Confidentiality agreement
♦ Restrictive-covenant agreement
♦ Employment agreement

- ◆ Purchase agreement
- ◆ Shareholder/operating agreement
- ◆ Amending entity organizational documents

As Giachetti has advised a number of clients, a sale to someone within the firm should be contemplated from the same legal perspective as selling to someone outside of it. A final agreement in writing is highly preferable to a series of undocumented conversations in which meanings and phrases may be either unclear or later forgotten. He also cautions that before negotiations begin, the firm should have a confidentiality agreement and a restrictive covenant agreement in place. It's especially important, he adds, that this be done before building a staff. These steps protect the firm's proprietary interests in its clients, referral sources, employees, technology, and operations in the event the sale is not consummated and any employees leave the firm.

Step 2: Operating Agreement

We have observed that in a number of practices, multiple shareholders lack formal shareholder or operating agreements. (Shareholder agreements exist for corporations; operating agreements are pertinent to limited liability companies). When none exists, it becomes very difficult to resolve disputes over termination, compensation, and valuation issues, and in some cases, even to be clear about who owns what. Shareholder or operating agreements in your business will help in a number of areas:

- ◆ Minimizing disputes among the owners
- ◆ Establishing a method of sale for the stock or membership interests at a fair price
- ◆ Keeping unwanted outsiders from acquiring interests in the business
- ◆ Providing guidelines to valuation on different conditions
- ◆ Defining the relationships of the officers, directors, and owners of the business

The operating agreement typically should accomplish the following:

- Define the financial structure
- Define the management structure
- Establish the business rules, thereby identifying which state's default rules apply
- Establish ownership percentages
- Delineate profit and loss distribution
- Specify voting rights
- Outline ownership succession

Taking the time to work through all these areas in the operating agreement is valuable because it creates a set of guidelines in the event of a dispute or other significant problem. In the absence of these customized rules for your business, the state rules will apply.

A Buy-Sell Agreement

A buy-sell agreement and a shareholder or operating agreement are not equivalent concepts. In other words, although they may occupy space in the same document, one is not an absolute substitute for the other.

Firms may have stock-redemption agreements or cross-purchase agreements, which spell out important conditions in the relationship among owners. When a business has two or more owners, it is important that an agreement be in place that clarifies key issues, including:

- What triggers a buyout—that is, death, disability, malfeasance, et cetera
- Whether a buyout is mandatory or optional when the triggering event occurs
- Who will buy the departing owner's interest and how
- What the value of the ownership will be

One example of an issue that can require clarification is the distribution of profits and losses. In a business with two owners, one may be a 60 percent owner and the other a 40 percent owner. It does not necessarily follow that profits and losses must be divided in exact proportion to the ownership interest of each party in the business, although that is the usual business practice. When that is not what the owners prefer, the operating agreement must be clear about special allocations. Keep in mind also that all owners will not be in the same income bracket or tax bracket, or share the same financial circumstances. Therefore, the allocation of profits and losses may need to be addressed or contemplated in more detail, with an eye toward the effects on each individual. These choices will depend on how the business is structured legally, because some business entities are legally required to distribute pro rata.

The buy-sell agreement (or the buy-sell provisions of the operating or shareholder agreement) needs to provide instructions regarding how an owner enters or exits the business. (Chapter 15, "Inside Stories: Buy-Sell Agreements—The Path to Happier Endings," provides more details on the buy-sell agreement.)

Step 3: Purchase Agreement

Once the letter of intent has been executed and the material terms of the operating agreement are established, the parties hammer out the final details of the transaction. These details are recorded in the purchase agreement. The purchase agreement is a legally enforceable document that details the sale of property (whether asset or stock) and includes the price and terms of the purchase.

Whether you're a buyer or a seller, you'll want to control the language of the purchase agreement. Authoring that document puts you at an advantage. Having your own attorney draft all the documents generally allows you to better control the language and puts the other party in the position of negotiating components of the contract. Any provisions that one party concedes during the contract negotiations should probably be reciprocated by the other party in some form, so authoring the agreement gives the buyer or seller greater leverage in achieving his or her goals with the transaction.

To write such documents, you should engage a qualified attorney who is familiar with the relevant business and tax laws that affect such transactions. In a letter or memo to your attorney (or to whoever is drafting the agreements), communicate in your own words what you believe you agreed to. This information will give the lawyer a stronger framework for crafting a document that expresses the intent of both parties. It should also help to minimize costs, as well as prevent any last-minute breakdowns in the deal itself. The issues described in the next section are typically covered in a purchase agreement.

Description of the Purchase and the Purchase/Sale Price

This part of the document describes the nature of the agreement and the names and addresses of the parties involved. It specifies the type of transaction—assets sale or stock sale—and establishes exactly what is being sold and the price that is being paid. For a stock transaction, it will set forth the number of shares being sold and the purchase price of the stock. For an asset transaction, it will identify the assets (or it may refer to an exhibit that will list the assets) and the purchase price of the assets. It also establishes the sale terms, including the conditions for contingent payments, interest rates on notes used as payment, et cetera.

Buyer and Seller Representations and Warranties

The purpose of representations and warranties is to protect each party and to allocate the risk in the deal. Warranties are guarantees that certain conditions exist, such as undisclosed pending lawsuits or compliance issues. Representations are factual statements made by both the buyer and seller, such as the completeness and accuracy of the financial information presented. For example, the parties to the transaction will need to represent that each is a registered investment adviser or registered representative in good standing, that their respective regulatory filings are current and accurately reflect their advisory operations, and that each is in compliance with applicable state and federal rules and regulations pertaining to investment advisers. There are other elements that should also be included, which an attorney experienced in both securities firms and transactions can help to draft.

Representations and warranties of seller. The seller of a business will typically make these warranties:

♦ The seller is a company (or a private individual, in the case of a sole proprietorship) in good standing.

♦ The seller has the authority to enter into the agreement and perform its obligations under the agreement.

♦ All financial statements of the business provided were prepared in accordance with GAAP and fairly present the financial condition of the business.

♦ The seller has provided a complete and accurate list of all tangible and intangible assets of the business.

♦ The business has good and marketable title to all tangible and intangible assets it claims to own.

♦ There are no undisclosed liabilities (such as lawsuits, arbitrations, or regulatory proceedings).

♦ There are no outstanding contracts except those that have been disclosed pursuant to the agreement.

♦ The business is in compliance with applicable federal, state, and local laws.

♦ If stock is being sold, the seller of the stock will further warrant and represent that the shares being sold were validly issued, fully paid, nonassessable, and issued in full compliance with all federal and state laws, and that the buyer will receive the shares free of any liens or encumbrances.

Representations and warranties of buyer. The buyer of the stock of a business will generally warrant the following:

♦ The buyer is a company (or a private individual) in good standing.

♦ The buyer has the authority to enter into the agreement and perform its obligations under the agreement.

♦ The buyer is in compliance with applicable federal, state, and local laws.

♦ The buyer will also make representations and warranties regarding its financial position. This will depend on whether the purchase is cash or noncash. Purchases for cash generally do not require the buyer to make representations concerning its financial means or ability to pay the purchase price. But if the purchase includes a promissory note or is to be paid in the future, then the buyer will typically make representations and warranties regarding its financial position.

Tax Considerations

Tax consequences of the sale of the stock of a business are different from the sale of assets. The seller will typically try to get capital gains treatment for the sale. The treatment of these types of tax matters should be addressed in the agreement. (More tax issues are covered in chapter 10, "Coming to Terms: Getting All the Way to Yes.")

Consent of Owners

If the sale is treated as a merger, then the consent of the owners and directors of the business will generally be required. In some cases, it may be necessary for all of the shareholders to sign the agreement, depending on the type of sale, asset, or stock.

Conditions to Be Met Before Closing

This section of the document specifies the conditions required for closing to occur. They may include these items:

- ◆ The sellers and buyers verifying the representations and warranties remain true
- ◆ Completing the transfer of the book of business
- ◆ Verifying that all applicable registrations and licenses are current
- ◆ Obtaining broker-dealer approval of the buyer, if applicable

Operations of the Business Between Agreement and Closing

Provisions for operating the business are installed to protect the value of the practice between the agreement and closing. These provisions typically require sellers to continue to service the firm's clients as they normally would and to avoid substantial capital expenditures or any other activities that may endanger the value of the business.

Employment Agreements and Restrictive Covenants

Among the big issues in finalizing the purchase will be the future role of the seller in the continuation of the business. Often, buyers want owners to stay on for a period of time in a consulting relationship, so the expectations and compensation for that work should be clear, as should be the limitations on what continued professional association or relationship the sellers may have with the clients once the transaction is completed and they leave the firm.

Corporate Liabilities

For asset sales, all the liabilities that the buyer assumes need to be described. This is also true in a stock sale. The buyer should require that the seller warrant that there are no other liabilities not specifically listed so that they may have recourse back to the seller for not having disclosed the liability.

Litigation

This is a provision that states the nature and extent of any litigation or any other adverse matter (such as arbitration or regulatory issues) affecting the company and generally serves to protect the buyer if unknown and unanticipated litigation or antitrust or other governmental regulatory problems arise in the future.

Closing Procedures, Expenses, and Reimbursements

These provisions specify the time and place for closing, the documents, and types of payment (typically cash, promissory notes, or stock) that will be exchanged at closing.

Remedies and Indemnification

Remedies for breach of representations, warranties, or covenants, and the scope of indemnification provisions, also need to be defined.

Rights and Obligations

Obviously, there is no guarantee a deal will succeed once the agreement is signed. Parties to the transaction will want a process by which to address the issues in the event of default, payment delinquencies, or extraordinary events that may impair the ability of the successor to continue as a going concern or to fulfill its payment obligations to the seller (for example, loss of key personnel, lawsuits, regulatory/disciplinary proceedings, et cetera).

Postclosing Issues

The parties will also want to address issues that may arise following consummation of the deal, including:

♦ The continued role of selling or retiring principal(s) during and subsequent to the transition process

♦ The buyer's obligation to provide information or notice to the seller as to ongoing business operations prior to the buyer's payment of the entire purchase price per the terms of the agreement of sale (financials, immediate notice and copies of lawsuits, regulatory proceedings, loss of key personnel, Form ADV amendments, et cetera)

Good Housekeeping

There are a number of other housekeeping issues that parties to the transaction should contemplate. These issues may include the following:

♦ Election of officers and directors and the schedule of annual meetings

♦ Filing a certificate of change with the state if the company's registered agent is no longer associated with the company or the registered office has changed

♦ Reflecting major company transactions (for example, sale of assets, stock, or interests) in an authorizing resolution.

To the extent a firm maintains a broker-dealer affiliation, it's important to coordinate with the broker-dealer, both before the sale and after, on matters such as certain transfers of registration, a change in errors and omissions insurance and related insurance issues (that is, coverage on prior accounts), and certain disclosures.

The parties to the transaction will also need to ensure that the appropriate filings are made. Especially in an environment of heightened regulatory oversight of advisers and registered representatives, both buyers and sellers should consult with competent compliance consultants or legal counsel to ensure issues such as ADV amendments relating to timing, client approval, and assignments are covered. They will also need to commit to maintaining books and records, maintaining errors and omissions insurance, and performing other corporate housekeeping tasks.

Key Documents

Both buyers and sellers always fare best having their own independent counsel rather than relying solely on an intermediary, especially if that intermediary is a broker facilitating the deal for both sides.

FIGURE 13.2 **Checklist of Closing Documents**

Document	Date	Status (Complete/ Pending)	Signed (Yes/No)

Settlement Sheet: Shows, as of the date of settlement, the various costs and adjustments to be paid by or credited to each party. It is signed by both the buyer and the seller.

_____   _____   _____

Escrow Agreement: Used only for escrow settlements, it is a set of instructions signed by the buyer and the seller in advance of settlement, which sets forth the conditions of escrow, the responsibilities of the escrow agent, and the requirements to be met for the release of escrowed funds and documents.

_____   _____   _____

Bill of Sale: Describes the physical assets being transferred and identifies the amount of consideration paid for those assets. It must always be signed by the seller and is often also signed by the buyer.

_____   _____   _____

Promissory Note: Used only in an installment sale, it shows the principal amount and terms of repayment of the debt by the buyer to the seller, specifies remedies for the seller in the event of default by the buyer, and is signed by the buyer (and the buyer often must personally guarantee the debt).

_____   _____   _____

Security Agreement: Creates the security interest in the assets pledged by the buyer to secure the promissory note and underlying debt and also sets forth the terms under which the buyer agrees to operate the assets that constitute collateral. It is used only in an installment sale and is signed by both parties.

_____   _____   _____

Document	Date	Status (Complete/ Pending)	Signed (Yes/No)

Covenant Not to Compete: Protects the buyer and his investment from immediate competition by the seller in his market area for a limited amount of time. The scope of this document must be reasonable for it to be legally enforceable. The covenant not to compete is sometimes included as a part of the purchase and sale agreement and is sometimes written as a separate document. It is signed by both parties and is not required in every transaction.

————— ————— —————

Employment Agreement: Specifies the nature of services to be performed by the seller, the amount of compensation, the amount of time per week or per month the services are to be performed, the duration of the agreement, and often a method for discontinuing the agreement before its completion. It is signed by both the buyer and the seller. Employment agreements are not required in all transactions, but they are used with great frequency. It is not uncommon for the seller to remain involved with the business for periods of as little as a week or as much as several years. The length of time depends on the complexity of the business and the experience of the buyer. For periods of more than two to four weeks, the seller is often compensated for his services.

————— ————— —————

Contingent Liabilities: Contingent liabilities must be taken into account and provided for when a business is sold. They most often occur because of pending tax payments, unresolved lawsuits, or anticipated but uncertain costs of meeting regulatory requirements. Contingent liabilities can be handled by escrowing a portion of the funds earmarked for disbursement to the seller. The sum escrowed then can be used to pay off the liability as it comes due. Any remaining money may then be disbursed to the seller.

————— ————— —————

Many investment bankers add value by identifying pitfalls in the agreements early, but any formal agreements will ultimately need to be drafted by a qualified attorney.

A number of documents are required to close a transaction. *Figure 13.2* is a sample checklist of closing documents along with a brief description of each one. Depending on the terms of the purchase agreement, some of these documents may not be applicable. Other documents not described in Figure 13.2 may also be needed, depending on the particulars of the transaction.

Inside
Stories

S OME YEARS AGO, we were working with a financial adviser whose business had reached a crossroads. He had to choose: should he keep the practice small and under his complete control, or should he add other advisers who could eventually become owners in his practice? Finally, he committed to his chosen path. "I've decided to add a partner," he told us. "I've found the right person. He'll bring the capital and I'll bring the experience." We asked him what tipped the scales toward this direction. "In three years," he said, "I'll have the capital and he'll have the experience."

The decision to add partners does not come easily. In fact, there are some legitimate reasons for fearing it. Partners are in a position to question what you're doing. They'll be drinking from the same profit trough as you. You have to share decision making. You have to navigate through conflicts instead of powering through them. You may add someone whose values, philosophy, and approach to business are different from yours. These pesky issues aside, adding partners is a pretty good idea.

That's because a partner can have a positive impact on your firm's growth, contribute meaningfully to the leadership of your business, and enhance your income. Partners will eventually want some stake in the business they're helping to drive. They provide you with an internal succession option, depth and continuity in the business, and the discipline that comes with having to be accountable to somebody else.

All the Right Reasons

When you weigh the pros and cons of adding a partner, it's important to balance the upside and the downside. Like almost every decision in managing an advisory firm, you must begin with the question, What problem are you trying to solve? Creating partnerships is an effective means of making an orderly transition of ownership from the founders to the advisers they've helped develop.

Advisers who add partners out of loyalty, a sense of obligation, or as a potential bonus should the business be sold or as a carrot to provide incentive for desired behavior may be asking the wrong question. They're certainly providing the wrong solution.

Most advisory firms that add partners do so through some means of internal promotion, although a fair number of firms create partners through mergers (see *Figure 14.1*). Either option works, but when grooming your partners it's important to have standards and thresholds for admittance.

A partnership—a term we use generically here for any form of ownership in the firm—should be something special. It should be reserved for those who contribute to the firm's financial success in a meaningful way. They may be lead advisers, rainmakers, or effective managers in an important area of your practice.

If you're tempted to share a stake in your business with someone who doesn't fit any of these profiles, you might consider alternative solutions, like granting phantom stock, stock appreciation rights, or participation in an employee stock ownership plan. Each of these perks provides a long-term incentive and an opportunity for big gains for employees should you sell the firm. But they do so without putting the individuals on the same footing as those who are significantly influencing the future direction of the firm.

When evaluating whether to make a person a partner in your firm, consider these four steps:

1. Define the business thresholds
2. Define the individual thresholds
3. Define the rights and benefits of ownership
4. Define the transaction

Source: © Moss Adams, 2003 FPA Compensation and Staffing Study, sponsored by SEI Investments (FPA Press, September 2003).

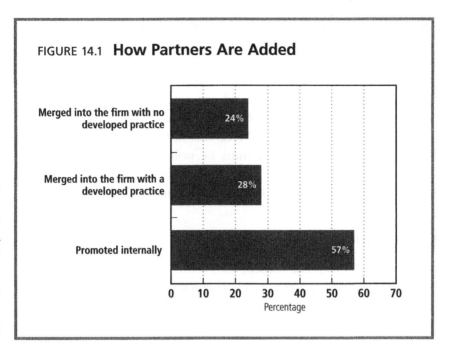

FIGURE 14.1 **How Partners Are Added**

A Threshold for the Firm

Before admitting a new partner, you need to make sure the choice is affordable for the practice. Dilution of ownership is one consideration, but dilution of income is an even more significant issue. Owners should ask themselves several key questions:

1. What is the desired average income per owner?
2. How much revenue does the firm need to generate to achieve that average?
3. How much revenue does the firm need to generate to maintain a reasonable level of profitability after fair compensation is paid to the owners?

The point of this exercise is to review the firm's revenue and understand the breakpoints that accommodate your adding a partner without diluting your own income. The addition of a partner should be a *consequence* of net income gains, not a cause of income reduction. Typically, we find that advisory firms need to generate between $400,000 and $750,000 of revenue per partner before it's economically viable to add a new one. Our studies for Schwab Institutional on the best-managed financial-advisory firms indicate that these firms have between $700,000 and $1,000,000 in revenue per partner.[1] By implication, if a firm has two partners and would like to add a third, the business should generate at least $2.1 million in annual revenue ($700,000 × 3 partners). In adding the third partner, existing partners need to be careful not to dilute their income. Therefore, the firm's revenue must be poised to move to a higher level. Understanding the economics of your business helps you evaluate whether your firm is ready to add a partner.

Individual Thresholds

The temptation to make someone a partner out of loyalty instead of evaluating the person's true contributions to the firm is difficult to overcome. Generally, if the person does not contribute meaningfully to growth, it probably is not a good idea to admit him as a partner. There are other ways for owners to reward loyal staff who are not growth drivers in the firm, and these ways may, in fact, be more in line with the person's expectations and risk tolerance. Remember that being a partner is a special role that entitles its holder to substantial income opportunities commensurate with the risk taken as an owner of the business.

In a data sample developed in the *2003 FPA Compensation and Staffing Study*,[2] we found that most owners who added partners did so as a result of some evaluation process. In digging deeper, we found the crux of this evaluation was revenue contribution and/or gut instinct. Both are vital indicators, but there are other factors that advisers should consider including in their evaluation of candidates:
- **Responsibility:** What else does the candidate do to influence the success of the business?
- **Staff development:** What is the person doing to help grow the next generation of advisers?
- **Performance evaluation:** How well has the person performed according to your annual or semiannual evaluations? And has the candidate responded well to counseling?

These three criteria are obviously subjective, but as your business grows, you'll develop more formal processes and protocols for evaluating employees in these areas. The performance evaluation may become the most important measure, which is one reason we encourage advisers to use upstream evaluations in which staff evaluate practice leaders, as well as downstream evaluations in which the leaders evaluate staff. These tools can be very insightful once you've created a culture of candid feedback without recrimination. (For more on staff evaluation and professional development, see *Practice Made Perfect: The Discipline of Business Management for Financial Advisers,* Bloomberg Press, 2005.)

Another benefit of using qualitative measures to screen prospective partners is that the approach allows you to build a culture you enjoy. Many advisory firms prefer to evaluate performance in purely financial terms, but in doing so, they run the risk of not balancing revenue growth with desired behavior such as respect, integrity, teamwork, and other concepts pulled straight from the Boy Scout manual.

This is not to minimize the importance of financial criteria. Obviously, if someone is not contributing to the growth of the business, it's hard to rationalize sharing profits with him. Further, if an individual is not growth oriented, this could undermine your succession plan if you expect her to eventually take over your practice through a buyout. You always need to ask whether the person has the ability to take on your ownership over time as you approach retirement (because it's rare to get cash on the barrelhead for your ownership at that point).

In judging a candidate's financial contribution, part of the equation should be a threshold of revenue that the individual is responsible for either managing or generating. You'll also want to make sure that the person is managing and adding clients that fit within your business model (optimal clients) and that the portion of the practice for which he's responsible is profitable to the firm.

Rights and Benefits of Ownership

Partnership in an advisory firm is a special position. It entitles the individual to profit distributions, a say in the direction of the enterprise, and usually a higher level of income than nonowners. With these benefits come certain risks and responsibilities:

♦ Partners are on the hook for any financial obligations of the firm.
♦ They are stewards of the business and must act in its best interest.
♦ Their actions should contribute to the continuity of the enterprise.
♦ They must create an environment in which other motivated people also can flourish.

Fair Compensation

Considering both the risks and obligations of becoming an owner, how should partners be compensated? Generally, we recommend rewarding partners first as key employees. In this regard, their compensation should be a combination of salary plus incentive. The base should be tied to reasonable market rates for the job they're expected to perform (for example, senior adviser, portfolio manager, CEO), and their incentive pay should be tied to exceeding the expectations of that job.

As a practice grows larger, it becomes easier to make this distinction and create a process for setting standards for both base and incentive compensation. A growing body of data is available on fair compensation for relevant positions, including the *FPA Compensation and Staffing Study* produced by Moss Adams and sponsored by SEI Investments every other year.

In addition to the base and incentive salaries, owners are entitled to a profit distribution. Although this share is usually based on their pro rata ownership interest, we've seen some clever compensation programs in which partners are awarded income units instead of equity units, and the number of units may fluctuate each year depending on a variety of factors related to an individual's contribution. The simplest form, however, remains treating the distribution as a dividend.

Setting the Terms for the Transaction

Advisory firms structure the transfer of ownership to new partners in many different ways. In many cases, they grant the new partner stock in lieu of cash, which is a practice we're not too keen on. That's because there's something about having to write a check or having bonuses garnished to pay this obligation that gives new partners—that is, nonfounders—a feeling of "skin in the game." Most firms establish a purchase price and may use a formula that sets the terms for both the buy-in and the buyout of partners.

A good way to set the purchase price initially would be either to do a valuation on your firm (as described in chapters 2 and 3) or to engage a professional appraiser to render an opinion of value. This can serve as your baseline for establishing a valuation formula. For example, once you arrive at a value, you could translate that value into a price to revenue, or a price to assets under management, or a price to operating profit. A common formula is to take the average of these three multiples and let it serve as the value in your buy-sell agreement. That value would then become the basis for all future transactions—both for buying in and selling out internally—that apply to new partners. Obviously, this does not have to be the price at which you would sell the company to an outside buyer, but it does serve as the market price internally and obviously would fluctuate as revenue, assets under management, and operating profits fluctuate.

In some cases, the current owners require that new partners come up with the money through borrowing or by cashing in investments to pay cash up front for their ownership. A more practical approach—and one more commonly deployed—is for the business itself to fund the transaction. For example, the new owner might be paid a base salary plus incentive. When the incentive is paid, the firm garnishes enough of it to pay down the purchase price, leaving a sufficient amount for the new partner to cover her taxes and perhaps have a little left over. In this way, the firm doesn't touch the new partner's base because that's likely what the individual is living on. And by creating an incentive plan with good upside, it gives the new partner the opportunity to pay down the obligation quickly. Typically, an interest rate is imputed in these terms.

In this circumstance, the new partner could vest over a period of three to seven years, depending on the transaction pricing and the deal's cash flow affordability. Owners must be careful not to make the buy-in onerous, but they should set the threshold high enough for the new partner to feel that she has skin in the game. Any profit distributions may be tied to the vesting so that the new partner doesn't get the full financial benefit of ownership until she's fully capitalized.

Some firms also have incentive plans that allow partners to purchase a larger stake in the business and oftentimes will have a provision in a buy-sell agreement that gives the individual the right of first refusal to buy the senior partner's ownership if he dies, becomes disabled, or retires.

As the practice grows and you clarify the career path for key individuals, it will become more important for you to clearly articulate what your partner admission policy is so that likely candidates have a framework for how to achieve it (see "Sample Partner Policy Statement," at right). Knowing that you're adding partners who can carry on the practice after you've retired from active participation gives you a strong option in your succession planning. Having internal buyers means you can walk away from any offer from an outside buyer if the terms are not sufficiently appealing.

Less-Than-Apparent Heirs

Financial advisers continue to struggle with what is clearly a fear of change in the admission of new partners to their practices either through merger or through internal growth and development of staff. We're seeing a widening gap between the owners of advisory firms and the staff they employ in terms of authority, accountability, responsibility, and contribution to growth. In the *2004 FPA Financial Performance Study* produced by Moss Adams, 20 percent of respondents said they wished they could change their staff (see *Figure 14.2*).

If you're among that unhappy 20 percent, you may find that the way you describe your staff betrays a lack of confidence in them: "They could never be owners; they don't think like entrepreneurs." Or, "They couldn't develop new business if their life depended on

Sample Partner Policy Statement

A partner policy statement provides a guideline to both current and prospective partners as to what should be considered. It helps maintain transparency in your career-development program for staff. The following statement outlines the firm's goals and procedures.

The selection of new partners is critical to achieving the firm's succession goals and sustaining professional pride and job satisfaction. The goal for the selection and admission of partners is to promote to the position of partner only those people who are expected to perform at a level equal to or higher than the firm's present effective partners. A partnership is in part a reward for past services, but it is primarily an indication of confidence in the future performance as a partner.

This policy statement is designed to accomplish the following objectives for the firm:
- Provide assurance to potential employees that they have adequate opportunity to become partners
- Retain personnel the firm needs to maintain its expected growth rate
- Reassure staff that they will have the opportunity to qualify as partner and outline the requirements for doing so
- Maintain a proper ratio of partners to clients and staff
- Replace retiring partners
- Encourage partners whose goals are no longer compatible with the firm's to withdraw from the partnership.

Standards for Partnership Admission
- Practice composition: a client base consistent with the firm's strategy
- Personal attributes: appropriate skills, attitude, and ability
- Economic considerations: new sales, retention, profitability of practice
- Marketing orientation: able to demonstrate business-development success
- Client management: maintains low client attrition and high client satisfaction
- Safety: prudent client acceptance and client management

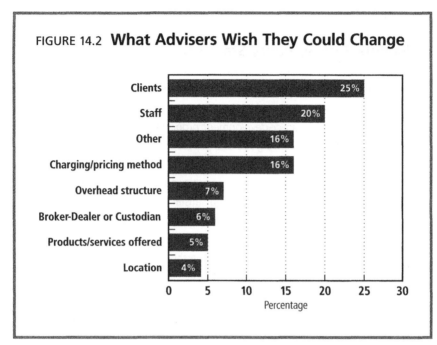

FIGURE 14.2 **What Advisers Wish They Could Change**

	Percentage
Clients	25%
Staff	20%
Other	16%
Charging/pricing method	16%
Overhead structure	7%
Broker-Dealer or Custodian	6%
Products/services offered	5%
Location	4%

Source: © Moss Adams, 2004 FPA Financial Performance Study of Financial Advisory Practices, sponsored by SEI Investments (FPA Press, September 2004), p. 15.

it." Or, "They're too raw; our clients wouldn't trust them or respond to them." If these comments echo your own, ask yourself why you hired these people in the first place. More important, why do you still employ them?

One adviser asked us to help his firm develop a practice succession plan. In the course of the engagement, he could not avoid criticizing the quality of the people who work for him. Bewildered by this, I couldn't help asking, "If something happened to you, would you encourage your wife [who was not financially sophisticated] to engage your staff to advise her on financial matters?" He answered, "Absolutely not!" With that much confidence in his own people, I began to understand why they were not developing. In fact, it appears they fulfilled his expectations completely.

Although this is clearly an extreme example, we continually hear practice owners express doubts about the people they've brought into their firms and whether they're trainable. Even when owners have great people, they tend to expect them to learn their advisory skills by luck or osmosis. And because of time or other resource constraints, owners often do nothing to train and develop employees' skills; rarely do they even set the expectations regarding what they expect from people. Unfortunately, this usually results in deterioration of the faith and trust owners have in their staff.

But what explains such neglect? Many attribute the widening gap in skills to the perceived values of the next generation (where have we heard that before?). We're not convinced that the weaker second tier indicates a younger generation of people who lack the same work ethic or the same sense of drive. We see too many examples

Beyond the Safety Zone

IN HER PROVOCATIVE BOOK *The Trouble with Islam: A Muslim's Call for Reform in Her Faith* (St. Martin's, 2004), author Irshad Manji relates a story about UCLA professor Khaled Abou El Fadl's lecture to Muslim students at a Toronto gathering. Among the points that stuck with me was a challenge the professor posed: "Have you ever known a civilization that grows on the basis of the lowest common denominator? A civilization that can be secure in the hands of its simpletons rather than its geniuses? Civilization is built by the artist, by the literary exponent, by the ability to generate beauty and music and new methods of expression. Civilization advances when there's a premium ... on originality of thought!"

Such profound observations make me wonder how I can apply them to my own life and work. Having been in and around the financial-advisory business for almost 30 years, I've come to appreciate two of the qualities that distinguish financial planners from so many other capitalists: introspection and intellectual curiosity. Of course, in response to such blanket pronouncements, someone will invariably point out the thousands of exceptions. But there does seem to be a certain type of person who is attracted to this profession.

Whereas fear of change consumes many, it is the fear of not evolving that seems to propel enlightened financial advisers forward. Perhaps that's because the business is still relatively new and has not yet established the kind of widely recognized practice-management techniques that exist in other professions. More likely though, it's because financial planners, by the nature of their work, must force clients to confront their anxieties and in doing so, advisers inevitably learn to pose the same questions to themselves.   —MT that contradict this premise. The many high-performing 20- and 30-something individuals who've had the benefit of mentoring from their practice leaders keep us from believing it's a generational pox. More times than not, the gap is widening because owners of advisory firms have not invested time, money, or trust in the development of those who work for them, and, in many cases, they live in fear that their employees might outshine them. Sadly enough, many financial advisers fear that providing professional development will indeed change underlings into peers.

Ensuring Success for Successors

Whatever the cause of inadequate professional development, the patterns we've seen have led us to conclude that part of the hiring process should include an assessment of whether the candidate could ever rise to be the owner's peer. As an owner of a business, your job is not to keep people down on the farm but to create an environment in which motivated people will flourish.

Part of your screening process when hiring entry level staff for your team is to evaluate whether or not you see the potential in this individual—with the right training and development—to become your partner. If you sense they don't have that kind of drive, don't hire them—even if they have the technical skills to be a good staff person. Our experience indicates that it's far better to invest your time and resources in developing people with long-term potential.

Can the investment backfire? Reluctance to make the commitment to professional development is deeply rooted in the psyche of most small-business owners, financial advisers included. If your people develop too well, will you be creating your own competition? Will they grow to the point of challenging you in terms of how many clients they serve and how much revenue they manage? If they become too successful, will they want to be owners? Can you bind them to your practice in any way? The most wary advisers are those who have been burned by staff who've left. Often they will say, "There's no loyalty in this business anymore." Yet, employees who have left firms tell us, "There's no opportunity in this firm anymore."

There is no perfect solution for protecting yourself from individuals who choose to "learn from the master" then replicate that practice on their own. Restrictive covenant agreements can help, but you can't truly prevent it from happening. Nevertheless, the reality is that advisory firms that create a career path, invest in the development of their people, and ultimately allow individuals to rise to become partners tend to be more effective in locking good people into their practices. The primary reason is that the value of being part of a larger, growing, successful team is far more rewarding than going it alone. At least it is for most people.

With this in mind, we recommend that advisory firms that wish to grow into dynamic practices with individuals who share the owner's values and contribute in meaningful ways to the firm's growth do so by rewarding those individuals with the opportunity for partnership. That goal is best achieved with a plan that encourages staff development. The plan should include a clearly defined career path, a framework for how partners are admitted, and clear guidelines on how ownership is obtained.

The Path to Ownership

In our semiannual studies on compensation and staffing for the FPA, we find that staff roles within advisory firms are being clarified and, consequently, the firms' expectations are clearer as well. Generally, an employee's career needs to progress through four distinct phases before the person will be considered for partner. Even in the smallest firms, such distinctions may be essential for measuring the progress of key people, but more important, they serve as markers that demonstrate to candidates the next hurdle they must clear on their road to partnership.

At most firms, the four phases logically separate into roles with the job titles of analyst, senior analyst, adviser or financial planner, and finally senior adviser or senior financial planner (see *Figure 14.3*). Following are the typical parameters for those positions.

Analyst. The analyst is a new hire whose primary job is to learn the job, perform the most basic tasks within the firm, and become grounded in the language, concepts, and applications of what an adviser does.

Senior analyst. After two to four years, once an analyst has demonstrated an aptitude and level of efficiency in performing the basics of the job, the employee might rise to the position of senior analyst. In this position, the person would begin to have more regular client contact, although he would not yet be expected to develop business.

Adviser/financial planner. After four to six years with the firm, an individual might rise to the position of adviser, or financial planner, depending on how well she performed in the senior analyst position. This position requires serving as primary liaison with clients and, in fact, may involve certain client-management responsibilities. The adviser begins to learn the ropes of business development and has a minimal goal of bringing in new revenue. The adviser would also share responsibility for supervising some of the younger staff.

Senior adviser/senior financial planner. After six to nine years, an adviser or planner would rise to the position of senior adviser, or senior financial planner. In this position, the employee's role would be heavily oriented toward business development, staff development, oversight of clients, and the client-management process. Ideally, the senior adviser would have a primary area of management responsi-

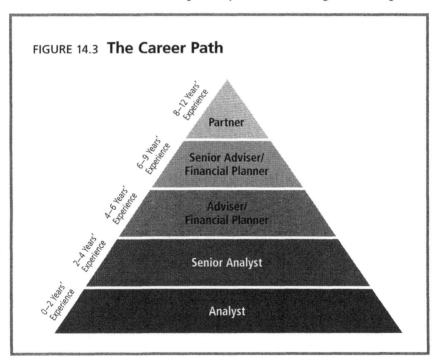

FIGURE 14.3 **The Career Path**

bility within the practice such as marketing, operations, investment policy, or financial planning.

Partner. Having achieved proficiency as a senior adviser, the employee would be considered for partner in the firm. A term of eight to 12 years is reasonable for the development of a homegrown partner. Becoming a partner, however, is not merely a function of proficiency in developing business. It must depend on the advisory firm's economics and on certain individual thresholds beyond business development that you as the owner have laid out.

In fact, many firms consider admitting as partners employees who are not responsible for business development, and many firms are successfully doing so. Advisers considered for this recognition should be contributing in some form to growth of the business, at least in terms of leadership if not in the number of active client relationships they manage. In other words, someone who is really skilled at delivering advice and keeping clients happy may be worth as much in terms of partner potential as someone who brings in new clients. That said, it's important in admitting partners that you have enough of them who can serve as a growth engine, or you will run the risk of creating a group of leaders who may not be able to perpetuate the firm's development.

An employee's ascension to partner should be based on whether that individual is contributing to your firm's culture as well as to its financial performance. Within Moss Adams, for example, we have been attempting to integrate our statement of cultural values into staff development and partner admission. In doing so, we've observed material improvement in the candidates we advance and have shared this principle with financial advisers struggling with the same issues. Our statement of cultural values revolves around the acronym PILLAR.

P —passion for excellence
I —integrity
L —lifetime learning
L —lead by example
A —a balanced life
R —respect for others

Advisers who've adopted similar principles have also developed a staff-evaluation process based on these concepts. They apply these principles in appraising their staff and in upstream evaluations that their staff performs. In our own case, PILLAR is the foundation on which we evaluate all candidates for partner. Violation of these principles is usually the reason an individual does not advance to ownership in the business.

Although revenue production is important, the risk every adviser takes in promoting coin-operated people without regard to values is that the resulting firm will be unlikable. Significantly, you will have created partners that you don't like. Your fears will be self-fulfilling.

Chapter Notes

1. Moss Adams and Market Knowledge Tools, *Best-Managed Firms: Recruiting and Retaining Top Talent* (Charles Schwab Institutional, October 2005).

2. Moss Adams, *2003 FPA Compensation and Staffing Study,* sponsored by SEI Investments (FPA Press, September 2003).

15. BUY-SELL AGREEMENTS: THE PATH TO HAPPIER ENDINGS

Inside Stories

IN CHAPTER 12, we discussed the agreements required in a sale and acquisition. When entering into an ownership relationship, however, a different kind of agreement is required: the buy-sell agreement. This document—sometimes referred to as a shareholder agreement or an operating agreement—spells out how the co-owners of an enterprise will address certain issues and, most important, how each will be bought out should the other leave. Sometimes, the buy-sell agreement provisions are contained in the operating or shareholder agreements, which cover more issues.

Taking the Marbles

Many financial advisers approach their buy-sell agreements and shareholder/operating agreements with a simplistic view that leaves out too many possibilities. For example, they might think, "We'll grow the business, then we'll exit and get paid a nice price." This gives an owner at least two options: sell to people on the inside, or find a buyer on the outside. But when the repurchase obligation becomes too onerous for the owners left behind, it's possible the departing owner could end up with little or nothing and may be forced to sell to somebody on the outside. That said, the quandary might not be about whether money is due to the departing shareholder, but rather about how the agreement is to be interpreted. The devil, as they say, is in the details.

And we've seen agreements within financial advisory firms that were quite devilish indeed. In one case, the largest shareholder and revenue producer was entitled to leave, get a multiple of firm revenue, *and* take his clients with him. By the terms of another agreement, the newest and youngest shareholder could actually be left having to buy out the veteran owners all at once (cash on the barrelhead), because any shareholder was free to leave the business with very short notice and without having prepared for succession. In another agreement, a departing shareholder could walk away from his share of the lease and other corporate obligations, right after the firm had made a significant commitment to very expensive office space and other infrastructure expenses.

Problematic as these provisions are, at least these firms had agreements in place. Unfortunately, many advisory firms we encounter are in the midst of contested valuations and no formal or signed agreement exists at all. And in the course of our engagement to perform valuations of advisory firms, we often discover that many buy-sell agreements are not quite complete or fail to address key issues that would give direction to appraisers who are attempting to value the ownership interests as provided for in the agreements. These agreements specify what should happen in the event of death or disability, but they are often less explicit about what happens when the partners no longer get along or when one of them decides to leave the business.

A buy-sell or other restrictive stock agreement has several purposes. It allows the remaining owners to acquire the interest of a withdrawing shareholder. A buy-sell agreement also restricts an owner's ability to sell or transfer his or her interest in the company, and it provides guidelines under which the company or other owners may or must acquire a departing shareholder's interest.

The triggering events for a buy-sell transaction usually include the following:
- Attempted sale or transfer
- Retirement
- Termination (voluntary and involuntary)
- Death or disability
- Divorce
- Bankruptcy
- Regulatory enforcement or disqualification

Headaches and Hindsight

EXPERIENCE TEACHES US many lessons, and sometimes they're lessons we wish we never had to learn. Some years ago, before we merged our firm into Moss Adams, I had to renegotiate a separation agreement with former partners. As in many firms with multiple shareholders, relationships were getting strained over the direction of the business, the performance of certain partners, and the misalignment of our individual goals.

When we first entered into the agreement, we made the same mistake that many new partners do in assuming that the strength of our friendships would override irrationality and that the protective language our attorney wanted to put in the agreements would prove to be moot. We weren't seriously thinking about things not turning out well, only about maximizing value when it was time to leave the firm. As with many assumptions, in hindsight these proved to be naïve.

It's funny how it works. When you're building the business, you think about how the shareholder agreement will translate into making all the shareholders rich. When you start pulling apart, you come to believe your so-called friends and colleagues are trying to stab you in the back. When one of our clients encountered a similar situation, a partner in my current firm explained the situation in clear but painful terms: "I guess you can't really hate somebody until you've loved them first."

In my case, the looseness in some of the language in the buy-sell agreement turned the forced termination of a partner into a poison pill for the business. If we adhered to the repurchase obligation spelled out in the agreement, it became clear that the firm could not afford to continue doing business. Our choices? Close it down, or redo the agreement. Either course of action was sure to destroy whatever remnants of a relationship still existed.

It's easy to get angry with the attorneys for how the documents were drafted or to be upset with yourself for not anticipating such a bad outcome, but if you didn't seriously contemplate the termination of a shareholder under stressful circumstances as you were drafting the agreement, it's easy to be caught off guard later on.   —MT

Many agreements contain specific language describing what would occur in the event of a shareholder's divorce. Many multi-owner firms are concerned that the owner's estranged spouse could end up having a stake in the company so the document provides language to mitigate this, especially under such negative circumstances. In the case of a divorce, generally, the divorcing partner should have first refusal rights to purchase any shares awarded to a nonowner spouse so that his shares are not diluted. Then the company and other shareholders can have the option (or obligation) to purchase the shares.

Buy-sell agreements are considered substitutes for market liquidity when any of these triggering events occur. The price paid depends on the terms of the agreement, but in general the shareholder knows he or she will receive something. Overall, a clearly written buy-sell agreement allows the company to continue operating smoothly during a transition.

Common Problems in Buy-Sell Agreements

If a buy-sell agreement is the instrument used to decrease uncertainty, increase liquidity, and allow the company to continue operating without affecting operations, why do problems, especially litigation, arise when there is a dispute? That's usually because the buy-sell agreement is ambiguous or lacks structure in certain areas. There are several key points that are considered when an expert is reviewing a buy-sell agreement or rendering an opinion on the value of a company that has a buy-sell agreement.

Members of Moss Adams's valuation consulting staff repeatedly encounter problems in shareholder and buy-sell agreements, some of which end up causing the legal fees and expert witness fees to spiral out of control. Calvin Swartley, one of our lead valuation consultants, points to six recurring problem areas that make the resolution of shareholder disputes so difficult:

1. **Standard of value:** How is value defined?
2. **Purchase-price standard:** What is being valued?
3. **Silence on key points:** What information is missing?
4. **Actions by shareholders:** How does management stay informed?

5. **Interpretations by courts or mediators:** Who else can influence the value?

6. **Valuation approaches:** How is value estimated?

Standard of Value

There are several standards of value that may be used in buy-sell agreements, including fair market value, fair value, and book value. The uninitiated mistakenly think that value is value, and that's one reason business owners get upset with appraisers. In the absence of a definition, the appraiser will need to exercise judgment as to which standard to use in arriving at an opinion, and often one party in the dispute will take exception to this choice.

Fair market value. The standard of value typically considered the most appropriate is fair market value, which is defined as the amount at which property would change hands between a willing buyer and a willing seller when the former is under no compulsion to buy, the latter is under no obligation to sell, and both parties have reasonable knowledge of relevant facts. Certainly, in real life, such conditions are rare. Fair market value is a hypothetical notion of value promulgated by the IRS for gift and estate tax purposes, but it's often used as a general guideline in buy-sell agreements.

Fair value. Fair value, on the other hand, is usually a legally created standard of value based on statutes and case law, which applies in dissenting shareholder disputes. Fair value is the value of shares immediately prior to an event to which the shareholder objects. The difficulty with fair value is that its interpretation and definition are not consistent across state jurisdictions. Some states, such as California, which has one of the most rigorous protections for minority shareholders in the country, have a process that allows the government to hire appraisers to determine the value in contested circumstances, and these states specify "fair value" as the standard.

Book value. Book value is simply the net worth on the balance sheet of the company at any date in time. The company's assets are stated at their depreciated historical cost. Net book value equals the company's total assets minus total liabilities. Book value, or net book value, is easy to calculate and easy to explain. Book value, however, does not provide a good indication of the company as a going concern. What's more, book value can be manipulated to create a low value. It is an especially irrelevant basis for value in a financial-services firm because in no way can it account for the inherent value in the practice's client list or the advisers' ability to generate cash flow.

Formula pricing. Formula pricing, which uses a simple calculation, is also used in some buy-sell agreements. A formula-pricing method (for example, a multiple of gross revenue) is usually objective and inexpensive, but as with book value, it does not represent fair market value. A buy-sell agreement that includes a formula-pricing method should be reviewed periodically to ensure the formula meets the changes the company undergoes.

Investment value. A concept often used in real-life transactions—though not used in such agreements—is the investment-value standard. Inevitably, when a business owner believes we have valued his business below its true worth, he points to what he understands are real-life market prices with strategic or financial buyers. But real-life transactions can take into account the benefit of synergy, operational cost savings, or discretionary expenses, whereas internal transactions cannot. So it's not uncommon for valuations determined under buy-sell agreements to be much lower than those one would find in the open market.

Purchase-Price Standard

Defining the purchase-price standard is a critical step in a buy-sell agreement. The total equity value (or controlling value) of a company is significantly different from a minority, noncontrolling interest in a company. An agreement that does not distinguish what standard should be applied leaves open the possibility a shareholder is entitled to something other than fair market value. For instance, an agreement stating that the price to be paid in the event of a transaction will be the fair market value of the company could be interpreted to mean the price per share for a minority shareholder is the same as the price per share for a controlling shareholder.

The purchase-price standard should also include a clear understanding of whether adjustments, if applicable, should be made for lack of control or lack of marketability. This problem is especially acute in buy-sell agreements for financial-advisory practices. Again, the seller or injured party in these transactions points to real-life market prices as indicators of what the value should be. But if he or she is giving up a minority stake (less than 51 percent in most states), then what is the true value of the interest? It's acceptable to state in the agreement that under certain circumstances, the value of the shares will be determined on an enterprise basis rather than a partial or minority ownership basis, or even an asset basis. And when you consider that the surviving shareholders may want to protect them-selves from a big repurchase liability, it may be wiser to state explicitly that the valuation will consider minority and nonmarketability inter-est discounts. This language will not bind the shareholders should they decide to sell to an outside party.

Remember, when drafting these agreements, you have to put yourself on both sides of the transaction. It may be tempting to gear the agreement to a higher value, assuming you're the first one out the door, but what if you're not? And what if multiple shareholders and advisers all decide to bolt at once, leaving you holding the bag?

Silent or Missing Information

Often, buy-sell agreements are silent on key points or neglect to con-sider all potential issues that may arise. For example, if the standard of value is missing, it may be the judge, mediator, state law, or even case law that will set a standard. To resolve silent or missing information, an expert is required to rely on state law, guidance from the company's counsel, and experience to resolve the resulting problems.

A good buy-sell agreement will also include a determination of the effective date of a triggering event. Without a clear determina-tion of the effective date, a moving target could be created, making resolution even harder. This becomes especially aggravating to the departing shareholder. Chances are hostility has developed long before the buy-sell agreement is triggered. If the fight goes on for months or years, the practice itself could suffer from all the distrac-tions, thereby undermining the firm's value.

Actions by Shareholders

Some buy-sell agreements state that the shareholders will determine the value of the shares annually (or at some other regular interval). The intention of this type of language is to ensure that shareholders are involved in the process of determining value and to ensure smooth transitions as they arise. Annual determinations are considered very beneficial. If the annual determination is not performed and a dispute arises, however, the chances of the parties agreeing on a value are not good. The dispute will require outside determination or resolution.

Having worked with hundreds of businesses, we find that annual determinations by the shareholders are, in fact, rarely done each year. They tend to be done the first two to five years; then they stop. In such cases, an evaluator is left wondering what to do when the last determination was five or 10 years ago and the agreement does not address what is to be done in the absence of a recent determination.

That said, we generally like the idea of financial advisers using an annual valuation as part of management deliberations, because the process prompts them to examine what's not working and to build on what is. Without the discipline to have management meetings that address these issues, however, the firm will face a bigger problem down the road should the buy-sell agreement be triggered.

Court, Mediator, and Other Interpretations

Ultimately, someone or some group will make a judgment on the value of the company or of a specific block of shares in the dispute. Although the buy-sell agreement was established to set a precedent, it may be given little weight or ignored in making a final determination. The courts have shown a dislike for book value in certain circumstances. What's more, attempts to buy out shareholders when a purchase of the company is imminent have been judged to be a breach of fiduciary duty.

Valuation

Determining the value of the company or its shares is an essential step in putting together a buy-sell agreement once a dispute is under way. Valuation of a closely held company is too difficult for the court to determine, and valuation specialists are usually called in to assist. Valuation specialists typically rely on fair market value and a combination of appraisal methods to determine the value of a company or a portion of it. In some instances, the valuation process can be highly complex as well as expensive.

Finding an Appraiser

SEVERAL REPUTABLE business-valuation or appraisal standards organizations are available, including the American Society of Appraisers (ASA, Accredited Senior Member) and the American Institute of Certified Public Accountants (ABV, Accredited in Business Valuation). When selecting or designating appraisers for your agreement, you may look to these groups for names of qualified experts. If you're not acquainted with them, you might interview them and ask for background. Firms who do appraisals of advisory firms should demonstrate an understanding of your business and describe for you a comprehensive process that will consider the earnings capacity of your business, market pricing, and comparable pricing analyses.

Investment bankers specializing in financial services, such as Berkshire Capital and Putnam Lovell, publish some data on mergers and acquisitions of larger advisory and wealth-management firms. FP Transitions publishes data on smaller practices that have been listed with them. Pratt's Stats, Bizcomps, Done Deals, and *MergerStat Review* are also sources of data on business transactions, although they tend to have limited data on financial-advisory firms.

In some situations, the opposing parties hire the same specialist and accept whatever value the specialist determines. That, however, is rare. Typically, anywhere from one to three valuations are performed, and each specialist weighs in on a final value. One specialist may perform an appraisal, with each side hiring another specialist to critique the value conclusion. Or each party may hire a specialist and have a third make the final decision based on the facts presented by the two valuations. In either case, the cost to complete the appraisal can escalate quickly. Clearly defining the "who" and "how" for the valuation of the company in the buy-sell agreement will greatly decrease the uncertainty of valuation when one is needed.

But even with excellent professional resources, it's very difficult to get solid comparable pricing on either broker-dealers or financial-advisory practices because the size, nature of the business, and terms of the transactions are not always fully disclosed. In any case, for internal transactions, you should not rely exclusively on external market prices because you will get some distortion, especially if the business is either underperforming or outperforming the industry. Certainly, give fair weight to market pricing, formulas, and valuation guidelines, but put greater emphasis on the underlying economics of the practice. Whenever possible formulas should also be expressed in easily measurable terms, such as price to revenue, price to assets under management or supervision, and price to operating profit (though this last one may be tough, depending on how you account for things).

A practical question in a buy-sell agreement is the lack of specificity as to when and how the redeemed interest is to be purchased. This stipulation is in place in some agreements but not in all. As practices get larger and more individuals are promoted to partner, become shareholders in the firm, or join as part of a merger—the need increases to establish an agreement with clear direction for those who must interpret it. Without careful planning, the intent of the buy-sell agreement could be lost. Granted, even the best-written buy-sell agreement cannot guarantee a smooth transition, but clearly defining the key aspects of a buy-sell and including all pertinent information will lessen the uncertainty surrounding the transition.

As the financial-advisory profession continues to evolve and attorneys become more familiar with the unique challenges facing advisory firms with multiple shareholders, such agreements will likely be written more tightly. In the meantime, cautious advisers should be alert to the questions to ask their counsel before entering into such agreements with their partners.

VI

The Marketplace

16. MAKING THE MATCH: INTERMEDIARIES
The Marketplace

I N THE LATE 1990S, leading broker-dealers such as SunAmerica Securities (now part of the AIG network of broker-dealers) and Mutual Service developed the concept of a Web-based platform for their registered representatives to sell their books of business. SunAmerica introduced IValue, and Mutual Service came out with Practice-Transitions.com. Other broker-dealers like American Express Financial Advisors (now Ameriprise), Raymond James Financial, and Western Reserve Life developed written manuals to guide their reps through the Web-based transition process.

Perhaps the most intriguing innovation came when a financial-services entrepreneur named David Goad created FP Transitions, an independent Web-based listing service for small advisory practices. A competing platform—SuccessionPlanning.com—opened for business about the same time. FP Transitions eventually took over SuccessionPlanning.com's business. In 2002, Goad sold his interest in FP Transitions to David Grau, who, together with his partner Bill Grable, has made it a resource for registered representatives and RIAs who are selling smaller books of business to interested buyers.

Broker-Dealers and Custodians

Schwab

The country's leading custodian for registered investment advisers, Schwab Institutional, has also created a Web-based platform for its

RIA customers (schwabtransition.com), although it is not intended to be an auction site. Schwab intends its Web-based platform to serve as a resource to provide access to professional advice for legal, accounting, due diligence, valuation, and investment-banking services, although buyers and sellers may work with Schwab's staff dedicated to helping them manage the sale process. One of the many appealing features of the Schwab Transition platform is that it provides confidential information on both buyers and sellers, who can then discreetly approach one another to explore a possible sale, merger, or acquisition, and the cost of this service is very low.

Schwab charges $100 per quarter for buyers; sellers list for free but commit to paying Schwab 1 basis point of their assets under management, and a maximum fee of $10,000 when a transaction is consummated. For the most part, Schwab's compensation for this service is a "speed bump" for buyers and sellers and helps Schwab cover the costs of maintaining the site to help their adviser clients identify interested parties and of providing dedicated staff to help advisers through the process.

Schwab has also embarked on a significant training effort for its advisers by creating a series of intensive workshops across the country that exposes advisers contemplating the purchase or sale of a practice to the insights of transition experts. One unique element of Schwab's training has been to feature a panel of top advisers—like Scott Roulston at Fairport Asset Management in Cleveland, Mark Soehn of Financial Solutions Advisory Group in Chicago, and Rusty Benton of Wealth Trust in Memphis—who share their experiences in navigating through a transaction. The firm has a continuing focus on preparing advisers for transitions whether internal or external.

For a custodian, such initiatives are cutting edge, both because they are a relatively inexpensive way for advisers to access professional consultants and because they bring together many of the country's leading experts on business transition and postmerger integration. Of course, Schwab has a vested interest in the orderly transition of its adviser clients. Studies show that the average age of advisers is now in the mid-50s and steadily moving up. Schwab has found it important to help these advisers to begin planning in order to ensure their continuity as clients. This shared interest in their advisers-clients' success allows Schwab to be a low-cost provider of the services while maintaining objectivity in matching up buyers and sellers. The firm's resource group, which assists both in succession planning and postmerger integration, now includes investment bankers, valuation experts, attorneys, CPAs, and management consultants.

Fidelity

Fidelity Registered Investment Advisor Group also has introduced a transition initiative for its RIA customers. Like Schwab's, the program offers access to professional resources but does not include a Web-based listing service. Fidelity features both access to FP Transitions and to Berkshire Capital, one of the country's leading investment bankers in the industry, as a way to offer full-service investment banking and brokerage to financial advisers. The firm is also populating its proprietary website with articles and reference material to assist advisers through the processes involved in purchases and sales.

Other Players

TD Ameritrade (née TD Waterhouse) is also embarking on a succession initiative for its affiliated advisers, though as of late 2005, the program had not yet been fully developed.

Many of the independent broker-dealers have both formal and informal programs for assisting their advisers through the transition. Most of the broker-dealers' efforts have been focused on setting up their older registered reps for succession, but in some cases, there is also an effort to assist the buyers to ensure that they don't overpay or overcommit to a purchase they cannot afford. Some of the broker-dealers have set up arrangements with consulting firms and intermediaries to assist in this transition so as to avoid liability for acting as an advocate for one side or the other.

The combination of broker-dealers and custodians insinuating themselves into the transition process is an important development among financial advisory firms. In all cases, these players see an aging population of advisers and recognize the need to help these firms achieve an orderly transition and position themselves to retain the assets upon sale.

Conventional Investment Bankers

As advisory firms get larger, they tend to seek guidance from experienced investment bankers and other professionals (attorneys or CPAs, for example) to help them seek a buyer or seller, negotiate the price and terms, and consummate the deal. The same principle is in play when wealthy individuals seek out financial planners and wealth managers for professional advice: there comes a point when the size of the mistake can be a career-defining moment.

The two leading investment-banking firms for financial-advisory businesses valued at more than $10 million are Berkshire Capital and Putnam Lovell NBF Securities. Prominent investment bankers such as Goldman Sachs, Merrill Lynch and Lazard Frères also serve the high end of this market. Filling the gap between the larger investment bankers and the auction market provided by FP Transitions, Moss Adams, one of the leading management consultants and accountants to the securities industry, has developed industry expertise within its investment-banking group—Moss Adams Capital—to provide investment-banking services to firms in the RIA market with less than $2 billion in assets under management. Moss Adams has been providing valuation and succession consulting services to both registered reps and RIAs since 1994; the investment-banking initiative was introduced in 2004.

To avoid conflicts of interest, investment bankers will represent only one side of the transaction and most prefer to work on behalf of the seller. That's because sellers tend to have a higher motivation to complete a transaction and it's generally easier to find buyers than it is to find sellers. This, of course, increases the probability that investment bankers will get paid for their efforts.

Costs

Most investment bankers receive a retainer and progress payments to cover their costs during the process of preparing a "book" (a profile of the seller's business) and seeking prospects; often these payments are offset against a success fee tied to the value of the transaction. Monthly retainers can range from $10,000 to $50,000 a month depending on the size of the firm being sold, and often these retainer fees do not offset the success fee. They are regarded as part of the cost of planning and searching. The success fee typically ranges between 1 percent and 3 percent of the purchase price, depending on a variety of factors including size, complexity, and the scope of the engagement and is paid in recognition of the banker's successful negotiation and consummation of the transaction for their clients.

When a buyer engages an investment banker, there may also be a monthly retainer to cover the time and cost of the search, plus a success fee. An acceptable success fee may be a flat amount that truly is tied to consummation of a purchase, but in some circumstances, the fee is tied to the value of the transaction, a practice that's a bit of a conflict of interest.

In relative terms, the cost of using an investment banker is less than the cost of using a business broker or FP Transitions, but since we're dealing in larger dollars, the actual dollar payment to an investment banker is larger. It's unlikely that a firm will pay less than $150,000 in fees when going this route, and if the business that's being sold is a substantial size, the investment-banking fees could be substantially more. Some investment bankers have a minimum fee of $500,000 on closing, so it's important to judge how well the firm can add value to the transaction (good ones can make this up by giving sellers peace of mind and confidence that their interests are being tended to).

Benefits

Buyers or sellers who use investment bankers should evaluate them on the basis of these factors:
1. Their contact list
2. Their relevant experience
3. Their track record with similar companies
4. Their success rate

Many sellers mistakenly think the contact list is key to selecting an investment banker, but frankly, with a good business to sell, developing a meaningful contact list of targeted buyers is not the biggest challenge. The tough part is negotiating a deal that's in the best interest of the client. Most investment bankers representing the seller begin the process with an assessment of the company and the preparation of a profile of the business, which is commonly called the memorandum, or book. The memorandum is essentially an offering document that features the more appealing aspects of the business such as financial performance, management depth, and market positioning.

The banker also works closely with the seller to understand the culture and philosophy of the firm. This helps the bank to cull its target list of prospective buyers to organizations that are both compatible and financially able to make the deal. A good banker will get the initial list down to six or seven target firms to engage in a discussion about the sale. From that list, it elicits firm expressions of interest before it goes any deeper into the discussions and negotiations. To encourage bidding and a better deal, the banker generally keeps several prospective buyers moving along at the same pace. Ultimately, the banker together with the client will decide on one firm with which to negotiate in earnest.

That's the point at which the investment banker delivers some of its greatest value. The intermediary's ability to help the seller negotiate the fine points in the letter of intent—and ultimately the purchase agreement—can considerably increase the money going to the seller. Throughout the negotiating process, the seller should expect frequent communication from the banker and see material progress within three to six months. The sale of a large advisory firm takes time, necessarily, but events can move fast at certain points in the process.

The advantage of engaging an investment banker is that you're hiring someone who is typically unemotional about the deal and motivated to help his client get the best deal. In evaluating offers made to four separate advisory firms by a consolidator, we saw that those who engaged an investment banker to assist them received a better offer and a better contract than the two that did it alone. Although this is a very small sample and anecdotal, the parallel for financial advisers is clear. As the millennium market crash proved, investors who did not consult or listen to their professional advisers tended to do worse than those who were guided by experienced and skilled investment managers, wealth managers, and financial planners.

Do-It-Yourselfers

One of the ironies of the financial-advisory business—an industry built on the wisdom of seeking professional advice—is the general reluctance of top-ranking people in this business to engage professional advisers to address issues outside their expertise. This may be a consequence of the innate confidence advisers have in their own ability to evaluate financial matters and their belief that they can read agreements as well as most financial professionals. Unfortunately, as do clients who think they can manage their own wealth without professional advice, many financial advisers fall into a trap that may cost them more than the money they saved by not hiring an expert.

Owners who attempt to negotiate a transaction on their own are often unaware of the nuances of the language in the letter of intent—subtleties that could cost them money once a transaction is consummated. They also may be less confident or objective in negotiating price and terms. Perhaps the most daunting challenge for advisers who eschew professional help is that they fail to anticipate the emotional tension tied up in the sale of a business and usually do not have a buffer between them and the other side when negotiating an agreement. They may attempt to resolve this by involving a lawyer in the negotiations. As attorney Tom Giachetti of Stark & Stark puts it, "Never let your attorney negotiate the economics of a transaction; that's not an attorney's skill set. The attorney's expertise is in negotiating and documenting the legal points."

For internal transactions, it may not be necessary to engage an investment banker. The services of an attorney, accountant, or succession consultant should be sufficient. In these cases, the issues that arise may involve how to prepare the successors for operating the business as well as for acquiring ownership. In addition, it may be necessary to build a partner plan, a valuation formula, and a career-development plan to ensure continuity of the enterprise. Advisers in these circumstances rarely if ever charge a success fee but often will charge project or hourly fees for their work. In addition to Moss Adams, which has been providing succession, career-path development, and valuation consulting to advisers since 1994, David Goad of Succession Planning Consultants is a resource to the profession in these areas. He has written a guidebook on this subject for the Financial Planning Association (*Succession Planning Strategies for the Financial Planner*, available at www.fpanet.org).

Business Brokers and Auction Markets

BUSINESS BROKERS ARE typically different from investment bankers in the types of services they provide, their experience, and the size and nature of their transactions. Most states require that business brokers have a real estate broker or agent license to be an intermediary for businesses in their jurisdiction. Even higher standards must be met by intermediaries seeking NASD licenses (commonly 7, 24, and 63). FP Transitions—which is well known in the securities industry as an intermediary for small books of business—is a combination business broker and auction market. The firm is not licensed as an NASD broker-dealer, but the firm says it does not position itself as a representative or an agent selling securities (that is, stock in a company), which is what the NASD and state securities commissions tend to scrutinize. For prospective buyers or sellers, the key when evaluating any broker is to know what licenses the brokers hold and whether it's appropriate for the job you're engaging the broker to do.

In any case, FP Transitions functions much like an auction market, with sellers posting their assets—their practices—on the site, along with an asking price, and prospective buyers responding, often with a bid above or below the offering price. FP Transitions then provides legal document templates and helps the parties through the process of escrow, due diligence, and deal structuring. In return, once a sale is consummated, FP Transitions generally gets paid a 7 percent commission based on the listing price, with both the buyer and seller each paying half in most cases.

Some industry observers believe it's a conflict of interest for a broker to be the listing agent for both the buyer and the seller, get paid by both parties, and draw up legal documents even though that appears to be common practice with other types of agency work such as home sales. The challenge for anyone serving the smaller end of the financial-advisory market is the cost, so organizations such as FP Transitions seek to use a template approach to gain efficiencies. Without such an approach—or the substantial financial incentive that comes with consum-mating a transaction—it would be neither practical nor economically feasible for

Most people get to buy or sell a business only once in their lifetime. Although they may have been adept at the management of the practice or in giving advice to clients, they face considerable risk in negotiating a deal without at least the help of a competent

FP Transitions to serve the lower segment of the market, in which the typical sales price is often well below $400,000. These relatively low selling prices are why this market is not effectively served by conventional investment bankers to begin with.

Benefits

Sellers. There are shortcomings in selling small firms in most cases, but some of these negatives are offset by the benefits of using a site such as FP Transitions. The site attempts to consolidate the marketplace for small books of business and provides templates for consummating transactions for both buyers and sellers.

The current relationship of supply and demand enhances the terms for sellers. Because they don't have to take the highest bidder but can pick the one they want, the size of the down payment and the terms of the transaction if the down payment is paid over time (and most are) can tip the seller toward one buyer over another.

Buyers. Buyers could benefit as well because they can shop for new business from the comfort of their homes or offices, although there do not appear to be too many new listings for a national marketplace. For example, a check of the site in November 2005 showed seven firms were currently available for sale and the sale of nine other practices were pending final negotiations.

Pitfalls

An auction market has some risks, particularly for those who enter the process without competent counsel to advise them. Both David Grau and Bill Grable of FP Transitions say the firm assiduously avoids being an advocate for either side. That means both parties—in addition to paying the brokerage fee—need to engage separate counsel to serve as advocate. Although buyers may understand the basic calculations involved in pricing the purchase or setting the terms, there are nuances to business transactions that they should be alert to if they choose to enter into negotiations without an independent professional looking over their shoulder.

and experienced attorney and CPA. But as the deals get bigger, it becomes even more prudent to engage a professional mergers-and-acquisitions adviser who's experienced in the art of deal making. The motivation of such professionals is to consummate the transaction in a way that fulfills the goals of the person they represent—whether a buyer or seller.

17. FINDING THE IDEAL BUYER
The Marketplace

I N HIS BEST-SELLING book *The Tipping Point: How Little Things Can Make a Big Difference* (Little, Brown, 2000), Malcolm Gladwell points out the phenomenon of "social epidemics," wild, raging trends triggered by a series of interconnected events. We're in the midst of just such an epidemic in the financial-planning industry: the sale of advisory practices. Two conditions have triggered this rush to the market:

1. Practice economics create a practical case for consolidation.
2. Very few aging advisers want to be left behind, for fear of seeing the window close.

Evidence of this epidemic in the profession is appearing in several forms:

♦ In 2004, Schwab introduced its new practice-transitions initiative and has since conducted a series of workshops throughout the country. The company put dedicated staff in place to manage the listings on its website.

♦ Fidelity came up with a response to this initiative with its own program in early 2005.

♦ J.P. Morgan updated the Undiscovered Managers white paper on the "Future of the Industry" and affirmed that there indeed is a trend toward industry consolidation and a need for it.

♦ National Financial Partners, the most successful consolidator of practices yet, had a very successful initial public offering that was also supported well in the aftermarket.

- ◆ There have been multiple announcements of banks in the hunt or having consummated transactions.
- ◆ New roll-up firms are appearing on the scene or are rumored to be on the scene already.

Adding to the drama is the frequency with which some of the most significant names in the profession are rumored to be either buyers or sellers of practices. Some of these rumors are even true. And all this activity is stirring up anxiety and excitement.

The Selling Season

One of the more sensational elements of the rumor frenzy surrounding buyers is that both buyers and sellers have a false sense of urgency, as if failure to come to an agreement means they'll miss the last plane to Shangri-La. Although it's true that merger and acquisition windows open and close, they are always ajar for the well-managed practices. Practices that have a clear strategy, strong profitability, systematic growth, built-in leverage and capacity, and an attractive client list have to swat away suitors like flies.

One adviser put it this way: "It's weird, I feel like I'm giving off inappropriate signals: I'm happily married, but I keep getting hit on." As guilty as one may feel about the temptation, there is nothing more flattering than being pursued. But eventually, I suspect, it gets old and annoying and not worth even a raised eyebrow. That's the point owners should try to get to—that stage in which you have both the emotional and financial security to walk away from any deal that doesn't fit your profile.

A confluence of interconnected events is driving this activity:

1. Rising costs among advisory firms are causing them to seek economies of scale.
2. Rising demand among wealthy individuals for professional advisers makes the business appealing to banks, accounting firms, financial buyers, and larger advisory firms.
3. Owners of practices on average are getting older and becoming interested in liquidity through the sale of all or some of their business.

4. In very few communities does one financial-advisory firm dominate the market, making this opportunity to compete even more viable.

There is considerable debate among investment bankers, business brokers, valuation experts, and advisers themselves as to whether this interest is causing prices to rise or to become more reasonable. One of the risks in making generalizations is that the trends often reflect a person's bias more than the reality of the marketplace. The truth is that prices are rising for the well-managed firms and falling relative to industry benchmarks for those that have less to offer. The price at which an advisory firm changes hands depends a lot on the motivations of both the seller and the buyer, the qualities of the firm being sold, and the financial strength of the buyer.

Serious Shoppers

As a seller, you are in control of the business you build, but you may not be in control of the buyer you choose. The good news is that financial-advisory practices are in a market where the choices are substantial and getting bigger. In a nutshell, there are three types of buyers:

1. Financial
2. Strategic
3. Individual

Financial Buyers

A financial buyer is often referred to as a roll-up firm or consolidator. Among the leading acquirers of investment-management firms using this model are Affiliated Managers Group, a publicly traded company headquartered in Boston; Wealth Trust, a well-funded, closely held acquisition group headquartered in Memphis; and Boston Private Bank, although all three do have characteristics of strategic buyers as well. Within the wealth-management and financial-planning segments of the market, the most prominent roll-up firms are National Financial Partners and Focus Financial Partners, both headquartered in New York. Other groups have entered this market or have expressed an interest in doing so. Each of them has different investment goals and parameters for the optimal acquisition and, like most successful consolidators, is well capitalized, has very sophisticated management, and is focused on the financial return of these investments.

Strategic Buyers

Typically, a strategic buyer is a bank, CPA firm, or a large advisory firm that's trying to consolidate its base, add new clients, or expand its sources of income from existing clients. Mellon Bank has been among the most active buyers, but there have been other significant entrants into the market including Harris Bank of Chicago; Compass Bancshares of Birmingham, Alabama; and Western Alliance Bancorporation of Las Vegas. Investment firms such as Lydian, United Atlantic, Convergent, and Rosemount all are strategic buyers in this space. Unlike financial buyers, who tend to use a more formulaic approach to structuring transactions, strategic buyers tend to be more flexible and focused on the synergy of a transaction. CPA firms entering this market are unlikely to pay as high a premium as banks, but often they're better at cross-selling the services after the acquisition. Large advisory firms tend to pursue mergers rather than acquisitions that require infusions of money, but the combined entities that typically emerge become much larger, thereby enhancing the value of a seller's ownership over time.

Individual Buyers

An individual buyer is generally someone a firm brings in from the outside as a buyer, though it could be someone from within who's been groomed as a successor. When larger advisory firms attempt to make these sales, it's usually to a group of individuals and is typically done over time. In smaller firms—with annual revenues less than $300,000—these transactions occur without much fanfare and are often facilitated by a broker-dealer or a business broker such as FP Transitions. In theory, individual buyers do not pay as much as institutional buyers, who have a financial or strategic motivation. Unfortunately, we've observed that many individual buyers lack experience, objectivity, and sophistication in making deals, which often results in their overpaying for a practice or structuring a deal

The Greater-Fool Theory

WHENEVER THE MARKETPLACE for businesses is active, sellers hope to find someone who will validate the greater-fool theory, which proposes that an unsophisticated or uncertain buyer will pay the highest price, based on the belief that because of his superior intellect he will transform a depleted oil well into a gusher.

Foolish Theories

Greater-fool theory. The theory that it is possible to make money by buying securities, whether overvalued or not, and later selling them at a profit, because there will always be someone (a bigger fool) who is willing to pay the higher price.

From Investopedia. When acting in accordance with the greater-fool theory, an investor buys questionable securities not with any regard to their quality, but with the hope of quickly selling them off to another investor (the greater fool), who might also be hoping to flip them quickly. Unfortunately, speculative bubbles burst eventually, leading to a rapid depreciation in share price due to the sell-off.

that benefits the seller in disproportion to the real value of the practice.

The mistake most of these buyers make is failing to think through in advance what they expect to accomplish with an acquisition, how much autonomy the acquired business should have, and how it will ensure synergy among the organizations. Problems are inevitable when banks, accounting firms, and law firms enter into the advisory business, because they do not always fully understand the nuances of the business and what the real economic drivers are. What's more, they often fail to anticipate the sticky cultural challenges that surface with such an acquisition, and they may not have the patience to stay the course. That doesn't mean selling to a bank or CPA firm is a bad idea; it just means that the challenges can make the transaction unfulfilling unless these issues are anticipated and addressed appropriately.

All of these buyers—financial, strategic, and individual—have
their places in the market and for different reasons can be appealing
as buyers. The goal of the seller should be to build a business that all
three types of buyers would seriously consider purchasing, thereby
creating a form of competitive bidding. Although the sale of a business is often a discrete process, whenever a seller can create multiple
bidders, the opportunity to maximize value increases.

Roll-up Firms

A roll-up is a technique used to consolidate a number of similar firms
in a fragmented marketplace. A fragmented marketplace can occur in
an industry when it comprises a number of small enterprises—with
few if any dominant companies—that are experiencing cost pressures
or are characterized by an aging population of owners. Roll-ups of
fragmented industries have occurred in such diverse businesses as car
dealerships, funeral homes, medical practices, and even accounting
firms to a degree. Under these conditions, the individual companies
merge in an attempt to transform smaller, private businesses into a
larger, more profitable one that eventually goes public—at least in
theory. The main appeal of such roll-ups is the promise of a public
offering, sale, or some liquidity event whereby owners can cash out
on a majority of their assets.

Even during the 1980s and 1990s there were buyers—firms
such as United Asset Management—that targeted larger investment managers for acquisition. There are also firms positioned
as consolidators, or roll-up firms, in the lower end of the investment-management and financial-advisory businesses. To owners
of smaller financial-planning practices, a roll-up offers a chance to
capitalize a portion of the value of their firm and gain liquidity on
their investment.

Typically, a roll-up firm will purchase a majority stake in the
acquired business and leave the owner in place to operate the business
under a management contract. Roll-up firms approaching smaller
practices will generally have a formulaic approach to valuation, with
the value based on some percentage of revenue, EBOC (earnings
before owner's compensation), or on EBITDA (earnings before

interest, taxes, depreciation, and amortization). They rarely use the traditional valuation methodologies described earlier in this book. Generally, an agreed-on portion of the transaction is paid in cash, with the remainder of the purchase price paid in the stock of the acquiring firm, in anticipation of an eventual IPO. Under the terms of the management contract, before receiving any distributions, the seller agrees first to make cash distributions to the roll-up firm based on a percentage of revenue or earnings, on a specified schedule. The seller is usually expected to stay with the company for some time.

Like any sale, a roll-up alternative should be examined closely. The key questions to ask when evaluating a roll-up opportunity include:

♦ What other companies have been rolled into this organization and is my business compatible with them?
♦ How much is the stock portion of the deal worth?
♦ What is the deal worth if the stock offering doesn't materialize?
♦ What are the tax consequences of the transaction?
♦ Who bears the risk and who gets the money according to the terms of the deal?
♦ Would I invest in this roll-up firm as part of my investment portfolio if I had cash available to invest?
♦ What alternatives to this roll-up are available?

The Bank as Buyer

Even advisers who would rather get root canal treatment done without anesthesia than work for a bank can be seduced by what looks like a large purchase price. Advisers often brag about offers from banks, ranging anywhere from three to five times the practice's annual revenues. Yet, under closer scrutiny, we see that as much as half of the purchase price is usually held back in these deals and tied to future performance. What's more, the currency for the purchase is often bank stock, not cash. Stock, especially if it's restricted or closely held, should be discounted by as much as 50 percent from its stated value when considered as part of the buyout.

Since the turn of the century, banks have been among the most active buyers of financial-advisory firms: both big banks such as Harris Bank, which acquired Sullivan Bruyette Speros & Blayney and

MyCFO, and little banks like Suislaw Valley Bank in Oregon, which bought Carter & Carter, are in the game. Sometimes financial institutions really do pay a premium over what the market will offer for such acquisitions, because they have a strategic motivation to expand their product line and increase their noninterest income. But can these deals actually work?

The short answer is, "Yes, they can." Banks can be a great merger partner, primarily because of their resources. But they don't always work. When the acquisitions do fail, it's often because the merging companies neglected to address the strategic, cultural, compensation, and integration issues that coincide with any merger. Ideally, these issues should be addressed before completing the deal. At the very least, addressing them should be a priority during the six months following the merger.

Seller Beware

Banks are notorious for following the herd. When they see their competitors introduce a new business concept, a mad rush to follow ensues. As a result, the impulse to merge with an advisory firm may be more reactive than strategic and it's important that a seller validate the solidity of the bank's motivation before proceeding.

In consulting with banks that have entered the financial-advisory business, we've seen some common institutional problems that can hinder success:

♦ The bank's financial-planning operations often lack critical mass. Because the advisory business is so foreign to a bank's leadership, the tendency is to start small. In an effort to manage risk, it may acquire a solo or small practice. However, many of these practices are already at capacity. These firms do not have the resources to respond to the bank's leads or even time to develop the internal relationships that are essential for growing revenues.

♦ A bank typically has no plan or feedback loop to expand banking clients into financial-advisory clients. Do the bank's customers truly come close to being the target clients the adviser seeks? Would those customers be comfortable asking for financial advice from the bank or its subsidiaries? Once compatibility is determined, both sides need to develop an action plan, accountability, and process for pursuing and managing relationships, as well as determining who gets paid for what.

Defining Success

During a merger transition, the leadership of both organizations should dedicate time for organized strategic planning. They must resolve questions surrounding client characteristics as well as which products and services to offer and why. They'll need to agree on goals and identify resource gaps that challenge the achievement of those goals. And they'll need to define the steps and designate accountability for moving the organization incrementally closer to its goals during the 12 months that follow.

It can take up to three years for an organized merger to meet the expectations of both parties; without a mutually established business and strategic plan, it will take far longer. Perhaps the biggest strategic issue that both the bank and the adviser need to resolve is how they define success. Will it be measured by the expansion of services to existing bank customers? Or by building a new financial-services brand in the market? How much weight should be given to return on equity? Or to an increased share of wallet? What measure will the adviser use: Liquidity? Market presence? Better management or more leads? Measures of success will help both parties direct the right resources to ensure a happy relationship.

Compensation

Compensation is another major obstacle to making a merger work. Compensation conflicts often arise when the newly acquired adviser makes more than the president of the bank. (Indeed, banks pay notoriously low salaries all the way to the top.) Whether it's ego or pay equity that gets in the way, the adviser's pay is frequently a cause of friction. More often, the tension surrounding compensation results from a lack of clarity regarding what the adviser and his team are getting paid to do. Is it production? Management? Giving advice? Portfolio management?

Surprisingly, these issues frequently are not resolved until after the price and terms of the acquisition have been negotiated, or in some cases, not until after the merger has been completed. How much the adviser will be paid under the new arrangement and how the profits of this new unit will be distributed can have a substantial impact on the overall economics of the deal. Clearly, the total compensation for all the adviser principals involved must be incorporated into the financial models from the beginning.

We recommend that after the advisory firm has aligned its organization to fit the agreed-on strategy, the parties set the compensation for each position. Incentive plans, benefit plans, and other factors that normally count toward an employee's reward should all be included. The bank may argue for lower levels of compensation to the adviser and his team because of a high purchase price. Seen in the proper context, that can easily be resolved. If the compensation model has been incorporated into the valuation analysis, both parties should focus on the right numbers. The bank will measure its return on equity from its income distribution from the advisory subsidiary as well as from the adviser's contribution to bank product sales or referrals such as those for loans back to the parent. The question becomes how these various revenue streams should be monitored and how the people producing these returns should be rewarded.

The bank may be concerned that the advisers, having been paid so much up front in the acquisition, will have little incentive to continue to drive the business forward. Because most such mergers involve the adviser principals staying with the firm for a considerable time, the merger is usually a growth strategy for the advisers, not an exit strategy. Consequently, the bank is likely to take care to have earnout clauses based on performance dictate the net purchase price. Although such terms are certainly appropriate, advisers should be careful to distinguish between the total buyout price and compensation for their labor. After all, the adviser's future task is adding additional value to the firm, and he should be paid accordingly.

Culture Shock

Perhaps the biggest hurdle in a bank-advisory merger is the problem of conflicting cultures. It's better, of course, if each side tries to understand the other's values, but the reality is that in most cases the advisers will eventually need to adapt to the parent culture of the bank. Although it's possible the larger entity—the bank in virtually all cases—will adopt some of the best elements of the advisory firm, it's far more likely that the advisory firm is going to have to do most of the bending.

Part of this bending comes from the reality that large organizations such as banks, with relatively rigid structures, have protocols on how they do virtually everything—from whom they hire to how they make decisions and where they focus resources. It's often difficult for independent advisers, once the biggest kids in their own sandbox, to find themselves having to share their toys with bigger kids in a much bigger playground. Such a new institutional decision-making process will seem glacial for the adviser who comes from an entrepreneurial environment. Issues such as coping with this kind of bureaucracy become more challenging if the adviser's "champion" within the bank—the person who pushed hardest for the merger to happen—does not end up being responsible for managing the new advisory affiliate after the merger, or worse yet, leaves the bank.

Advisers would be wise to spend time talking to principals in other firms about their experiences of having merged with a bank, as well as to employees who joined a bank from another company. Don't expect employees of a bank to show all the dirty laundry; nevertheless, asking them about their transitional experiences and how the bank compares with their old planning firm or with other companies can be revealing. The goal is to get a better understanding of how to work successfully within that particular institution.

Nearly everyone has something derisive to say about the politics and bureaucracy within larger companies like banks (these antics are brilliantly captured in the Dilbert comics). Certainly, if the parties are bogged down in negatives, the merger will not work. In a larger sense, company politics are also about the art of getting along with coworkers in any setting—it's something all people must achieve, whether with clients, vendors, staff, friends, or even children. Position and leverage often dictate who prevails when conflicts arise, but in a respectful culture, there is always opportunity for compromise.

All these problems seem tactical, but their roots are strategic. Before merging with a bank, understand what the vision is for the firm, what resources the bank will commit to realizing that vision, and how the bank defines success. Any merger can be made to look

good on paper, especially when it adds up to high six or seven figures, but between the idea and the reality, there is plenty of room
for failure.

The Accountant as Buyer

Accountants typically merge with advisory firms rather than buy
them, although there are exceptions. In some cases, the accountants
buy a stake in the practice so that the advisers in the firm can continue to see their equity build. In the case of a more modest financial-advisory practice, they'll recruit the adviser as an employee and
integrate him or her into the accounting firm's wealth-management
practice.

Either way, it's no secret among independent financial advisers
that accounting firms, a traditional source of client referrals, have
been steadily making inroads into the advice business. The AICPA
has been seeing a mad rush for the personal financial specialist (PFS)
designation, which can be conferred only on certified public accountants. The number of broker-dealers dedicated to the CPA market,
such as First Global and H.D. Vest, is growing. Many advisory
broker-dealers like FNIC and Raymond James have successful CPA
partnering programs, and platform providers like BAM and Terra
Financial continue to attract high-end CPA advisers.

Bad Advice

Although the number of CPAs entering the advisory business has
increased, accounting firms have not made as much of an impact
in terms of assets gathered as one would expect. Many CPAs find
that branching into financial advice is not the transitional slam
dunk originally anticipated. In response, many accounting firms
have been adding units to do financial planning and staffing them
with—you guessed it—genuine financial planners. This approach
promises to be much more effective, but it still presents considerable
challenges to both the CPAs and the financial planners with whom
they partner.

The effectiveness of CPAs in financial planning can be clearly
seen in the results of the *2004 FPA Financial Performance Study*,

produced by Moss Adams, which examined the operating performance of participants in the financial-advisory profession, including CPAs:

♦ CPA advisers on average generate $234,000 per professional, compared with $391,000 per professional at elite ensemble advisory firms.

♦ CPA advisers generate $120,000 per staff person on average, compared with $244,000 per staff person at elite ensemble firms.

♦ CPA advisers generate an average of $3,890 in revenue per client from wealth management, compared with $6,690 generated at elite ensemble firms.

♦ CPA advisers on average generate $109,000 of income per partner from wealth management, compared with $327,000 per partner within elite ensemble firms.

There are exceptions to these averages—for example, Plante & Moran, a regional accounting firm in Michigan, has more than $4 billion in assets under management—but the figures show that most CPA firms who have gotten into the advisory business have, for the most part, done poorly. Their numbers are below those of elite ensemble firms in all regards, and the tension that builds up between the accountants and the nontraditional practitioners in the office often becomes acute. Most accountants who have not brought financial-advisory professionals into their practices are merely harvesting opportunities when their busy season has passed, rather than sustaining a focus on the advisory business.

Accounting for Failure

Why haven't accountants been more successful in the financial-advisory business? The reasons are complex: the skills needed often aren't there, the strategies required up front are half-baked or absent entirely, and when it comes to wealth management, many accountants have a problem with their image—and their attitude. When the CPA profession began entertaining the possibility of entering the adviser market two decades ago, most of the interest came from accounting firms with client bases consisting substantially of business owners. After all, these were clients with substantial net worth and complex planning issues that would challenge and therefore reward advisers who could combine expertise in tax, estate planning, and business finance with classic wealth management.

As it turned out, however, most business owners had neither the liquidity nor the inclination for comprehensive wealth management. Consequently, most of the relatively few wealth-management clients that accounting firms attracted came accidentally from their tax-preparation work. When a business owner became liquid through the sale of an enterprise, he often had difficulty viewing the CPA as a wealth manager. The owners tended to seek alternative assistance for allocation of their investable assets.

It appears from the operating performance of CPAs who've entered into the financial-advisory market that most have taken what might be described as an opportunistic approach: they viewed the sale of insurance products, annuities or mutual funds as a quick-buck opportunity at a low cost, allowing them to capitalize on existing relationships. This approach creates many problems, but critical among them are the following:

1. **Lack of a coherent strategy:** When a CPA firm and an advisory practice fail to commit to the development of a coherent vision for the business or agree on timing and accountability for implementation, the relationship usually falters or fails completely.

2. **Incompatible culture:** When it comes to nontraditional business, accountants break down into three camps: the early adapters, the wait-and-seers, and the never-wills. The best mix for a CPA firm is to have about one-third of the partners in each camp, but often the never-wills dominate. They see financial advice as all risk and the rewards as pie-in-the-sky. In their minds, expanding to financial advice only dilutes the focus of the practice.

3. **No consensus on benchmarks for success:** Measures of success often become a moving target—with both parties feeling confused and misled. If the leadership of the CPA firm and the leadership of the advisory practice can agree, then it becomes easier to understand each party's position. The measures might be related to the number of referrals from one side to the other (referrals should be reciprocal, not one-sided), additional fees generated from tax-preparation

clients, gross profit margin, operating profit margin, and a variety of productivity measures.

4. **Lack of linkage between financial-planning and accounting services: How integrated are the two practices?** Do both parties use a comprehensive approach to serving clients, drawing on each other's expertise, or is the financial planning viewed merely as an asset collector? Is there a protocol and process in place for involving clients with professionals from both disciplines? Is there a framework for taking an integrated approach with clients, for example, when both parties are focused on the closely held business market? Some estate-planning and business-transition issues naturally fall within the realm of the CPA, and some personal financial-planning, liquidity, and wealth-management issues naturally fall within the realm of the financial adviser.

5. **A failure to systematically harvest the tax database:** The real opportunity for business growth in this arrangement lies in the data from the firm's tax-return database and the opportunity that information creates to go back to clients to discuss their situation. Most accountants do not go back to the tax returns once they've been completed and filed, but in reality they're chockful of insights.

6. **Failure to systematically survey the firm's clients on their wants, needs, and perceptions:** Firms that regularly survey their clients in a format that's structured and positioned correctly tend to build longer-lasting relationships and harvest many more opportunities than those who don't. An excellent firm in Toronto—Advisor Impact—conducts such surveys inexpensively and effectively.

7. **Failure to view non-CPAs as equals:** Many CPAs do not see financial advisers as equals in terms of capability and value to the clients. "Advisers are just trying to sell them something," suspects the CPA. It's often a frustrating, absolute truth that the nontraditional practitioner within a CPA firm will not be valued as highly as a practicing accountant. This doesn't mean financial advisers cannot demand respect for their work or that they alone should assume the burden of making the venture succeed. But an elevated view of financial advisers will come only through demonstrations of excellence on their part.

Getting It Right

If you manage a CPA firm and are contemplating an acquisition, or if you manage an advisory firm and are contemplating merging into an accounting firm, there are some elemental things that you should make part of your early negotiations.

♦ **Define a joint strategy:** The nature of a joint venture is that there is a shared commitment to success. This shared commitment must be fostered. The best beginning is for key partners to agree to a structured process of strategic planning regarding the advisory business and then jointly commit to an action plan. If there's no agreement, the party is not serious about the business.

♦ **Make a commitment:** If an accounting firm is getting into financial planning part-time just to make a few extra bucks, it's better all around that it stay out of the business. To do otherwise is a disservice to clients, who deserve an adviser with a full-time commitment to the discipline. Equally questionable is whether such half measures make for a sound business practice for the accounting firm. Accountants already wear a large, tempting target on their chests; liability exposure is even greater for dabblers. For CPAs to fancy themselves financial advisers merely because they work well with numbers is folly.

♦ **Define the optimal client:** Instead of seeking ready-made opportunity, the CPA firm should identify which clients would be best served by a wealth-management practice and build a needs-based approach to serving them. This includes creating a protocol for approaching them, a process for advising them, and a system for communicating with them—and for the accountant to be in charge of the relationship.

♦ **Create a leveraged business model:** If CPAs are serious about making this a meaningful business line, they need to get away from making it a "hobby business" that relies on one or two people. They should build an organization that will allow the firm to serve clients systematically—similar to an audit or tax practice—and provide a career path for the professionals working within the practice. The leveraged model could be either multidisciplinary to better integrate all of the services of the firm or vertical to allow other resources to be used as needed.

♦ **Align compensation to support the vision for the firm:** Too many CPA firms have a compensation program that reinforces the wrong behavior or is too expensive for the advisory side of the practice. The compensation model should be aligned with the rest of the firm's reward structure but should resolve the questions as to how much is variable versus fixed, how much is paid for sales or referrals versus for service, and how much is tied to the profitability of the overall enterprise.

♦ **Merge with practices compatible with the accounting firm's values, client focus, and quality control:** Accountants can typically merge with an advisory firm rather than buy one outright, because the venture provides the opportunity for both parties to increase their income. But an adviser selling to an accountant may want to have an exit strategy in its operating agreement if it appears that the CPA is giving only lip service to the business model.

Opportunities for CPAs in the financial-advisory business are enormous. Even when independence or conflict issues exist (these arise primarily for firms providing audit services), CPA firms often have many other clients in their stable that would be very suitable candidates for a comprehensive approach to financial planning and wealth management. With an integrated approach, the CPA can actually drive its own billable revenue up when it links financial planning and wealth management to its service offering. The combination drives tax planning, estate planning, and ownership-transition planning. From business owners, the expanded services can generate management-consulting work because the biggest investment these clients have is usually their business, which might not be performing well.

Economics dictate that sooner or later CPAs and advisers will get this model right. The firms that do it sooner, of course, will have a tremendous advantage.

The Individual as Buyer

Although the conclusion is difficult to validate, anecdotal evidence suggests that most financial-advisory firms transfer ownership to other individual advisers. The transaction takes the form of an outright sale or the creation of partners over time.

When adding partners, owners of advisory firms are not typically motivated to maximize value but rather to optimize it. Here's the difference: owners may command a higher price by selling to an outside buyer, but often they're motivated to leave a legacy, ensure continuity of quality service with their clients, and reward employees for their loyalty and commitment while the firm was growing. A good example of this is Blankinship & Foster, a Southern California advisory firm. The two founders of that firm set up a plan to transfer equity to younger partners over a five-year period. This process allowed the older partners to wean themselves from the business, receive a reasonable value for their shares, and provide enough time for the younger partners to learn how to manage and finance the transaction.

An equally common way for individuals to buy an advisory firm is to acquire the practice on some earnout basis, wherein they pay a percentage of the future gross revenue for a defined period of time. Many advisers see such transactions as a quicker way to build their practices than more conventional marketing. They're buying into an enterprise that has recurring cash flow, a built-in client base with individuals who already value the service, and, in some cases, a staff to help in the transition. Often, the seller will commit to a transition period to ensure most of the clients come over to the buyer of the practice.

Selling to individuals rather than institutions allows sellers to influence the processes and services being offered and, in some cases, allows them greater flexibility in terms of how long they may continue to work in the business themselves. However, individuals usually do not have the resources to pay maximum value, and because such deals are structured on an earnout, they tend to carry more risk. An earnout ties the ultimate purchase price to what actually transfers. If the buyer doesn't pay much of a down payment, then the seller assumes most of the risk in this transaction.

That said, a large proportion of advisory firms are not large enough to command the attention of a bank or consolidator, so individual buyers become the best marketplace. In such transactions, individual buyers should be careful to apply the valuation concepts described earlier in this book and be conscious of the tax treatment their deal will require.

Obviously, one of the downsides of an individual sale, whether by an internal or external buyer, is that such buyers often can't pay as much as institutional buyers. We believe that owners of practices who wish to avoid institutional buyers should be grooming at least two internal successors for every owner of the practice. This approach will allow a sale to groups of two or more who collectively may be better able to afford the purchase price. This preparation also provides for continuity when the owner is ready to execute the sale. In other words, it provides a more liquid market and gives the owners a bona fide option for selling if they choose not to go the strategic or financial buyer route.

Ultimately, the question of fit is what matters most for both buyers and sellers regardless of the identity of the purchaser or the size of the transaction. Given rising costs in the industry, pressure on compliance, a growing talent shortage in the advisory business, and other elements, the appeal of making acquisitions in this business can be questionable. But the rising demand for advisory services, the growing transition of wealth, and the desire of individuals to work with trusted advisers also make this a compelling business.

The advisory business has tremendous appeal for both buyers and sellers. In spite of the pitfalls and challenges, it's a business that has proved to be rewarding for its founders and can be equally rewarding for its successors

Opportunities for Buyers

Sellers have several avenues to choose from. But what are the options for buyers of advisory firms? Again the economics of advisory firms, with increasing strain caused by regulatory compliance and the need to have resources dedicated to this effort, as well as the aging adviser population provide opportunities.

Depending on which resource you use, somewhere between 15,000 and 150,000 potential targets are ripe for acquisition. The challenge for the buyer is to discern a business from a book of business, that is, an advisory firm from a book of business owned by a registered representative of a broker-dealer. In terms of potential assets to acquire, the marketplace is huge. As part of a research project

FIGURE 17.1 **Sizable Opportunities**

♦ **Broker-dealer–affliated RIAs:** $116 billion

♦ **Middle-market independent RIAs:** $90 billion

♦ **Large investiment managers:** $561 billion

♦ **Wealth-management firms:** $232 billion

Moss Adams was engaged to conduct in 2005, we estimated that as much as $1 trillion of assets was being managed or supervised in four key segments of the advisory world: broker-dealer–affiliated RIAs, middle-market independent RIAs, large investment-management firms, and large wealth-management practices (see *Figure 17.1*).

In an update in 2005 on the study on the future of the industry by Undiscovered Managers (published in 2000), Sharon Weinberg, the managing director of J.P. Morgan/Fleming evaluated the size and characteristics of the RIA world. It showed a much smaller universe of firms with more than $1 million in annual revenues, but an impressive list nonetheless. In J.P. Morgan's analysis, there were 810 RIAs with between $1 million and $3 million of revenue, 139 firms between $3 million and $5 million, 23 firms between $5 million and 8 million, and 88 firms over $8 million. Weinberg also noted in her study that just 15 percent of all RIAs manage 85 percent of the assets in this category, which demonstrates the size of the opportunity. One of Weinberg's interesting observations is that most of the firms with revenues between $3 million and $8 million in revenues are mature and their owners may not have prepared well for their eventual transition. But such practices make up the sweet spot of firms targeted by banks, roll-up firms, and other wealth managers who wish to consolidate.

Of course, there are literally thousands of registered reps associated with independent broker-dealers, wirehouses, and regional firms, who manage billions in assets for millions of households.

These smaller practices represent an opportunity for buyers who want to bulk up their client list and add assets, assuming buyers can find them and coax them into selling—or in the case of the wirehouse brokers, pry them away from these firms, given the tight constraints on moving assets out of employer-based relationships.

Although the choices vary depending on which type of advisory enterprise buyers are seeking, the market potential across the board is tremendous. The difficulty is in how to find motivated buyers. Sellers try to be discreet and often are reluctant to use listing services. Some will engage investment bankers, but it appears that many transactions occur as the result of buyers searching their target markets, winnowing the list of firms in that market to the ideal firms, and then approaching candidates directly.

The key to success for both buyers and sellers is to be clear about who the ideal partner in the transaction would be. The search can be long and tedious and, in some cases, expensive. But the opportunity for sellers to maximize value and for buyers to build a larger, more sustainable enterprise is huge. Demographics and economics in the advisory business are changing the way buyers and sellers evaluate their options. But as with any industry entering into a maturing phase in its life cycle, the market for transactions will likely be active for some time to come.

18. BUILDING VALUE: THE FIRM THAT SELLS ITSELF
The Marketplace

THE MOTIVATIONS FOR considering a sale or merger can be varied and compelling, but we're concerned that owners of wealth-management and investment-advisory firms will let emotion rather than logic rule their decisions. Clearly, sophisticated (and some not-so-sophisticated) buyers see tremendous growth opportunities in the wealth-management and investment-management business, given economists' predictions of a pending tsunami of liquid wealth over the next 20 years as baby boomers retire and die. As a result, buyers are offering extraordinary prices, but it's questionable whether the average or less-than-average firms will command these multiples going forward.

No doubt there will always be a market for well-managed firms. But firms caught in the limbo between being too big and too small, that are overly dependent on one owner, that struggle with weak profitability or growth, or that have an aging client base will likely see values decline over time. The fork in the road for many advisers is clear. Should they choose the option of managing and maintaining the business they have, or should they structure a business that will give prospective buyers an opportunity for material growth after acquisition? Neither decision is necessarily wrong, but those who choose not to invest will need to be prepared for lower valuations. By understanding this dynamic, owners can make clear choices about what they need to do to build value for their firms.

A Question of Readiness

A decision about an appropriate transition will inevitably come, either voluntarily or involuntarily. In the meantime, preparing your business strategically, organizationally, and financially will give you more options. The optimal strategy is one that allows you to achieve certain goals, recognizing that you may have a set of restrictions such as the desire to remain small, to protect the jobs of key employees, or to leave a legacy. Adhering to these restrictions, of course, may mean that you don't get the highest price.

If your goal is to maximize value, you will need to execute strategies that will help your practice to demonstrate strong growth in revenue and profits within a business model that can sustain that growth. If your goal is not to maximize value but rather to optimize it in order to achieve certain other objectives through the sale, it's important to position your firm so that an individual buyer from within the firm, whom you've groomed, can be almost as appealing as an institutional buyer, who may offer you more money but perhaps less fulfillment. You may still choose to sell to the highest bidder, but at least you'll know you've considered all your options with both your clients and your staff in mind.

Many advisers have a choice of both internal and external buyers, and they appear to be in a tug of war with themselves as to which course to follow. If they sell to an outside buyer, can they get the best price? If they sell internally to members of their team, can they better ensure continuity of their practice and the care of their clients? In preparing the guidebook titled *Succession Planning Strategies for the Financial Planner* for the Financial Planning Association, David Goad, president of Succession Planning Consultants in Newport Beach, California, received some interesting responses from financial advisers regarding choices they're contemplating. In this sample, an incredible 66 percent indicated a preference toward an internal transition (see *Figure 18.1*).

If you extrapolate this response over the entire population of financial advisers, you'll see it has profound implications for the industry. Where is the talent going to come from to accommodate this preference for internal transitions? And how will these individuals be able

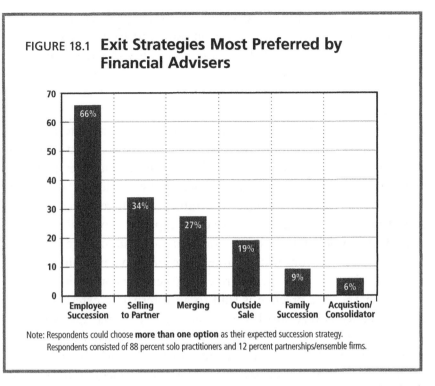

FIGURE 18.1 **Exit Strategies Most Preferred by Financial Advisers**

Note: Respondents could choose **more than one option** as their expected succession strategy. Respondents consisted of 88 percent solo practitioners and 12 percent partnerships/ensemble firms.

Source: 2005 survey by Succession Planning Consultants, Newport Beach, CA.

to pay the high prices owners are asking for their practices? Individual firms can shape their own solutions, but such transitions will require planning. Advisers who are contemplating an internal succession will need to look at three key transition issues in particular:

1. Client succession
2. Management transition
3. Ownership transition

Client Succession

In a professional-service business, success is determined by how well relationships are managed. A vital question to address in selling a practice is whether those clients will continue to be managed well or even continue their relationship with the adviser who acquires the firm. Key to determining the outcome will be the buyer's capacity to handle these relationships and the buyer's experience and expertise, as well as the chemistry between the buyer and the clients. One advantage to grooming successor client-service professionals is that you can observe and coach people on how best to work with those clients, a process that helps to ensure continuity of the relationship once the business is sold.

Management Transition

The second critical element in the effectiveness of an internal successor is management transition. Most people who are attracted to financial planning are not interested or skilled as managers; yet, to run a practice well, certain "muscles" need to be developed. To ensure continuity of the business once you transition out, you need to have confidence that your successors have the capability to think strategically, deal appropriately with operational issues, and manage the business wisely. Again, committing time and energy to developing people inside the firm to serve in these roles helps ensure continuity regardless of whether the practice is sold to an internal or external buyer. If the practice is very small, the buyer's ability to manage both the clients and the practice is especially important because the purchase of the practice will likely be completed over time, with the final price based on how many clients stick and how the business performs (see chapter 10, "Coming to Terms: Getting All the Way to Yes").

Ownership Transition

Ownership transition is the third and final element of the transition process. Although it's not only possible but likely that many practices will transfer without their owners having addressed either the client succession or management transition issues, failure to pay attention to those first two steps can result in a lower value. Some practices are better prepared to be transferred to a new owner simply because clients are prepared for the change, as are the staff and leadership of the practice. That said, we find many sellers of advisory firms are under the mistaken impression that all practices sell for the same multiple regardless of quality. The reality is quite different, and that is the beauty of effective succession planning. Your business is one of the few investments whose value you can influence through your management actions.

Transferable Value

The key to raising the value of your business is to deploy a process that will make that value transferable. When you give yourself enough lead time, you can transform the quality of your business and change the way prospective buyers view it. The tighter your management process and the more consistent your results, the less risky the acquisition of your company will seem. This translates into meaningful multiples and higher values.

Nevertheless, when eager shoppers approach advisers, almost without exception the first question prospective sellers ask is "What's the price?" That's an important question—and, ultimately, the right question—but it's usually the wrong question to ask *first*. Of course, it's a difficult question to answer, because each firm is unique and has its own value drivers, and each buyer has his own motivation for a merger or acquisition, which may affect the price and terms of the offer.

Valuable Preliminaries

Advisers must step away from the excitement of being courted for a moment and ask questions more relevant than "What's the value of my firm?" Key personal questions need to be addressed first:

◆ What will I receive beyond price in terms of future compensation and future opportunities?

◆ If I sell to this buyer, will I be required to stay with the firm?

◆ If I'm not required to stay, what will I do?

◆ How much money do I want and need from the sale?

◆ If the buyer wants me to stay, for how long will it be, in what role, and for how much additional pay?

◆ Is the timing right for a sale, in light of the stage I've reached in my career?

◆ Will the sale allow me to focus on my unique abilities and interests? Or will it force me to function in a role I won't enjoy—for example, managing and growing a bigger business?

◆ What is my motivation for selling? Liquidity? Taking some chips off the table? Boredom? Burnout?

Important business questions must also be addressed:

- ◆ What is the buyer's motivation for wanting to acquire my business?
- ◆ If the buyer is a consolidator, how compatible with my own are the other firms it's rolling up?
- ◆ If the buyer is offering stock as part of the offer, is this a company that I want to invest in?
- ◆ Will the sale or merger help me solve my internal management and client-succession plan or does it deflect the problem onto somebody else?
- ◆ If I'm going to stay active in the business and the business is growing, does the deal make economic sense?

If you're contemplating a transition within five years, it's a good idea to begin thinking about what that afterlife will look like and how the business transition will help you get there. Will it provide the cash or the resources to grow even further? Will it allow you to focus on the things you want to do from that point forward?

As you think about these questions, you can take steps to enhance the transferability and therefore the value of your practice to prospective buyers. Chapter 1, "Defining Value: Uncovering True Worth," can serve as a good organizing principle for building value. *Figure 18.2* frames the issue clearly.

The formula for determining value via the capitalization of cash flow approach has three basic elements: cash flow (the numerator) divided by the discount rate minus the growth rate. The discount rate is another way to express "risk rate," meaning the degree of uncertainty surrounding the likelihood that the business will achieve the cash flow number. The growth rate refers to the long-term rate of expected growth in cash flow. In management terms, it's clear that if you take steps to enhance cash flow (going forward), minimize risk or uncertainty, and build a business that can sustain a reasonable level of growth for a long time, you will increase the value of the business.

Having looked at hundreds of advisory firms throughout the United States, Canada, and Australia, we've observed that the elite-performing firms have six distinguishing characteristics that

FIGURE 18.2 **Capitalization of Cash Flow Calculation**

$$\text{Value} = \frac{\textbf{Adjusted Cash Flow}}{\textbf{Capitalization Rate}}$$

(Discount Rate – Growth Rate)

contribute to enhanced cash flow, lower risk, and a sustainable growth rate:

1. Clear positioning
2. A systematic approach to operations
3. A human capital plan that's aligned with its business strategy
4. Effective financial management
5. Built-in leverage and capacity
6. Systematic client feedback

It's no coincidence that these are also the firms that tend to command the highest values, because they tie together dynamics that make their businesses more transferable. As an owner, consider how you might address these issues in your practice to begin building value.

Clear Positioning

Clear positioning means having a well-defined idea of who your optimal client is and what your client-service experience should be. These elements are the essence of your business strategy. That understanding provides a framework for how you will invest in your business in sales, marketing, operations, staffing, and service offering. Strategy is about deciding on the basic value you want to deliver to clients and the type of clients you want to serve. Every firm needs to clearly define both.

Sound strategy begins with the right goals. If you do not have the right goals to direct your efforts to begin with, you'll quickly move to actions that will undermine your strategy. Strategy should also have continuity and not have to be continually reinvented. Changing direction makes it difficult for your firm to grasp what the strategy is and for clients to know what your firm stands for.

The following steps can help you develop a sound strategy:

1. **Understand and evaluate choices:** Define your strategic choices and prioritize them in a way that builds on your firm's capabilities, responds to your market, and differentiates your firm from the competition.

2. **Focus:** Apply strategic questions to selecting your optimal client and building your client-service experience.

3. **Assess the current situation:** Perform a SWOT analysis—that is, determine the firm's strengths, weaknesses, opportunities, and threats. Use the analysis to determine what you need to invest in to build value in your business.

4. **Execute:** Brainstorm ways to achieve goals; select the best ideas; identify appropriate measurements; and create SMART objectives—that is, specific, measurable, attainable, related to overall objective, and time sensitive. Finally, employ resources to implement the SMART objectives.

As discussed in *Practice Made Perfect: The Discipline of Business Management for Financial Advisers* (Bloomberg Press, 2005), we've identified eight leading strategies that financial advisers use to differentiate their businesses. None of them by itself necessarily leads to a higher value, but the existence of a clear strategy does. That's because the strategy gives advisers focus. This results in greater efficiency in operations, effectiveness in client service, and enhanced profitability.

Systematic Operations Process

A systematic approach to operations gives firms the ability to monitor capacity at each step, budget and plan for upcoming workloads, and seek additional resources if demand exceeds capacity. In a study titled *Mission Possible,* which Moss Adams conducted for Pershing Advisor Solutions in 2005, we observed that advisory practices go through three major transformations in which they need to deconstruct then reconstruct their operations in order to evolve with their changing practice. These transformations are often a function of size measured in revenue, but they're also a function of the number of clients the business is serving. At about $300,000 of revenue, again at about $2 million, and yet again at $5 million, advisers experience financial distress and a dramatic change in their span of control—with both clients and staff.

Expressed in nonfinancial terms, the three stages of transformation are

1. when an individual adviser or small firm hires the first few administrative staff;
2. when the firm realizes that it needs to add capabilities and expertise to its operations;
3. when the firm turns into a large organization, with departmentalized expertise, running multiple processes at the same time.

Clearly, the importance and strategic value of operations—meaning everything from client intake to execution of the plan, to trading and reporting, to compliance and financial management—is rising for many advisers. However, we have observed through our studies and through detailed interviews with advisers at 41 leading advisory practices that their processes can't keep pace with client demands and firm growth. Most of these advisers tell us they are mainly reactive and not strategic about how they address operations issues, and that their staff is overwhelmed.

Ultimately, growth-oriented advisory firms need to think more strategically about how they're integrating their technology and their administrative staff into their client-service experience. This process begins with several key acknowledgments:

♦ **Technology does not drive firms; people do:** Technology must be combined with the right people—those with a specialty in operations and the skills and experience to lead in that critical area. The heart of the challenge is for firms to build a human capital plan that enables them to maximize the technology applications.

♦ **More-sophisticated technology requires more-sophisticated staff:** An administrative staff with minimal training can no longer handle the complex applications coming out of the industry's research and development departments. Firms must consistently and continually upgrade the knowledge and skills of their operations staff in tandem with evolving technology.

♦ **Your investment in operations talent will affect your bottom line and growth prospects:** Attitudes toward operations staff should change from expense reduction to investing in talent and experience.

♦ **The goal is not to manage overhead; the goal is quality:** Too often, when management focuses on operations, the goals are how to minimize costs or reduce overhead. The emphasis should be given to quality, consistency, and safety. No matter how low their costs, no firm can be successful without maintaining the highest quality of client service and regulatory compliance. Neither is possible without a culture of quality in operations.

Ultimately, the holy grail of operations is not best-of-class technology but rather the inspired leadership of an experienced and dedicated chief operations officer (COO) supported by a talented team of operations specialists. Currently, the biggest weakness in advisory firms is the lack of leadership and career track in operations. Turnover is high, and the price of experienced talent is only increasing. With their energy focused on client relationships and business development, principals rarely have the time or direct experience to devote to operational issues. The elite firms are changing this dynamic by recruiting experienced operations people to help them systematize their approach so that the advisory staff can remain focused on client service. (See *Figure 18.3.*)

Human Capital and the Business Strategy

The term *human capital* usually is associated with large organizations, but even small advisory firms have this asset. The moment you hire an administrative assistant, you have human capital. For many advisory firms today, the size of the staff can be substantial, growing as the business grows. Growth is important, but the most critical concept in the development of a human capital plan is to ensure its alignment with the business plan (for more on this subject, see *Practice Made Perfect*).

FIGURE 18.3 **Capitalization of Cash Flow Calculation**

Is it time to change your approach to operations?

1. Have you reached or are you nearing the critical revenue marks—$300,000, $2 million, and $5 million?

2. Are most advisers at or near capacity?

3. Is there low morale and high turnover among operations staff?

4. Are you frustrated with your technology or vendor support?

5. Has your overhead increased?

6. Was your last review of operations more than two years ago?

A human capital plan addresses issues such as a career path for staff, compensation schemes that reinforce the right behavior, a partner track for prospective successors, and an evaluation process that allows leaders of firms to counsel and develop employees of the firm.

The reason human capital has become a buzzword in the profession and such a critical issue for advisory firms trying to build value is that advisers don't have time to manage their businesses *and* serve clients. The staff is becoming inefficient because of the lack of clarity in defining their roles and the overwhelming demands for their attention. As a result, firms lack capacity to grow. In many cases, turnover among staff is high because employees know it's a tight market for talent and often they can name their price to a new employer.

What's more, hiring good people is becoming an even greater challenge for those who've been in the business for a while, because new generations of employees have a different attitude and approach to work than their predecessors have. An article in *USA Today* in November 2005 noted five characteristics of the Generation Y workers—traits that seem to irritate many owners of practices today:

1. **Highly competitive standards for themselves:** They aim to work faster and better than other workers.
2. **High expectations of their employers:** They want fair and direct managers who are highly engaged in employees' professional development.
3. **Ongoing learning opportunities:** They seek out creative challenges and view colleagues as vast resources from whom to gain knowledge.
4. **Immediate responsibility:** They want to make an important difference to the firm from day one.
5. **Goal oriented:** They want small goals with tight deadlines so they can build up ownership of tasks.

"They're young, smart, brash," stated *USA Today*. "They want to work, but they don't want work to be their life." Citing research from RainMakerThinking, an organization in New Haven, Connecticut, that studies the behavior of young people, the article suggests the adviser's working relationship with staff is going to have to change. Others in the profession share many of these characteristics, regardless of when they were born, and so understanding these drivers of behavior may help you to create a better structure and process to enhance future value in your business.

A Career Path

When people chafe within the confines of their job, we find that it's frequently because they're not clear on how they're being evaluated or how long they'll need to toil in one particular role before they're given another challenge. This eagerness does not entitle them to be disrespectful to their bosses, but it can help you to recognize that when you hire motivated people and they get restless, they're only doing exactly what you hoped they would do—asking for another challenge.

The question is whether you're prepared to let the employee move up a step or whether such a move threatens or confuses you. It may be that because it took you 15 or 20 years to finally achieve the momentum that comes with recognition as a leading adviser in your community, you're reluctant to share that glory with your underlings for fear it might overshadow your accomplishments. We've encountered this attitude among owners. Indeed, in helping one advisory firm design a compensation plan to help lock in their employees for the long term, we found that the biggest impediment to getting the plan to take root was the resistance of the principals. "These are my clients," the principals reasoned, "so why would I want to share ownership in them?"

Of course, the point of adding staff in the first place is to provide leverage, continuity of practice, enhanced expertise, and a better client-service experience. It's not a question of whose clients they are but rather what kind of business you're trying to build. It's important not to resent staffers who want to be challenged and be an integral part of the business. Frankly, they see no reason to reinvent the wheel anyhow; you already own that patent.

So when it comes to the first action step of harnessing the power of good staff hires, we recommend that you create a career path with measurable expectations. Firms that first offer entry positions requiring new staff to learn the fundamentals of the job and that create metrics to move staff up the ladder tend to keep everyone focused on the goals. We also find that this process tends to vest responsibility in individuals at different levels, provides a framework for learning, and serves to fulfill the expectations of both the staff and the employer. (See *Figure 18.4.*)

Compensation

Aligning human capital to your business strategy also means aligning compensation to the behavior you seek. Although the temptation is strong to pay all new hires on a variable basis so they can earn their keep and minimize your costs while you're developing them, you may not want the result such a pay structure can create. Typically, when individuals are in sales positions, their compensation should be highly variable and short term. When they're in service positions, their compensation should be more fixed, with incentives tied to the result you're seeking, such as minimizing client turnover or increasing client satisfaction. So ask yourself what it is you're hiring them to do. Many new hires in advisory firms are brought in for service roles so that the principals can develop business from among the firm's optimal target clients.

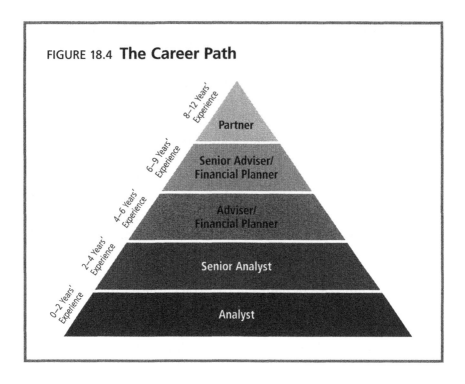

FIGURE 18.4 **The Career Path**

8–12 Years' Experience — Partner

6–9 Years' Experience — Senior Adviser/Financial Planner

4–6 Years' Experience — Adviser/Financial Planner

2–4 Years' Experience — Senior Analyst

0–2 Years' Experience — Analyst

Measuring Performance

Developing human capital requires a regular and systematic perfor-
mance-evaluation process. Ideally, you would be checking in with the
staff regularly, but doing so formally at least twice a year is essential.
This evaluation process allows you to reinforce your expectations,
evaluate how individuals are meeting those expectations, and counsel
them on how they can move up to the next level.

The most important asset of a financial-advisory firm is its talent base. High employee turnover, especially in the service industry,
equates to higher risk and significant costs. Talented people are
retained by encouraging them to invest their time and energy in the
firm, not by issuing legal threats or by overpaying them. Employees
in turn will feel that they can create more value by staying with
the firm than by going elsewhere. What's more, this process allows
you to build a firm that has not only transferable clients but also a
transferable staff.

When you sell a book of business, meaning a client base, you're selling an asset of a business. When you sell a business, you're selling an enterprise and all of its systems, processes, people, structures, and brands. If you choose to build a business and not just an asset to sell, then over time you'll find that investing in good people is as important to enhancing value as acquiring your very best clients.

Financial Management

Throughout this book and in *Practice Made Perfect*, we've emphasized the need to manage both the gross profit margin and the operating profit margin. Even in a world where buyers and sellers are approaching transactions as a multiple of revenue or a multiple of assets under management, the more economic sense the business makes, the more successful the transaction will be for both sides.

In chapter 2 we discussed business analysis and demonstrated the forces that affect both of these margins. The questions for buyers will always be whether the business can ultimately provide a return on investment and whether the profitability is sustainable. The best firms use these metrics to evaluate how they're building value.

The Story the Numbers Tell

If you use the organizing principle that the value of a business equals cash flow divided by capitalization rate (that is, risk minus growth), you'll continually be seeking ways to maximize the bottom line while minimizing uncertainty and enhancing the growth potential of your business. As explained in chapter 2, the ideal financial model for the financial-services industry is:

Revenue

− **Direct expense**

= **Gross profit**

− **Overhead expense**

= **Operating profit**

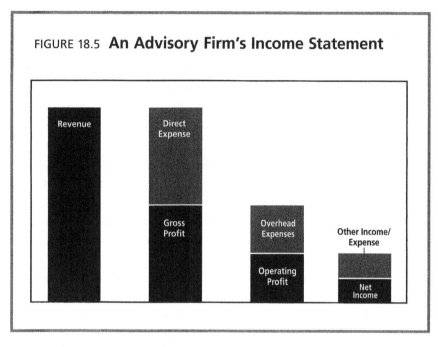

FIGURE 18.5 **An Advisory Firm's Income Statement**

In *Figure 18.5,* the direct expense represents fair compensation for professional labor and the operating profit represents the return to owners after fair compensation. When you subtract direct expense from revenue, you arrive at a gross profit. When you divide gross profit by revenue, you arrive at a gross profit margin.

Managing the gross margin is the single most effective financial-management tool for financial-advisory firms. Cutting overhead costs can provide dramatic results in the short term, but effectively managing gross profitability will produce better long-term results. The following factors affect gross profitability:

♦ Pricing
♦ Productivity
♦ Product or service mix
♦ Client mix

Pricing. Financial advisers have the ability to control fees for assets under management, financial planning, and consulting, and retainers and fees for other services. Although it's important to understand what fees are being charged in the marketplace, having a fee schedule that's in line with your strategy is appropriate. You may have the ability to charge higher fees if your firm is perceived to have more experience or greater technical ability in your niche. To price appropriately, it's essential to understand the costs of servicing the client.

Productivity. Advisers need to manage the productivity of the staff. In chapter 2, we discussed measures of productivity, evaluating productivity trends in the firm itself, and comparing productivity measurements with benchmarks. Ideally, the productivity measurements improve over time and are at least similar to the benchmarks. Managing for productivity is never easy, but the payoff is well worth the effort.

Product or service mix. The type of products and services you provide should fit your strategy and provide profitability. Any products or services you're providing that don't meet those criteria should be outsourced or eliminated so that your focus is not unnecessarily diverted from your goals.

Client mix. After working through your strategy, you'll know who your optimal clients are and understand how to service them appropriately. In many financial-advisory firms, 20 percent of the revenues account for 80 percent of sales. The theory behind this 80/20 rule comes from Pareto's constant, derived from a study that contended that 80 percent of the wealth was held by 20 percent of the population. Essentially, the top 20 percent of clients are subsidizing the remaining 80 percent of the clients. Optimally, the reverse would be true, and 80 percent of your clients would account for most of your revenue. You may be willing to accept a client that is a loss leader, such as a woman in her 70s who has a son or daughter who fits within your optimal client matrix. But the number of suboptimal clients you're willing to accept—say, 20 percent—should be predetermined so that you can maintain the integrity of your firm's strategy and sustain profitability.

Ultimately, value is determined by whether your business is profitable and whether the profitability is sustainable. If you can manage your overhead expense to align with industry benchmarks or with your own best year and continue to improve your gross profit margin through better pricing, better client selection, and improved productivity, you'll see the value of your business increase over time.

Built-in Leverage and Capacity

If you agree with the premise that there is a physical limit to the number of active client relationships an adviser can manage well, you'll recognize that for your firm to grow, you'll need to add capacity—more people—and leverage your business better. From a value standpoint, the most valuable financial-advisory firms are those that are not substantially or solely dependent on the owner for success. Such dependence marks the difference between a business and a book of business.

One of the questions buyers will want to explore is which is more valuable—your people or your clients. Clients offer a firm a finite opportunity and a degree of certainty. The right staff doing the right things efficiently and effectively becomes a growth engine for a firm, a means to take the business to a new level.

Using a firm's professional staff to build leverage is also appealing because it provides an internal transition option. For many sellers, transferring ownership to someone outside the firm is not the best choice. The reasons have to do with the seller's continued role, the commitment to ensuring that clients are tended to properly, the desire to reward loyal staff with this opportunity, or a desire to leave a legacy. By building a leveraged organization with other professional staff, these goals can be achieved more readily.

Leverage and capacity also allow an adviser to build a business to critical mass—that point at which the firm achieves optimal efficiency, effectiveness, and profitability. Larger firms command higher values not just in terms of real dollars but also in terms of higher multiples. That's because they become more appealing to institutional buyers, who may be inclined to pay a strategic price if the business has the capacity to grow beyond its current limits.

Systematic Client Feedback

Organizations that provide professional services, especially financial services, need to build better relationships with their clients. By strengthening client relationships, firms are better able not only to identify ways in which to improve their business practices but also to identify cross-selling, consolidation, and referral opportunities to grow those relationships.

Client-satisfaction surveys are also an effective tool in building client relationships. Indeed, prospect and customer surveying can provide valuable information about prospects' and customers' expectations, customer satisfaction, and strategies for improvement. Client surveys should have the following outcomes:

♦ Identify specific clients who are willing to provide referrals
♦ Identify specific cross-selling and marketing opportunities on a client-by-client basis
♦ Help advisers gauge satisfaction among existing clients and identify specific gaps
♦ Demonstrate commitment to existing clients
♦ Provide data to build deeper relationships with centers of influence and prospects
♦ Track progress and changes over time

Identify the information requirements that will enable you to make decisions and take the actions necessary to enhance how you serve and procure clients. Doing some homework on the front end regarding the feedback desired and the actions the firm is willing to take as a result of what it learns will ensure the most useful survey

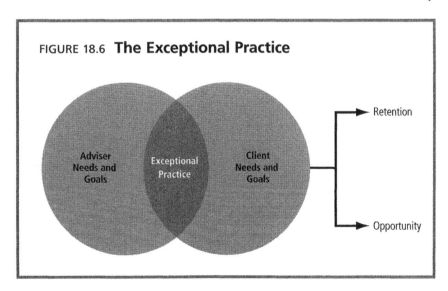

FIGURE 18.6 **The Exceptional Practice**

results. Survey goals and objectives are the key to the entire effort. Taking the time to strategize and develop a plan of action will make the feedback provided by prospects and customers that much more meaningful and worthwhile.

A well-designed client survey process also can help a buyer evaluate the client-retention possibilities as well as the opportunities for additional business. Both of these make a better case for a higher value because they convey the impression of an exceptional practice (see *Figure 18.6*).

Building Value

In real life, the price paid for a firm will be governed not by a formal valuation but by a buyer's perspective on the opportunity for financial return and the seller's need or desire to cash out. Still, it's best not to leave the process to such whims or to chance.

By understanding value drivers and the factors that separate the elite advisory firms from other firms, sellers of practices enhance their chances of dictating the price and terms. At a minimum, these owners put themselves in a position to walk away from any deal that doesn't fit their parameters for the sale of their business. They've structured the enterprise in a way that produces consistent income, reduces the dependency on owners, and helps it continue to grow. These factors result in better cash flow, lower risk, and a business that is built to last as well as one built to sell.

Appendix of Sample Documents

Document Request List

1. Copies of the company's articles of incorporation, bylaws, and any amendments to those documents

2. Copies of any other agreements or documents dealing with shareholder rights (for example, buy-sell agreements, options, or rights of first refusal)

3. Copies of the company's annual financial statements (audited, if possible) for the for the past four years

4. Copies of the company's interim statements as of the valuation date and for the same period in the prior year

5. Any business plans, future projections, and budgets that are available

6. Any contingent or off-balance-sheet assets or liabilities (pending lawsuits, compliance requirements, et cetera)

7. A complete list of stockholders and number of shares held as of the valuation date

8. Documentation with respect to any transactions in the company's stock in the past three years

9. A list of any options or warrants outstanding as of the valuation date, including exercise price and remaining life

10. A list of the company's competitors, with location, relative size, and any other relevant factors

11. Schedule of insurance in force (key person, life, property, and liability)

12. Any information you have from trade associations that describes the industry or forecasts trends

13. Any company or industry literature that will provide some background on the business

14. A list of key members of management including title, age, year hired, and a brief description of their areas of responsibility

Due-Diligence Document and Information Checklist for Investment Adviser Representative Compliance

1. If the individual is an existing registered investment adviser (or a principal thereof), obtain current Form ADV (Part 1, Part II, and Schedule F) and proof or confirmation of current registration status with the **U.S. Securities and Exchange Commission** and states, as applicable.

2. (a) Items 6–11 on pages 9–15 of Part 1A of Form ADV and (b) items 2C–2H on pages 2 and 3 of Part 1B of Form ADV. Item 11, beginning on page 13 of Part 1, will provide important information relative to disciplinary matters.

3. For the purpose of determining the appropriate qualifying examinations and/or state registration filings that may be required by the investment adviser representative (IAR) (and/or notice filings required of the adviser as result of becoming engaged by existing clients of the IAR), the adviser should obtain from the IAR: (a) a list of all current clients of the IAR by state of residence; and (b) a list of all locations (that is, city/town and state) where the IAR maintains or plans to maintain an office (that is, principal, branch, or otherwise) while acting on behalf of the adviser.

4. To the extent that any IAR is or was a registered representative of an NASD broker-dealer, obtain a current Central Registration Depository (CRD) report for each such person to ascertain additional information, and to confirm the information previously reported on Parts 1A and 1B of Form ADV.

5. To the extent that any IAR is or was currently an IAR for another adviser and is in a state that requires IAR registration on the Investment Adviser Registration Depository (IARD) system, obtain a current CRD report for each such person to ascertain additional information, and to confirm information previously reported on Parts 1A and 1B of Form ADV.

6. By obtaining the above information, an adviser will be able to determine that the IAR or RIA (a) is not subject to an order issued by the SEC under Section 203(f) of the Investment Advisers Act of 1940, as amended; (b) has not been convicted within the previous 10 years of any felony or misdemeanor involving conduct described in Section 203(e)(2)(A)–(D) of the Investment Advisers Act; (c) has not been found by the SEC to have engaged, and has not been convicted of engaging, in any of the conduct specified in paragraphs (1), (4), or (5) of Section 203(e) of the Investment

Advisers Act; (d) is not subject to an order, judgment, or decree described in Section 203(e)(3) of the Advisers Act; and (e) is otherwise involved in any activity or proceeding that an investment adviser would determine as disqualifying the IAR from becoming associated with the adviser.

7. Obtain a list of all outside investment-related and financial-services industry activities so that an adviser is informed of any such services, affiliations, et cetera, so that it can determine if those affiliations or services warrant enhanced ongoing due diligence or disqualification from serving as an IAR of the adviser.

8. Obtain written verification of current examinations (for example, Series 6, 7, 65, 66) and designations (for example, CFP, CFA, ChFC) for each prospective IAR.

All of the above should be maintained in the IAR due-diligence file. In addition, the information and responses should be codified in the representations section of the investment adviser representative agreement, which agreement should be executed by the IAR prior to becoming associated with the adviser and should require the IAR to immediately notify the adviser of any change in his or her response to any previously provided information.

As part of the investment adviser representative agreement, the IAR should acknowledge his or her duty of confidentiality and prohibition from soliciting or serving clients of the adviser in the event of termination of the IAR's association with the adviser. These obligations should be set forth in a separate confidentiality and restrictive covenant agreement to be executed by the IAR in favor of the adviser, which agreement may exclude from the solicitation or service prohibition specific current clients of the IAR that transferred their accounts to the adviser.

Source: Thomas Giachetti of Stark & Stark

Key Documents for RIA Internal Transition

♦ **Investment adviser representative (IAR) questionnaire.** This initial document is to be completed by the IAR candidate prior to his or her becoming an employee of, or associated with, the company, pursuant to which the IAR candidate shall answer various background questions regarding his or her relevant experience, designations, disciplinary history, potential conflicts of interests, et cetera, so as to allow the company to perform initial due diligence on the IAR candidate.

♦ **Restrictive covenant agreement.** This is a critical initial document (preferably to be executed upon commencement of the IAR's employment or association with the company), pursuant to which the IAR shall agree (among other covenants and restrictions), upon termination of his employment/association with the company, to maintain all company information confidential, not to render services to the company's clients, not to induce any company employees to leave the company's employ.

♦ **Investment adviser representative agreement.** This document must also be executed by the IAR (preferably upon commencement of the IAR's employment or association with the company), pursuant to which the IAR acknowledges the terms and conditions of his or her employment or association with the company.

♦ **Purchase agreement.** This document is to be executed between the company and the IAR, setting forth the terms and conditions of the IAR's prospective purchase of a company ownership interest (that is, as a shareholder, member, or partner).

♦ **Shareholder or operating agreement.** This document is to be executed by the company and each of its owners, setting forth, among other substantive provisions, the terms and conditions for the disposition of each owner's ownership interest upon the occurrence of various events, such as death, disability, statutory disqualification, employment termination.

♦ **Insurance trusts.** The shareholder agreement must also set forth any insurance trusts pursuant to which insurance would be purchased (the amount of which would be routinely evaluated) by the company (or its owners) on the lives of the company's owners, the proceeds of which insurance policies would be used by the company (or its owners) to fund the purchase of the ownership interest from the deceased owner's estate.

♦ **Regulatory filings.** Regulatory filings refer to (a) the filing of individual IAR registration documents with each state requiring the company to do so, as generally required by each state—with certain exceptions—in which the IAR maintains a place of business; and (b) amending of the company's IARD filing to disclose new owners.

Source: Thomas Giachetti of Stark & Stark

Document Checklist for Mergers and Acquisitions

Confidentiality agreement. This document should be executed before the letter of intent if the parties intend to exchange information or documentation about each other before entering into a letter of intent. The purpose of this document is to protect each party's proprietary interest, confidential information, and documents and to provide for the immediate return thereof (including any copies) in the event that a transaction does not proceed within a specified period of time (for example, 90 days).

Letter of intent. This document is a prelude to commencing the agreement of sale preparation stage. The letter of intent should set forth the basic terms and understandings of the parties, which should include the initial understanding as to the basic terms of the prospective transaction, such as payment terms, due-diligence review, continued employment, restrictive covenants. Although the letter of intent will usually be drafted by legal counsel, the parties should attempt to arrive at the basic terms independent of legal counsel's direct involvement, including a preliminary due-diligence schedule. It must also contain a confidentiality provision as discussed above.

Purchase agreement. This agreement is a comprehensive document to be executed between the seller and buyer, setting forth the terms and conditions of the purchase of the investment-advisory entity, including but not limited to representations and warranties, purchase price and payment terms, remedies in the event of violation, continued employment of key personnel, restrictive covenants, indemnification.

One of the most critical purposes of this document is to indicate what happens in the event that the purchase or transition does not go as planned due to various events, including but not limited to failure to have certain clients transfer or maintain accounts (that is, purchase-price setoff), breach of material representations or warranties (for example, recapture of business, further setoff of purchase price or repayment of monies previously paid).

Shareholder or operating agreement. This document—to be executed by the surviving advisory firm and each of its owners—sets forth, among other substantive provisions, the terms and conditions for the disposition of each owner's ownership interest upon the occurrence of various events, including death, disability, statutory disqualification, and employment termination.

Restrictive covenant agreements. In this critical document, the principals and associated persons of the selling firm agree (among other covenants and restrictions) that upon commencement of their employment or association with the acquiring firm, they will maintain all the buyer's information confidentially, will render no services to the buyer's clients (including those clients that he or she previously serviced when employed by or associated with the seller), will not induce any of the buyer's employees to leave its employ. It is critical for the selling firm to have these agreements already in place before the letter-of-intent stage (preferably always upon commencement of employment or association with the firm) so that the seller does not run the risk of clients' leaving the firm during the transition process with employees or associates who are not subject to any such restrictions.

Regulatory issues and filings. These requirements include but are not limited to (a) amending the company's ADV filings as required; (b) filing, maintaining, or withdrawing notice filings with each state that requires the company to do so; (c) filing, maintaining, or withdrawing individual IAR registration documents with each state that requires the company to do so; (d) making the announcement to clients; (e) obtaining client approvals (negative consent letters); (f) eliciting assignments under the Investment Advisers Act of 1940 (change of management or control); (g) obtaining advisory agreements (assignment vs. execution of new agreement); (h) withdrawing the seller's registration (pros and cons); (i) retaining the books and records; and (j) maintaining or supplementing errors and omissions insurance.

Source: Thomas Giachetti of Stark & Stark

Operating Due-Diligence Checklist

BUSINESS AND FINANCIAL INFORMATION

Responsible Party	Date	Task
_____	_____	Three to five years of financial statements
_____	_____	Breakdown on revenue, quality, quantity, and type
_____	_____	Copy of business plan and marketing plan
_____	_____	Copies of any leases or contracts
_____	_____	Licenses
_____	_____	Total assets under management
_____	_____	Mix of business
_____	_____	List of clients on retainer
_____	_____	Credit history and bank references

MARKETING INFORMATION

Responsible Party	Date	Task
_____	_____	Press releases
_____	_____	Advertisements
_____	_____	Promotional materials
_____	_____	Other public relations
_____	_____	Centers of influence—transferable
_____	_____	Client-satisfaction surveys
_____	_____	Newsletters and client communications
_____	_____	Seminars
_____	_____	Office locations and logistics
_____	_____	Special markets, niches, positioning

OPERATIONS AND COMPLIANCE

**Responsible
Party**   **Date**   **Task**

_____ ____ Policies and procedures manuals

_____ ____ Errors-and-omissions insurance records

_____ ____ Complaint files

_____ ____ Software and technology

CLIENTS

**Responsible
Party**   **Date**   **Task**

_____ ____ Client file review and client statements

_____ ____ Complaint files

_____ ____ Client profile and demographics

_____ ____ Average size

_____ ____ Largest clients and their percentage of total revenue

_____ ____ Strength of relationships

_____ ____ Intervals of service and review

_____ ____ Average time with the firm

_____ ____ Investment policy statements

_____ ____ Client survey results

_____ ____ References

PERSONNEL

**Responsible
Party**   **Date**   **Task**

_____ ____ Personnel manual for the practice

_____ ____ Employee census

_____ ____ Employee retention

_____	_____	Employment contracts, if any
_____	_____	Morale
_____	_____	Skill levels
_____	_____	Employee written reviews
_____	_____	Benefit programs and insurance records
_____	_____	Payroll records
_____	_____	CRD/U4 review of licensed personnel

PLANNING/ADVISORY

Responsible Party	Date	Task
_____	_____	Assets under management
_____	_____	Breakdown
_____	_____	Software and technology
_____	_____	Investment style and philosophy
_____	_____	Investment performance

Offering Memorandum
"The Book"

This Confidential Memorandum (the "Memorandum") has been assembled by Moss Adams Capital LLC ("Moss Adams") exclusively from information supplied to Moss Adams by the Apex Advisers LLC ("Apex" or the "Company") and is being provided to potential purchasers by Moss Adams, as Apex's agent, solely for use by potential investors in considering their interest in purchasing the Company.

Neither Apex nor Moss Adams makes any representation or warranty as to the accuracy or completeness of this Memorandum; nor shall either of them assume any liability for any of the representations (expressed or implied) contained in this Memorandum or any other written or oral communications provided to the recipient during its evaluation of Apex.

By accepting this Memorandum, the recipient agrees and acknowledges that: (1) all of the information contained herein is highly confidential, and the recipient will keep all such information and all other information made available to the recipient in connection with any further investigation of Apex confidential; (2) none of the information will be used by the recipient or any of its employees or representatives in any manner whatsoever, in whole or in part, other than in connection with its evaluation of Apex for the purpose of considering its investment in Apex; (3) the recipient will not reproduce this Memorandum, in whole or in part, and will not distribute all or any portion of this Memorandum to any person other than a limited number of the recipient's employees or representatives who have a clear need to know such information for the purpose set forth above, who are informed by the recipient of the confidential nature of such information, and who have executed written covenants to maintain all such information in the strictest confidence; (4) if the recipient does not wish to pursue this matter, it will immediately return this Memorandum to Moss Adams, together with any other material relating to Apex which the recipient received from Moss Adams or Apex and will destroy all memoranda, analyses, compilations, studies, and other documents containing or reflecting information set forth in this Memorandum or otherwise received from Moss Adams or Apex that relates to Apex and will confirm such destruction in writing to Moss Adams; and (5) any proposed actions by the recipient which are inconsistent in any manner with the foregoing agreement will require the prior written consent of Apex.

Apex reserves the right to negotiate with one or more prospective buyers at any time and to enter into a definitive agreement for the sale of Apex without prior notice to you or other prospective purchasers. In addition, Apex reserves the right to terminate, at any time, further participation by any party and to modify data and other procedures for any reason. Apex intends to conduct its business in the ordinary manner during the evaluation period; however, Apex reserves the right to take any action, whether in or out of the ordinary course of business, which it deems necessary in the conduct of such business.

Moss Adams Capital LLC

1001 Fourth Avenue, 27th Floor

Seattle, Washington 98154-1199

Phone: (206) 223-1820

Fax: (206) 652-2096

Wiley Kitchell

Managing Director

(206) 652-2024

wiley.kitchell@mossadams.com

CONTENTS

EXECUTIVE SUMMARY

Founded in San Jose, California, in 1982, the Apex Advisers LLC ("Apex" or the "Company") provides fee-only, personal financial-counseling services to corporate executives and high-net-worth individuals. Apex's service combines superior, highly quantitative investment-management expertise with outstanding, individually tailored financial-, tax-, and estate-planning advice. The Company's approach has quickly earned Apex a reputation as a client-focused firm, providing proactive, creative solutions to a broad range of its high-net-worth clients' financial needs.

Today, Apex is a major regional provider of financial services to the high-net-worth market. According to the 2004 survey results published in *Bloomberg Wealth Manager* magazine, Apex ranked No. 1 in California, No. 5 on the West Coast, and No. 30 nationally for the performance of its assets under management ("AUM").*

What's equally important, Apex is currently in a position to aggressively expand its AUM with little additional overhead. Until recently the Company preferred to focus on developing the analytical tools and technology required to provide the highest level of service possible for its high-net-worth clients. Traditionally, Apex relied almost exclusively on word-of-mouth referrals to attract new clients. Now the Company's proven systems and its highly experienced management team are well positioned to aggressively pursue new business, both from Apex's existing client base, as well as new, high-net-worth targets.

Apex currently has $2.1 billion of AUM. For the current fiscal year ending December 31, 2004, the Company expects to report gross revenues and earnings before interest, taxes, depreciation, and amortization (EBITDA) of $17.5 million and $4,200,000, respectively. Gross revenues in 2003 and 2002, were $17.1 and $16.4 million, respectively; EBITDA for the same periods were $3,591,000 and $3,280,000, respectively.

Apex's management strongly believes one of the Company's primary competitive advantages over its peers is the Comprehensive Wealth Solutions it pioneered long before the practice became popular. Apex's unique approach to wealth management, which has continually evolved since its initial implementation in 1982, has been a major contributor to Apex's success. Today, Apex's comprehensive approach to providing financial services allows the Company to service clients throughout the full array of financial disciplines. Further, the service model makes Apex a one-stop service provider, thereby fostering greater client loyalty and retention and allowing Apex to capture a greater percentage of its clients' investable assets.

Apex is owned by the Company's founder and chief executive officer, Mr. David Borden. The Company continues to be headquartered in San Jose, California.

---

*Based on average client account size, in *Bloomberg Wealth Manager* magazine's 2004 national survey of privately held wealth-management firms, Apex ranked No. 1 in California, No. 5 on the West Coast, and No. 30 nationally among firms that provide a full range of wealth-management services.

SUMMARY OF FINANCIAL AND OPERATING DATA

(1)   Summary Income Statements

Provided in the table below is a summary of Apex financial data for the years 2002–2003 actual, and 2004 estimated.

The Apex Advisers LLC

Summary Income Statements
($ in thousands)

For the Year Ended December 31	2004(E)	2003	2002
Gross Revenues			
Gross Profit			
Gross Margin			
Operating Expenses			
Operating Income			
Other Income (Expense)			
Pretax Income			
EBITDA			
Adjustments:			
Owner's Salary			
Owner's Bonus			
Total Adjustments			
Adjusted EBITDA			

Additional financial data are provided in Appendix A of the Memorandum. Appendix A reflects the strength and quality of both Apex's gross revenue and its EBITDA. The historical 2002 and 2003 results reflect actual expenses and staffing for those years.

The analysis in Appendix A also reflects Apex's 2004 full-year run rate, assuming no additional assets under management. In addition, the analysis projects Apex's potential to the extent the Company effectively implements its Strategic Growth Initiative. If Apex is able to execute all elements of its Strategic Growth Initiative at the low end of the estimates provided, Apex should be able to increase its gross revenues by approximately $1,375,000 per year. If Apex executes its plan at the high end of the estimates, the Company will increase gross revenues by approximately $2,500,000 per year.

Appendix A projects the results of both these scenarios, less corresponding expenses, for 2005 through 2008.

(2) AUM Fee Schedule

Apex's basic fee schedule for its Comprehensive Wealth Solutions services is as follows:

**The Apex Advisers LLC
AUM Fee Schedule**

AUM	Management Fees
Up to $3 million	0.950%
$3 million–$5 million	0.750%
$5 million–$25 million	0.500%
$25 million–$50 million	0.375%

Apex's size and scale allow it to aggressively negotiate fees with its selected money managers to institutional levels. Apex's equity managers generally manage Apex clients' assets for fees of 0.5 percent or less; Apex's fixed-income managers generally manage Apex clients' assets for 0.3 percent or less; and Apex's fund-of-funds managers typically waive any performance incentive fees for Apex clients. In addition, for actively managed accounts, Apex clients pay the lowest brokerage fee available.

The combination of Apex's competitive compensation structure, combined with the institutional-level fees negotiated with third-party money managers makes Apex's Comprehensive Wealth Solutions services a compelling value in the marketplace. The combination of Apex's fees and third-party manager fees is more than competitive with fees charged by wrap accounts at major wirehouses. Yet, for a similar fee structure—or lower in the case of larger relationships—Apex offers clients a level of professional, personalized services that few major institutions can match.

KEY INVESTMENT CONSIDERATIONS

Provided below are key operating attributes and strategic goals that Apex's management believes are critical to the Company's prior growth and development, as well as to its ongoing expansion.

(1) Apex's Strategic Growth Initiative

Apex is committed to long-term strategic growth, whether as an independent entity or as part of a larger organization. Apex's strategic vision for growth rests on four independent pillars and does not rely on any single engine for its continued success. The four pillars are as follows:

(a) Asset Harvesting From Existing Client Base

Substantial additional near-term value exists for Apex within the Company's existing client base, since Apex's current clients have substantial additional assets on which the Company is not currently earning any fees. This pool of investable assets comprises unexercised stock options, deferred compensation accounts, and 401(k) plans, as well as stocks, bonds, and cash held at third-party managers not under Apex's active management. Apex estimates this pool of assets to be between $500 million and $650 million.

Apex's continued ability to harvest assets from its client base over the recent past is illustrated in Exhibit 6 of the Memorandum. Apex is confident that it will continue to harvest at least $50 million to $100 million per year from existing clients for the foreseeable future. Assuming that assets harvested from existing clients earn an incremental .5 percent per year, asset harvesting should generate $250,000 to $500,000 of additional annual revenue for the foreseeable future.

(b) Alternative Investments

As illustrated in Exhibit 1, only a small percentage of Apex's current AUM is in hedge funds or other alternative investment products. To date, this has been a conscious decision because Apex's clients were slow to adopt alternative asset classes. In addition, Apex has recognized the potential to earn premium fees on alternative assets to the extent the Company can add value to its clients in this area.

As a result, Apex is in the process of creating an alternative multistrategy fund with a low correlation to the Standard & Poor's 500 index. Unlike traditional fund-of-funds offerings, the fund will offer Apex clients:

- *Full transparency,* since each strategy is managed in a separate account, not in a partnership
- *Monthly liquidity* with no lockup
- *Low internal fees,* since underlying managers will not charge typical 1 percent base and 20 percent performance hedge fund fees
- *Preferential fee structure for Apex clients*

(c) Apex's New-Client Development Team

As discussed above, Apex has enjoyed substantial growth in its AUM by harvesting assets from its existing client base. Although Apex anticipates it will be able to do so at substantial levels for some time to come, Apex also recognizes the need to build a new pipeline of prospects and future clients. To this end, during mid-2003 Apex began to build a New-Client Development team through a combination of professional business developers and existing technical staff.

Apex recognizes that the job of building a pipeline of prospects and converting these prospects to clients is a time-consuming process, especially with high-net-worth and ultrahigh-net-worth families for which the relationship-building process can take an extended period of time. Recognizing the nature of the effort, Apex has instituted a multifaceted approach with the following areas of focus:

- *Geographic focus:* Western U.S. area ranging from Apex's home base in northern California to San Diego, California
- *Industry focus:* Concentration on Apex's core expertise in the biomedical and technology manufacturing arenas
- *Leadership and management wealth counseling focus:* Having corporations hire Apex to counsel groups of their senior executives

♦ *Event-driven focus:* Where a change in control, or other liquidity event, occurs in areas of Apex's geographic or industry focus

(d) Appreciation of Existing AUM

One of Apex's major current assets is its billable AUM in excess of $2 billion. Apex recognizes, however, that it is unrealistic for a strategic growth plan to rely merely on market appreciation to generate ever-increasing revenues. Conversely, a strategic plan that ignores long-term market appreciation, at least at some modest level, is equally unrealistic, because markets appreciate over time. However, to become less market dependent, Apex continues to refocus its investment efforts on managers that provide steady and consistent growth and not merely index-like returns.

Although growth in AUM cannot be made completely independent of the financial markets, it can be made less dependent on market performance. Therefore, Apex believes given its evolving asset mix, and the ongoing migration into non-index-like investments, over time Apex should average at least 5 percent to 7 percent increased revenues from appreciation of its AUM. Based on Apex's 2004 run rate for gross revenues generated by AUM, even such modest market appreciation will increase Apex's gross revenues by $325,000 to $400,000 per year.

(2) Geography—Located in One of the Premier High-Net-Worth Target Markets in the United States

Apex is headquartered in one of the most desirable locations in the country for identifying and servicing high-net-worth clients. Situated in the San Francisco Bay area of California, Apex is at the center of a 40-mile radius covering some of the most affluent communities in California.

Although much of Apex's business was originally concentrated in Northern California, today the Company services clients located throughout the United States.

(3) Synergistic Benefits With Strategic Partner or Institutional Parent

Apex's client-service model is highly leverageable. To the extent Apex partners with an institutional parent that wants to create or add to a Comprehensive Wealth Solutions service, Apex's services can be broadly leveraged into the client base of its new parent.

Apex also recognizes the potential to leverage products and services offered by a new parent into Apex's high-net-worth client base. Apex clients currently use a wide array of financial products and services offered by third-party providers. These products and services range from asset management to a wide variety of alternative investments: unsecured loans to secured mortgages; money market accounts to mutual funds; property and casualty insurance to life insurance; and nearly every other investment product or service imaginable. Apex's client-service model is based on open architecture and bringing its clients best-of-breed products and services.

Some of the areas in which Apex can provide immediate synergistic benefits to a new parent include the following:

(a) Apex Assets Held by Third-Party Custodians

Apex currently uses third-party brokers and custodians. As such, Apex forgoes substantial revenue earned by these third-party firms on its asset base. Given access to a robust brokerage platform covered by a parent company, Apex can further enhance the revenue of its new parent. During 2003, third-party brokers and custodians generated commissions and fees totaling millions of dollars safeguarding Apex's clients' assets. In 2004, this total amount should be even higher as AUM continues to increase.

(b) Municipal Bonds

Apex manages only a small percentage of its clients' municipal bond investments. Given the lower returns on bonds, clients historically have been reluctant to pay asset-management fees on actively managed bond portfolios, especially since Apex must levy its own fee on top of any fee charged by a separate account manager. If Apex had access to a brokerage platform, its new parent could generate all of the brokerage on the unmanaged bonds currently held at third-party brokerage firms.

(c) Cash

As illustrated in Exhibit 1, Apex's current AUM includes high levels of cash in money market funds and cash alternatives such as short-term bond funds. In addition, Apex controls substantial additional client cash not under its active management. This cash could be transferred to in-house money market funds and other short-term vehicles to generate additional fees on these high-margin products. In addition, if Apex directly controls the cash held by its clients, the likelihood of transitioning this money into active management at a more accelerated rate would be increased.

(d) Insurance

Apex has never sold insurance products to its clients. However, given the wealth and estate-planning needs of Apex's clients, insurance sales to support estate planning is a significant untapped market available to a new parent.

(4) Historic Focus on Business Management and Profitability

Since inception, Apex has been managed as a business with a strong profit orientation. Apex's culture has developed around the principle that the Company must deliver excellence in everything it does while maintaining a focus on organizational efficiency, the generation of strong EBITDA, and margins that are above industry norms.

Rather than spending money on expensive offices and leasehold improvements, Apex maintains convenient, professional, and functional offices and prefers to invest in technology or other areas that create increased efficiency and direct or indirect client benefits. Rather than entering into a "talent auction" or becoming the high bidder to buy employees away from larger firms, Apex's most loyal and valuable colleagues have proved to be those who have been developed through the years since they started with the company. Apex has had its greatest success in hiring smart, talented, and motivated professionals, either upon graduation or early in their careers, then assisting them with graduate education or relevant professional certifications.

The Company is committed to hiring talented individuals and providing them with the superior training and work environment necessary to become outstanding employees—and eventually owners—for many years to come.

(5) Corporate-Sponsored Leadership and Management Wealth-Counseling Programs

Apex is well known for the particular expertise it has developed in providing corporate-sponsored leadership and management wealth-counseling programs to many notable corporations.

Apex has been one of the leading independent firms to successfully serve the corporate fee-only marketplace and continues to pursue the business aggressively.

Apex also has substantial expertise in the creation, preparation, and presentation of large-scale seminars to corporate executives. Apex's seminar skills can be leveraged into a marketing function, an additional fee service to a broad market segment, or used as an ancillary service to support a mid- to lower-tier Web-based corporate-counseling program.

OTHER COMPANY MATTERS

(1) Growth of Apex's AUM

Exhibit 1 illustrates the total client assets currently under Apex's active management and on which Apex earns a fee based on a percentage of assets under management. Apex also supervises a substantial amount of additional client assets for which it does not currently earn a fee, but which represents a potential source of future asset-based fee growth.

Exhibit 2 illustrates the growth of Apex's assets under management between January 1997 and the end of the prior calendar quarter. This strong record of growth is a testament to Apex's value proposition in the marketplace. The Company's growth in AUM is even more impressive in light of the macroeconomic climate in which it occurred. Neither Apex nor its clients were immune to the millennium bear market. A large percentage of Apex's assets were gathered either immediately prior to or in the early stages of the unprecedented 2000–2002 bear market. It is a testament to Apex's strong client relationships and the loyalty promoted by the Company's client-service model that Apex's AUM reached an all-time high only one year after the end of the bear market.

(2) Apex's Comprehensive Wealth Solutions

Apex's services have continually evolved over the years to keep ahead of the needs of its clients. Today, Apex provides Comprehensive Wealth Solutions services that integrate all financial- and estate-planning disciplines with asset management and tax compliance. As such, Apex provides clients with a comprehensive level of wealth-management services previously available only to those with long-established wealth.

Apex delivers this unparalleled level of service by combining expertise in financial, tax, and estate planning, along with investment management and technology. Each element of Apex's Comprehensive Wealth Solutions services represents a high level of service in its own right. But the true value of Apex's comprehensive planning approach lies in the integration of these varied services. As a client-focused firm, Apex provides its clients with the customized blend of services they want or require.

Apex's professional team serves all of the needs of Apex's clients as they pass through the life-cycle stages, from wealth accumulation to wealth management to intergenerational wealth transfer—when the cycle begins all over again. Apex's approach to wealth management is unique due to the depth of the analyses, breadth of topics covered, innovative recommendations, and personalized attention and follow-up. In addition to investments, Apex specializes in providing integrated advice on a broad range of financial disciplines, including compensation and benefits for corporate executives; personal income taxes; cash flow and budgeting; investments; estate planning; education funding; retirement planning; and life, disability, and personal insurance; as well as any other topic related to a dollar sign. These skills form the foundation for Apex's Comprehensive Wealth Solutions services.

As part of its comprehensive client-service model, Apex provides its clients with cutting-edge estate-planning and intergenerational wealth-transfer services. The sophistication of the estate-planning advice provided by Apex is comparable to that provided by any leading law firm. Yet the Apex advantage is the Company's ability to see and understand a client's complete financial picture and actually implement this advice through correct asset location within a client's portfolio.

Apex also integrates expert tax compliance with the other elements of its wealth-management services. High-net-worth individuals have complex tax situations that require the attention of a specialist. This complexity can create demands that exceed the abilities of all but the most sophisticated tax preparers. Apex knows the finances of its clients intimately and is expert in the tax laws that affect them. Therefore, Apex's clients are ensured a level of accuracy and the convenience of "one-stop shopping" not otherwise available in one-dimensional law, accounting, or investment firms. As part of its tax-compliance services, Apex professionals also deal directly with all tax authorities to relieve its clients of these otherwise stressful encounters.

(a) Investment Management

Although Apex's Comprehensive Wealth Solutions services form the primary basis for the Company's client-service model, Apex's Investment Management services are its major revenue-generation mechanism. Today, the majority of Apex's AUM is custodied at Charles Schwab and Pershing. However, true to its legacy of objective advice and putting clients first, through a combination of technology and its dedicated investment-implementation team, Apex has created a completely open architecture that allows it to work with virtually any money manager and any custodian. True to its culture of continuous improvement, Apex's investment platform and process is continually evolving to meet ever-changing client needs and market conditions.

(b) The Apex Investment Committee and Due-Diligence Process

Apex has a five-member investment committee with more than 100 years of combined experience. The Apex investment committee meets weekly and implements a formal, rotating agenda covering all aspects of the investment and portfolio-construction process. The investment committee conducts an ongoing manager search, due diligence, and selection process, so that it can identify best-of-breed managers in all investment disciplines and continue to expand its investment platform. Apex's investment strategy, which focuses on risk control and tax minimization, is designed to maximize after-tax returns while reducing risk by providing consistent performance over time.

The investment committee is governed by a series of philosophies and pro-cedures. These philosophies and procedures are codified and are accessible to Apex colleagues on Apex's intranet and in bound printed form. These procedures are reviewed regularly and modified as needed to meet the challenges of an ever-evolving world environment and clients' changing circumstances.

The following areas of the Apex investment committee policies and proce-dures have been codified:

♦ Apex investment philosophy that governs Apex's approach to portfolio construction and investment selection.
♦ Rotating weekly agenda
— Decisions are made on a wide array of topics aided with help of proprietary "financial dashboard" of key indicators
— Committee members stay abreast of market and manager perfor-mance trends
♦ Model portfolio
— Represents Apex's "best thinking"
— Used as a starting point but may be tailored to specific client needs and goals
— Procedures for engaging investment managers
— Procedures for disengaging investment managers
— Proprietary internal reports to assist with decision making
  • Investment managers' performance reports

- Investment managers' survey forms
- Assets under management by asset class, investment style, and investment manager
- Financial-planning models and portfolio-construction models
— Proprietary research reports and other communication medium

(c) Apex Client-Service Teams

Multiple cross-discipline client-service teams, as illustrated in Exhibit 3, serve Apex clients. As such, each client has access to the best of Apex. The multiple Apex client-service professionals, with whom each client interacts, foster the development of deeper, interdependent relationships with the entire Apex organization, not a single individual. The Company's team approach provides clients with seamless service continuation in the absence of any single individual. Over the years, this model has insured that Apex's high-net-worth client relationships are easily transitioned among client-service professionals.

As reflected in Exhibit 4, Apex clients are serviced by a broad cross section of senior financial advisers, with no single financial adviser controlling a dominant number of clients. Apex's growth-oriented client-service model is designed to enable senior vice presidents to work as a team with vice presidents to continually transition those clients with lower investable assets, or less complicated situations, where appropriate. This structure serves all parties well. The vice presidents are better able to provide their new clients with more focused attention while they gain professional growth as they build their own client base. In addition, the senior vice presidents benefit by creating more leverage and becoming able to take on more-profitable clients. The fact that this system has worked well over the firm's history has allowed Mr. Borden, the firm's founding shareholder, to limit his client-service role to a select number of clients.

(3) Apex's Innovative Use of Technology

Apex has always relied on technology to enable it to compete effectively with brand name firms many times its size. As a result, Apex has developed a particular expertise in using technology to solve problems creatively and to foster an efficient, highly effective client-service model.

(a) Scalable Portfolio-Management and Reporting System

Apex maintains its clients' investment data on the Advent Axys portfolio-management system. Data from all custodians where the Company's client assets are held are downloaded into the system and reconciled by 12:30 p.m. each day. Asset positions are posted to Apex's secure Website by 2:30 p.m. each day. Performance is calculated on each of a client's accounts and on consolidated groups by the 21st day of each month. In developing this process, Apex has chosen to partner with Advent Back Office Service (ABOS) to ensure unlimited scalability in terms of the number of accounts consolidated into our system and to access the greatest number of prebuilt custodial feeds. In addition to the many checks and balances in place at ABOS, Apex maintains an internal group that employs its own series of data-checking procedures.

(b) Apex Online Account Access

Apex's online account access puts clients in control of their finances and enhances Apex's personalized service. As noted above, asset positions and values are posted daily to Apex's secure website. Monthly, as well as year-to-date, performance is posted by the 21st day of each month. One Apex username and password brings users secure access to their Apex managed accounts together with information about their other online accounts. In addition, www.Apexgroup.com securely organizes Apex's client communications and investment reports, as well as copies of Apex clients' wills, trusts, and any other important documents.

Apex's online account access is built on the Charles Schwab Advisor Web Center platform and leverages the technological skill and resources that are needed for scalability and to support and further develop this technology. Among many other features, Apex's website ensures secure access to clients' asset-management and consolidated asset-management (CAM) accounts. All the information is presented separately for each custodial account and consolidated across all Apex managed accounts regardless of account custodian, including:

◆ Daily updates of holdings
◆ Drilldown into research on holdings
◆ Unrealized gains/losses by tax lot
◆ Allocations by security type and asset class
◆ Transaction details
◆ Monthly performance calculations
◆ Apex's My Whole View—Account Aggregation

Apex's clients can also view their non-Apex online accounts by aggregating them through more than 5,000 data providers, including:

E-mail	Mortgages
Banking	Bill payment
Credit cards	Research
Financial tools	News
Investments	Travel-reward programs
Loans	

If clients choose, they can grant their Apex advisers access to this information to streamline the financial-planning process.

(c) Apex's Custom Reporting Package

Apex has created a custom reporting package based on the needs of its high-net-worth clients. These reports are mailed on the 21st day following the close of each calendar quarter and provide Apex clients with:

♦ Individual account information

♦ Information consolidated across accounts

♦ Performance

♦ Performance composition and activity summary

♦ Asset allocation

♦ Style allocation

♦ Benchmark return comparison

♦ Fixed-income holdings

♦ Equity holdings

♦ Definition of key terms

(d) The Apex Financial Planner

Apex has consolidated its years of technical financial-planning efforts into a single database-driven financial-planning system. Because a comprehensive computer-based financial-planning system to service high-net-worth and executive clients did not exist, Apex created its own, highly leveraged internally developed program. The comprehensive computer program dramatically decreases analytical preparation and client response time, provides more-focused client reports, and facilitates the fact-finding process to further leverage professional time. This unique system can also facilitate the management of a large financial-planning practice providing standardization and quality control. The program also increases the firm's internal asset-gathering opportunities, with numerous cross-client reporting capabilities. This proprietary financial-planning system can be an important part of building a highly leveraged personal financial-counseling platform.

(e) Practice-Management Tools

In the course of providing service to its clients, Apex has maintained a specific focus on technology to increase the efficiency of its operations. Apex has created many technological solutions to practice-management issues.

In addition to Apex's cross-client reporting capabilities discussed above, Apex's internally developed wealth-management database application is another example of a successful development effort by Apex. The application allows Apex's client-relationship managers to communicate new investment strategies, and changes to existing investment strategies, to Apex's financial advisers. Once communicated, the progress toward completion of each request is monitored through various stages. In addition to tracking progress and avoiding errors, the application also allows team members to prioritize tasks, and their time, to ensure that the clients receive the best possible service.

MANAGEMENT AND PROFESSIONAL STAFF

The table below provides information on Apex's management and key professional staff. A brief biography on each of the Company's primary officers is included.

The Apex Advisers LLC
Management and Key Professional Staff

NAME	TITLE	AGE
David Borden	Chief Executive Officer	

David Borden, CEO

Mr. Borden is Apex's founder, CEO, and sole shareholder. Prior to founding the Company, Mr. Borden …

Prior employment

Educational degrees (where, when)

SUGGESTED EXHIBITS

1. Assets Under Management
2. Growth of Assets Under Management
3. Organization Chart
4. AUM by Adviser
5. Staff Tenure
6. New and Committed AUM
7. New-Client Development Pipeline

This document is meant to serve as an example and is intended only to aid discussion. The terms and condtions herein will change depending on the parties to an actual negotiation and on applicable state law. Do not use or otherwise rely on this document without consulting an attorney.

Adviser Roll-Up, Inc.
11 Delirium Lane
Edina, MN 55439

September 1, 2005

Mr. Fred Williams
Ziti Wealth Management, LLC
600 University Park Place, #501
Muskegon, MI 49442

LETTER OF INTENT

Dear Mr. Williams:

This letter sets forth our proposal for a mutually beneficial and rewarding transaction among Adviser Roll-Up, Inc. ("Adviser Roll-Up"), Ziti Wealth Management, LLC (together with its subsidiaries and affiliated entities, the "Company"), and the principals of the Company (the "Principals"), comprising, among other things, (i) the acquisition of the Company by Adviser Roll-Up, and (ii) a concurrent management agreement that would entitle the Principals to a substantial portion of the future earnings of the Company.

Adviser Roll-Up was founded by highly experienced financial-service executives and will be funded by premier private equity investors. Adviser Roll-Up has developed a model that allows independent financial advisers to access capital for growth, tap into shared resources, and leverage the resources available to a large firm while maintaining control of their practice and entrepreneurial culture. Shareholders of Adviser Roll-Up will have the opportunity to participate in the anticipated growth of a portfolio of leading advisory firms.

I. PROPOSAL

1. Acquisition

The current owners of the Company (the "Owners") would sell all of the outstanding equity securities of the Company to Adviser Roll-Up. The closing of the proposed acquisition (the "Closing") will occur simultaneously with other Founding Partners on or about January 1, 2006. Adviser Roll-Up is willing to explore with the Owners tax-efficient structures for the proposed acquisition.

2. Purchase Price

The purchase price for the outstanding equity securities of the Company would consist of the following components:

(a) Basic Purchase Price

Adviser Roll-Up would pay to the Owners $3,675,000 (the "Basic Purchase Price"), of which

> (1) the sum of $2,000,000 would be paid at closing; and
>
> (2) the sum of $1,675,000 would be paid through the issuance of restricted shares of common stock of Adviser Roll-Up, valued at $10.00 per share.

The Basic Purchase Price was determined by

> (i) estimating the projected revenues of the Company for the current year to be $3,500,000, based on the Company's most recent projection;
>
> (ii) using the Company's future expenses forecast for 2004, arriving at an adjusted projected earnings before interest, taxes, depreciation, and amortization (EBITDA) for the current year of $875,000 (the "EBITDA Target");
>
> (iii) multiplying the EBITDA Target by 60 percent (the "Acquisition Percentage") to arrive at the sum of $525,000 (the "Acquired Earnings"); and
>
> (iv) multiplying the Acquired Earnings by 7.0.

The Acquisition Percentage reflects the portion of the future earnings stream of the Company acquired by Adviser Roll-Up, whereas the other portion of such earnings stream (100 percent minus the Acquisition Percentage) will be retained by the Principals under the Management Agreement referred to below (the "Principals' Percentage").

The Basic Purchase Price assumes that at Closing the Company will be free of long-term debt, with a minimum cash balance of $50,000.

(b) Earnouts

The Owners would also be entitled to two earnout payments based on the compounded growth rate of the Company's adjusted EBITDA over the two successive three-year periods following the proposed acquisition, not taking into account any add-on acquisitions. Each earnout would, at the option of the Company, be payable in cash or shares of common stock of Adviser Roll-Up at its then current value.

3. Management Agreement

At the Closing, the Company would enter into a Management Agreement with the Principals or an entity designated by them. The Management Agreement would provide for the following terms:

(a) The Principals would be responsible for the management of the Company under the general supervision of Adviser Roll-Up. Significant decisions would require the approval of Adviser Roll-Up, such as acquisitions, new lines of business, major capital expenditures, incurrence of debt, and transactions with the Principals, their family members, or related entities.

(b) If the Principals provide their services through a management company, they would be free to design its internal governance structures in accordance with their individual preferences. The transfer of ownership interests in the management company would require the consent of Adviser Roll-Up, but Adviser Roll-Up would cooperate with the Principals in connection with any generational transfers.

(c) The Principals would be entitled to an annual management fee consisting of the EBITDA of the Company for each year in excess of the Acquired Earnings.

If the Company consummates any add-on acquisitions, Adviser Roll-

Up and the Principals would jointly redefine the EBITDA Target for the purpose of calculating the management fee.

(d) The Management Agreement would have an initial term of six years, with automatic, subsequent renewals. After the initial term, the Principals could terminate the Management Agreement upon 12-month prior notice. Adviser Roll-Up can terminate the Management Agreement only for cause ("Cause") as defined in the paragraph below.

Cause, as referred to in the Management Agreement, above, shall specifically be limited to actions by any Principal that involve

(i) the conviction of a felony or willful gross misconduct that, in either case, results in material and demonstrable damage to the business or reputation of the employer; or

(ii) engaging in fraud, embezzlement, theft, or other materially dishonest conduct related to the Principal's performance hereunder.

Further, to the extent any of the Principals is fired for Cause, it is acknowledged that Cause shall not exist unless and until Adviser Roll-Up has delivered to the Principal a copy of a resolution duly adopted by a majority of the Board of Directors ("Board") and an opportunity for the Principal to be heard before the Board, finding that Cause exists in the good-faith opinion of the Board and specifying the particulars thereof in detail.

The Company may at its option unwind the transaction for Cause, as defined in the paragraph below.

Cause, as referred to above, shall specifically be limited to actions by the management of Adviser Roll-Up that involve

(i) the conviction of a felony or willful gross misconduct that, in either case, results in material and demonstrable damage to the business or reputation of Adviser Roll-Up; or

(ii) engaging in fraud, embezzlement, theft, or other materially dishonest conduct related to Adviser Roll-Up's performance hereunder.

4. Additional Agreements

(a) The Owners and the Principals would enter into standard noncompetition and nonsolicitation agreements.

(b) The Owners would enter into the stockholders' agreement of Adviser Roll-Up, which will contain customary transfer and voting restrictions and provide for "piggyback" registration rights.

5. Incentive Programs

(a) Employees of the Company, based on recommendations made by the Principals, would be entitled to receive stock options under the stock option plan of Adviser Roll-Up. The grant of any options would be in the discretion of the Board of Directors of Adviser Roll-Up. All options would be subject to customary vesting provisions.

(b) Principals determine incentive programs for key employees of the Company as a component of their ongoing management responsibility.

6. Other Terms

(a) The Company and Adviser Roll-Up would make customary representations and warranties to, and would provide customary indemnities for the benefit of, the other party.

(b) The consummation of the proposed transactions by Adviser Roll-Up and the Company would be subject to various conditions, including

(i) the completion of all financial, business, and legal due diligence by Adviser Roll-Up and the Company;

(ii) the absence of any material adverse changes;

(iii) the receipt of all required consents and approvals; and

(iv) the negotiation and execution of definitive agreements and other legal documentation in form and substance satisfactory to Adviser Roll-Up.

(c) All disputes would be resolved by arbitration.

II. GENERAL PROVISIONS

7. Access

The Company and Adviser Roll-Up shall provide each other with all information reasonably requested by it or its respective representatives in connection with the due-diligence review of the Company, Adviser Roll-Up, and their businesses. The Company and Adviser Roll-Up shall, upon reasonable notice and at reasonable times, afford each other access to each other and each other's personnel, books, records, contracts, and other documents and data. Adviser Roll-Up and the Company will use reasonable efforts to minimize any disruption to the business of the Company in connection with its due-diligence efforts.

8. Exclusivity

For a period of 90 days after the date hereof, neither the Company nor any Seller shall directly or indirectly through any representative solicit or entertain offers; initiate, continue, or engage in discussions or negotiations; in any manner encourage, consider, discuss, or accept any proposal; or enter into any agreement or understanding relating to any (i) acquisition of the Company or its equity securities or assets, in whole or in part, whether directly or indirectly, through merger, consolidation, purchase of equity securities, purchase of assets, or otherwise, or (ii) any joint venture or similar arrangement providing for a sharing of the Company's revenues or earnings.

9. Confidentiality

The parties acknowledge that they have previously signed a Mutual Nondisclosure Agreement dated June 1, 2005, which shall remain in full force and effect. This letter and the terms, conditions, and other aspects of the transaction proposed in this letter shall constitute confidential information under such Mutual Nondisclosure Agreement.

10. Publicity

Except as and to the extent required by law, neither party shall—and each party shall direct its representatives not to—make, directly or indirectly, any public comment, statement, or communication with respect to, or otherwise disclose or permit the disclosure of, the existence of discussions regarding a possible transaction between the parties or any of the terms, conditions, or other aspects of the transaction proposed in this letter. Further, following the closing of the transaction, and except as required by law, no public discussion of the transaction shall occur until both parties agree to such disclosure.

11. Conduct of Business

The Company shall conduct its business only in the ordinary course consistent with past practice without distributions or dividends.

12. Expenses

Each party shall bear its own costs and expenses in connection with the transactions contemplated by this letter.

13. Termination

This letter shall terminate on the earlier of (i) January 1, 2005, or (ii) the execution and delivery of definitive agreements relating to the transactions contemplated by this letter.

14. Governing Law

This letter shall be governed by and construed in accordance with the laws of the State of Minnesota, without giving effect to principles governing conflicts of laws.

15. Counterparts

This letter may be executed in one or more counterparts, each of which shall be deemed to be an original of this letter and all of which together shall constitute one and the same instrument.

16. Binding Effect

Part I of this letter shall not constitute a binding agreement between parties but merely express their intent with respect to the proposed transactions. Neither party shall be obligated to proceed with the transactions contemplated by this letter until the execution and delivery of definitive documents. Part II of this letter constitutes the legally binding and enforceable agreements of the parties.

Please indicate your agreement to the foregoing by signing this letter in the space provided below. We appreciate the opportunity to work with you and are confident that the proposed transactions will be mutually beneficial and rewarding.

ADVISER ROLL-UP, INC.

By: _____
    NAME

_____
    TITLE

Agreed and accepted:

ZITI WEALTH MANAGEMENT, LLC

By: _____   By: _____
    NAME   NAME

_____   _____
    TITLE   TITLE

[PRINCIPAL OWNERS]

Nondisclosure and Confidentiality Agreement

This document is meant to serve as an example and is intended only to aid discussion. The terms and conditions herein will change depending on the parties to an actual negotiation and on applicable state law. Do not use or otherwise rely on this document without consulting an attorney.

This nondisclosure agreement (the "Agreement") is made this ____ day of _____, 20xx (the "Effective Date") by and between _____ _____, (the "Recipient"), and _____, (the "Company").

WHEREAS the Recipient has requested and/or has been provided certain confidential and proprietary information for the sole purpose of evaluating a possible acquisition of or investment in the Company by the Recipient (the "Purpose"); and

WHEREAS the parties desire to protect the confidential and proprietary nature of the information disclosed by the Company to the Recipient;

NOW, THEREFORE, in consideration of the mutual promises and covenants contained herein and other good and valuable consideration, the receipt of which is hereby acknowledged, the parties agree as follows:

1. Confidential Information. The Company may find it beneficial to disclose to the Recipient certain information and material of a confidential, proprietary, or secret nature, whether written or oral, tangible or intangible, including but not limited to existing or proposed business or products, technology, trade secrets, discoveries, ideas, concepts, know-how, methods, techniques, designs, patterns, styling, markers, structure, marketing and distribution methods, plans, and efforts; the identities of and the course of dealing with actual and prospective customers, contractors, and suppliers; specifications, drawings, maps, blueprints, diagrams, analysis, compilations, studies, and other technical, financial, or business information that has not been made available to the general public ("Confidential Information"). Confidential Information shall include the terms of this Agreement and the existence and nature of the parties' negotiations. Any information of third parties furnished or disclosed in the behalf of the Company shall be deemed the Company's information, subject to the terms and conditions of this Agreement.

2. Marking. If such Confidential Information is provided in written, encoded, graphic, or other tangible form, the Company shall make commercially reasonable efforts to clearly mark it as "confidential." If such Confidential Information is provided in oral or intangible form, the Company shall make commercially reasonable efforts to orally identify it as "confidential." Any failure by the Company to so identify Confidential Information shall not relieve the Recipient of its obligations hereunder.

3. Information Excluded. This Agreement shall not apply to any information that (a) has been or becomes publicly known through no wrongful act of the Recipient; (b) was previously and lawfully known to the Recipient without obligation to keep it confidential; (c) is rightfully received from a third party who received the information lawfully and under no obligation to keep it confidential; or (d) which is independently developed by the Recipient without use of or reference to the Confidential Information that has been disclosed pursuant to this Agreement.

4. Limited Use and Distribution. The Confidential Information will not be used by the Recipient, its employees, or its representatives in any manner whatsoever, in whole or in part, other than for the Purpose contemplated in this Agreement, and the Recipient shall hold such Confidential Information in confidence, except to the extent that disclosure of such Confidential Information is (a) consented to in writing by the Company; (b) required by law, as provided in Paragraph 7 below; or (c) made to the Recipient's employees, agents, consultants, advisers, subcontractors, and entities controlled by it (collectively, "Personnel") who have a need to know such Confidential Information in connection with the Purpose and who have been informed by the Recipient of the provisions of this Agreement and agree to keep such Confidential Information confidential and the Recipient has advised the Company in writing of the names of such personnel. The Recipient shall be responsible for any breach of this Agreement by its Personnel. The Recipient and its Personnel will not disclose to any third party (including, without limitation, any employee, customer, supplier, or vendor of the Company) the fact that discussions or negotiations are taking place concerning a possible transaction, or any terms or conditions or other facts relating to a possible transaction.

5. Reproduction. The Recipient will not reproduce the Confidential Information, in whole or in part, and will not distribute all or any portion of this Confidential Information to any person other than the Recipient's Personnel for the purpose set forth above in Paragraph 4(c).

6. Nonsolicitation. The Recipient agrees that for a period of two (2) years from the date of this letter agreement, it will not, without the prior written consent of the Company, directly solicit for employment or hire any person employed by the Company. This obligation does not apply to solicitation by an employee of persons whose employment with the Company has terminated or to solicitations or advertisements for employment in publications or other media or by employment search firms not focused on Company employees.

7. Required Disclosure. If the Recipient is required to disclose certain Confidential Information in order to comply with applicable law or regulation or with any requirement imposed by judicial or administrative process or any governmental or court order, the Recipient shall promptly notify the Company prior to such disclosure to allow the Company to seek protection of the Confidential Information. Confidential Information so disclosed shall continue to be otherwise considered confidential under this Agreement.

8. Proprietary Rights. Any and all proprietary rights, including without limitation patent rights, inventions, copyrights, trademarks, service marks, and trade secrets, in and to Confidential Information shall be and remain with the Company. The Recipient shall not have any rights, by license or otherwise, to use the Confidential Information except as expressly provided herein. To the extent that the Recipient acquires any proprietary rights in Confidential Information disclosed by the Company, the Company shall own and retain all such proprietary rights and the Recipient hereby assigns and agrees to assign all such rights to the Company.

9. Return of Confidential Information. Within ten (10) days following the request by the Company, the Recipient shall return all Confidential Information to the Company or to its authorized representative, together with any other material relating to the Recipient that the Recipient received from the Company or from its authorized representative, and will destroy all memoranda, analyses, compilations, studies, and other documents containing or reflecting the Confidential Information or material otherwise received from the Company or from its authorized representative that relates to the Company and will confirm such destruction in writing.

10. Publicity. Neither party shall in any way or in any form distribute, disclose, publicize, issue press releases, or advertise in any manner the discussions that gave rise to this Agreement or the discussions or negotiations covered by this Agreement or the information provided pursuant to this Agreement without first obtaining the prior written consent of the other party.

SAMPLE 8: NONDISCLOSURE AND CONFIDENTIALITY AGREEMENT

11. No Commitment or Exclusivity. Neither this Agreement nor any discussions or disclosures hereunder shall (a) be deemed a commitment by either party to any business relationship, contract, or future dealing with the other party or (b) prevent either party from conducting similar discussions or performing similar work as that contemplated hereunder, so long as such discussions or work does not violate this Agreement. Any acquisition or other business relationship between the parties regarding the subject matter hereof shall be the subject of a separate agreement to be negotiated and executed by the parties.

12. No Warranty. The Confidential Information provided to the Recipient has been prepared exclusively from information provided by the Company to assist interested parties in making their evaluation of the Company and does not purport to contain all of the information that a potential purchaser or investor may need to complete its analysis. In addition, the Company makes no representation or warranty as to the accuracy or completeness of the Confidential Information, nor shall either party be liable for any statement contained in the Confidential Information or any other written or oral communications provided to the Recipient during its evaluation of the Company (except as may otherwise be expressly provided in any definitive purchase agreement between the Recipient and the Company). It is expressly understood that it is the obligation of the Recipient and any other prospective purchaser to conduct its own due diligence regarding the Company, its business, and its industry. The Recipient hereby waives any conflict of interest that may now or hereafter exist between the Recipient, on the one hand, and the Company or any of its respective officers, directors, or shareholders, on the other hand.

13. Assignment. Neither this Agreement nor any rights hereunder, in whole or in part, shall be assignable or otherwise transferable by either party.

14. Injunctive Relief. The Recipient acknowledges that disclosure or use of Confidential Information in violation of this Agreement could cause irreparable harm to the Company for which monetary damages may be difficult to ascertain or be an inadequate remedy. The Recipient therefore agrees that the Company shall have the right, in addition to its other rights and remedies, to seek and obtain injunctive relief for any breach or threatened breach of this Agreement, and waives the claim or defense that the Company has an adequate remedy at law.

15. Attorneys' Fees. If either party brings any action, suit, counterclaim, appeal, arbitration, or mediation for any relief against the other in connection with this Agreement, the substantially prevailing party shall be entitled to recover all reasonable fees and costs incurred in connection therewith.

16. Term. The term of this Agreement shall begin on the Effective Date and shall continue for three (3) years, unless terminated sooner on thirty (30) days' written notice by either party. Paragraphs 4–10, 13–15, 19, and 20 shall survive the termination of this Agreement.

17. Relationship of Parties. Nothing herein contained shall create or be construed as creating a partnership, joint venture, agency, or employment relationship between the parties, and no party shall have the authority to bind the other in any respect.

18. No Waiver. Failure to enforce any of the terms or conditions of this Agreement shall not constitute a waiver of any such terms or conditions, or of any other terms and conditions.

19. Applicable Law and Venue. This Agreement shall be governed by and construed in accordance with the internal laws of _____, without regard to any conflict of law principles. The venue of any proceedings regarding this Agreement shall be in the state and federal courts in _____ _____ [City], _____ [State].

20. Severability. If any term or provision of this Agreement shall be declared invalid, illegal, or unenforceable, the meaning of said provision shall be construed, to the extent feasible, so as to render the provision enforceable, and if no feasible interpretation would save such provision, it shall be severed from the remainder of this Agreement, which shall remain in full force and effect. In such event, the parties shall negotiate, in good faith, a substitute, valid, and enforceable provision that most nearly effects the parties' intent in entering into this Agreement.

21. Entire Agreement. This Agreement represents the entire understanding between the parties with respect to the subject matter herein and cancels and supersedes all prior agreements and understandings, whether written or oral, with respect thereto. This Agreement may be modified or amended only by an instrument in writing signed by duly authorized representatives of the parties.

IN WITNESS HEREOF, the parties hereto have caused this Agreement to be executed by their duly authorized representatives as of the date and year written above.

Company: **Recipient:**

_____   _____
SIGNATURE   SIGNATURE

_____   _____
PRINT NAME   PRINT NAME

_____   _____
TITLE   TITLE

Index

fair, 6, 7, 217
fair market, 6–7, 217
investment, 7, 218
standards, 6–9, 217–219
transferable, 261–263
what is being valued, 8–9

warranties, 146–147, 187–188
Wealth Trust, 111, 226, 237
Weinberg, Sharon, 254
Western Alliance Bancorporation,
     111, 238
Western Reserve Life, 225
working capital analysis
   multipartner firm example, 62–
     63
   solo practitioner example, 84–89

About Bloomberg

Bloomberg L.P., founded in 1981, is a global information services, news, and media company. Headquartered in New York, Bloomberg has sales and news operations worldwide.

Serving customers on six continents, Bloomberg, through its wholly-owned subsidiary Bloomberg Finance L.P., holds a unique position within the financial services industry by providing an unparalleled range of features in a single package known as the Bloomberg Professional® service. By addressing the demand for investment performance and efficiency through an exceptional combination of information, analytic, electronic trading, and straight-through-processing tools, Bloomberg has built a worldwide customer base of corporations, issuers, financial intermediaries, and institutional investors.

Bloomberg News, founded in 1990, provides stories and columns on business, general news, politics, and sports to leading newspapers and magazines throughout the world. Bloomberg Television, a 24-hour business and financial news network, is produced and distributed globally in seven languages. Bloomberg Radio is an international radio network anchored by flagship station Bloomberg 1130 (WBBR-AM) in New York.

In addition to the Bloomberg Press line of books, Bloomberg publishes *Bloomberg Markets* magazine.

To learn more about Bloomberg, call a sales representative at:

London: +44-20-7330-7500
New York: +1-212-318-2000
Tokyo: +81-3-3201-8900

About the Authors

Mark C. Tibergien, formerly a principal in Moss Adams LLP, is CEO of Pershing Advisor Solutions LLC. At Moss Adams, his responsibilities included management consulting, business valuations, and business-owner succession. *Accounting Today* has recognized Tibergien as among the "100 Most Influential" in the accounting profession. *Financial Planning* magazine has listed him as a "Mover & Shaker" in its annual review of industry professionals, and *Investment Advisor* has included him as among the "25 Most Influential" in the financial-services industry. He is coauthor of *Practice Made Perfect: The Discipline of Business Management for Financial Advisers.*

Owen Dahl is a principal in the Valuation and Litigation Services group of Moss Adams LLP. He has provided commercial litigation, damages, asset-allocation, and acquisition consulting services to small and large corporations alike. Dahl specializes in issues relating to intellectual property and works with firms for which such issues are key. He has more than 17 years' experience in the investment-advisory industry. A native of Canada, Dahl is a chartered financial analyst and a member of the CFA Institute and the American Society of Appraisers.

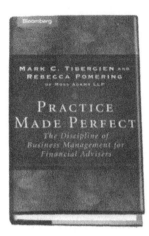

Printed and bound by CPI Group (UK) Ltd, Croydon, CR0 4YY

24/04/2025

14661391-0001